GRAPHITTI DESIGNS AND
VIEW ASKEW PRODUCTIONS PRESENT

Clerks.

(The Comic Book)

Kevin Smith

Jim Mahfood

Phil Hester

&

Ande Parks

S0-BDT-543

image

CLERKS: THE COMIC BOOK™

written by
Kevin Smith

"The Comic Book" &
"Holiday Special"
illustrated by
Jim Mahfood

"The Lost Scene"
pencilled by
Phil Hester
inked by
Ande Parks

lettered by
Sean Konot

back cover art by
Chris Bailey

chapter breaks by
Gilbert Hernandez
Arthur Adams
Duncan Fegredo

book design by
John Roshell of Comicraft

edited by
Jamie S. Rich

original comic books edited by
Bob Schreck and Jamie S. Rich

This collects the original
Oni Press comic books
Clerks: The Comic Book,
Clerks: Holiday Special &
Clerks: The Lost Scene.

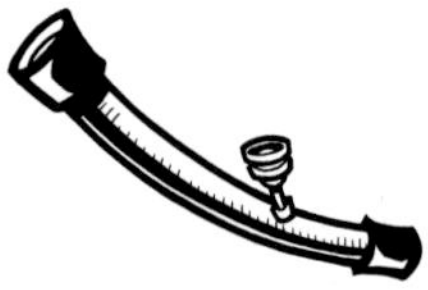

Published by

Image Comics
www.imagecomics.com

Jim Valentino
Publisher

Anthony Bozzi
Director of Marketing

Brent Braun
Director of Production

Doug Griffith
Art Director

Traci Hale
Controller

View Askew Productions, Inc.
www.viewaskew.com

Kevin Smith
& Scott Mosier
Producers

Gail Stanley
Bryan Johnson
Walt Flanagan
Jason Mewes
Staff

Graphitti Designs, Inc.
www.graphittidesigns.com

Bob Chapman
Producer

Gayle Blume
Max McBurney
Adrian Romo
Kevin Chapman
Staff

CLERKS. THE COMIC BOOK TRADE PAPERBACK. JULY 2001. FIRST PRINTING. Published by Image Comics, 1071 N. Batavia Street, Suite A, Orange, CA 98267.

ISBN 1-58240-209-4
PRINTED IN CANADA.

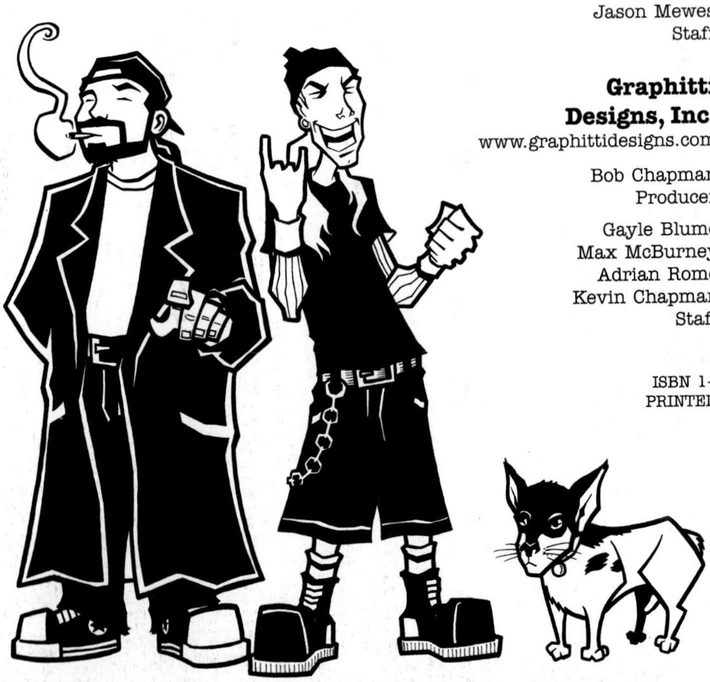

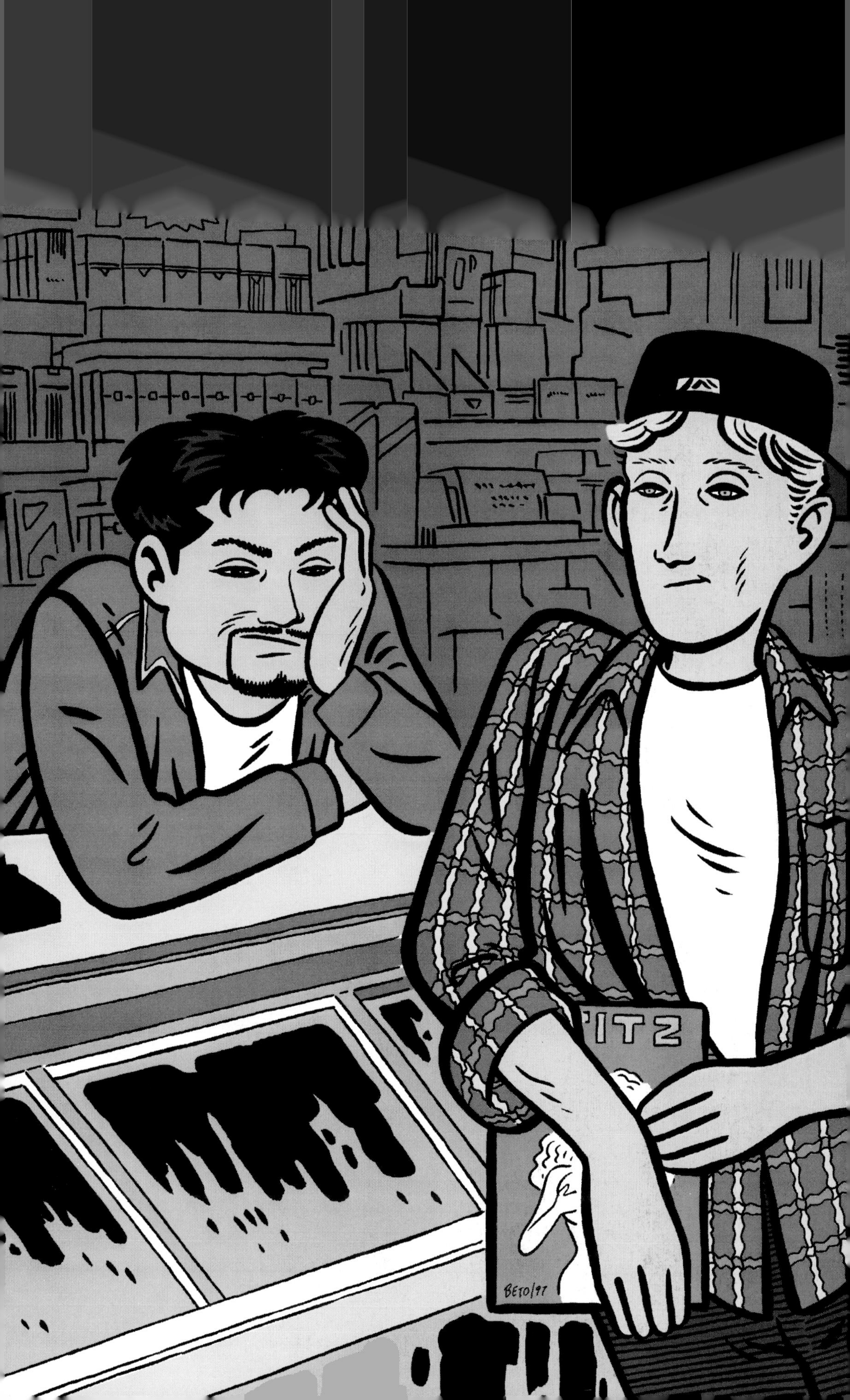
ITZ
BETO/97

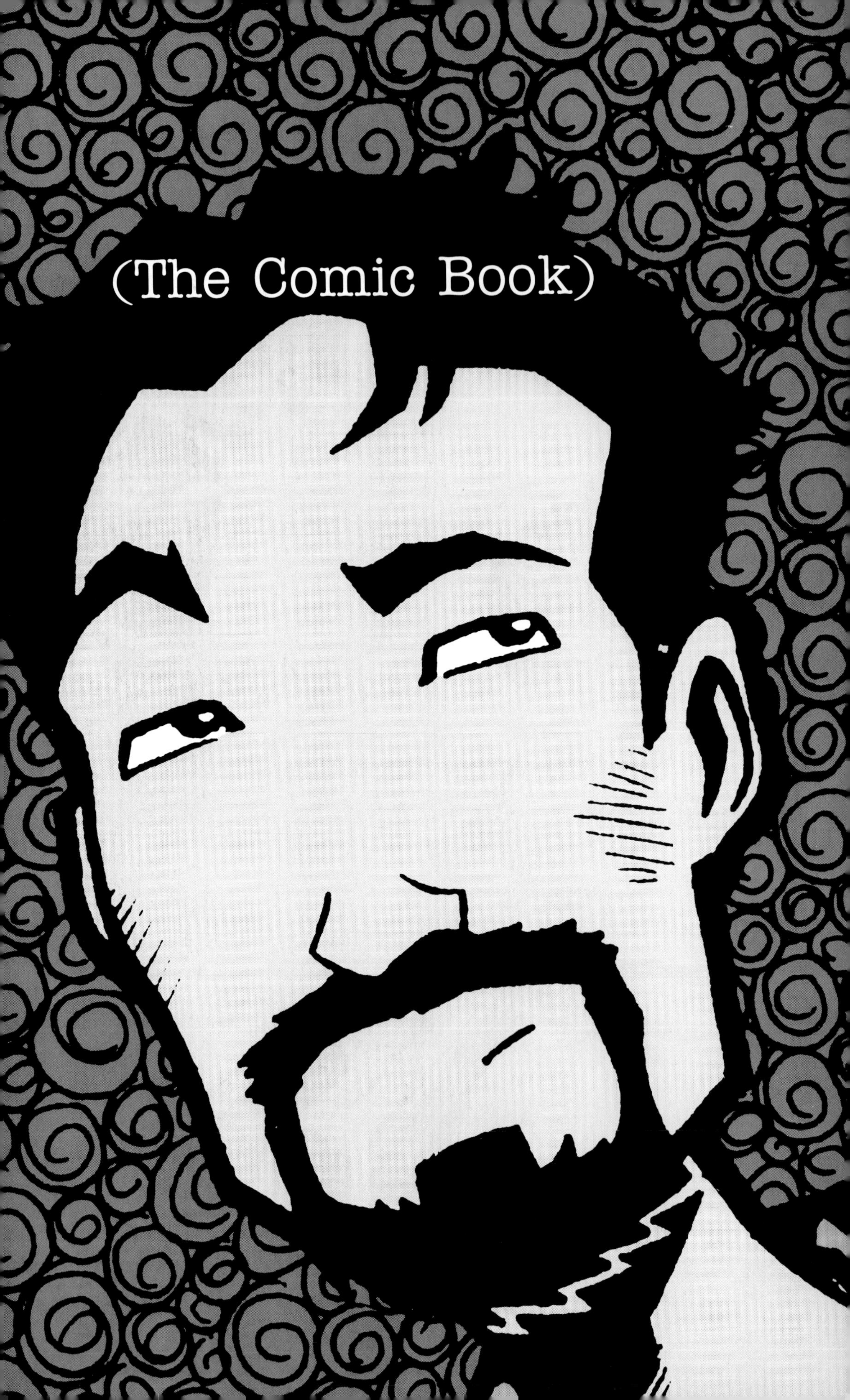
(The Comic Book)

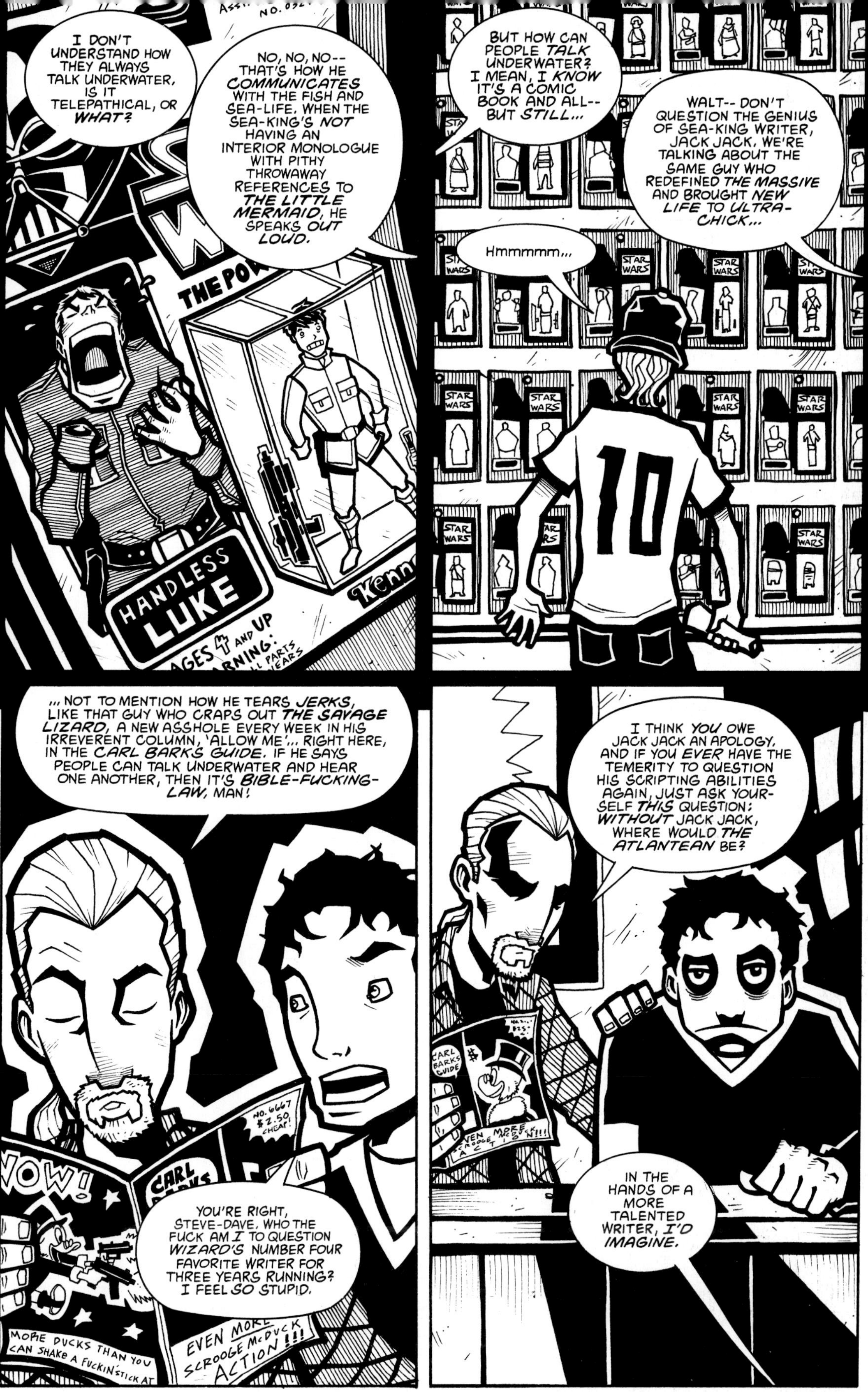
I DON'T UNDERSTAND HOW THEY ALWAYS TALK UNDERWATER. IS IT TELEPATHICAL, OR WHAT?
NO, NO, NO-- THAT'S HOW HE COMMUNICATES WITH THE FISH AND SEA-LIFE. WHEN THE SEA-KING'S NOT HAVING AN INTERIOR MONOLOGUE WITH PITHY THROWAWAY REFERENCES TO THE LITTLE MERMAID, HE SPEAKS OUT LOUD.
HANDLESS LUKE
BUT HOW CAN PEOPLE TALK UNDERWATER? I MEAN, I KNOW IT'S A COMIC BOOK AND ALL-- BUT STILL...
WALT-- DON'T QUESTION THE GENIUS OF SEA-KING WRITER, JACK JACK. WE'RE TALKING ABOUT THE SAME GUY WHO REDEFINED THE MASSIVE AND BROUGHT NEW LIFE TO ULTRA-CHICK...
Hmmmmm...
...NOT TO MENTION HOW HE TEARS JERKS, LIKE THAT GUY WHO CRAPS OUT THE SAVAGE LIZARD, A NEW ASSHOLE EVERY WEEK IN HIS IRREVERENT COLUMN, 'ALLOW ME'... RIGHT HERE, IN THE CARL BARKS GUIDE. IF HE SAYS PEOPLE CAN TALK UNDERWATER AND HEAR ONE ANOTHER, THEN IT'S BIBLE-FUCKING-LAW, MAN!
NO. 6667 $2.50 CHEAP!
CARL BARKS
YOU'RE RIGHT, STEVE-DAVE. WHO THE FUCK AM I TO QUESTION WIZARD'S NUMBER FOUR FAVORITE WRITER FOR THREE YEARS RUNNING? I FEEL SO STUPID.
MORE DUCKS THAN YOU CAN SHAKE A FUCKIN' STICK AT
EVEN MORE SCROOGE McDUCK ACTION!!!
I THINK YOU OWE JACK JACK AN APOLOGY. AND IF YOU EVER HAVE THE TEMERITY TO QUESTION HIS SCRIPTING ABILITIES AGAIN, JUST ASK YOURSELF THIS QUESTION: WITHOUT JACK JACK, WHERE WOULD THE ATLANTEAN BE?
CARL BARKS GUIDE
IN THE HANDS OF A MORE TALENTED WRITER, I'D IMAGINE.

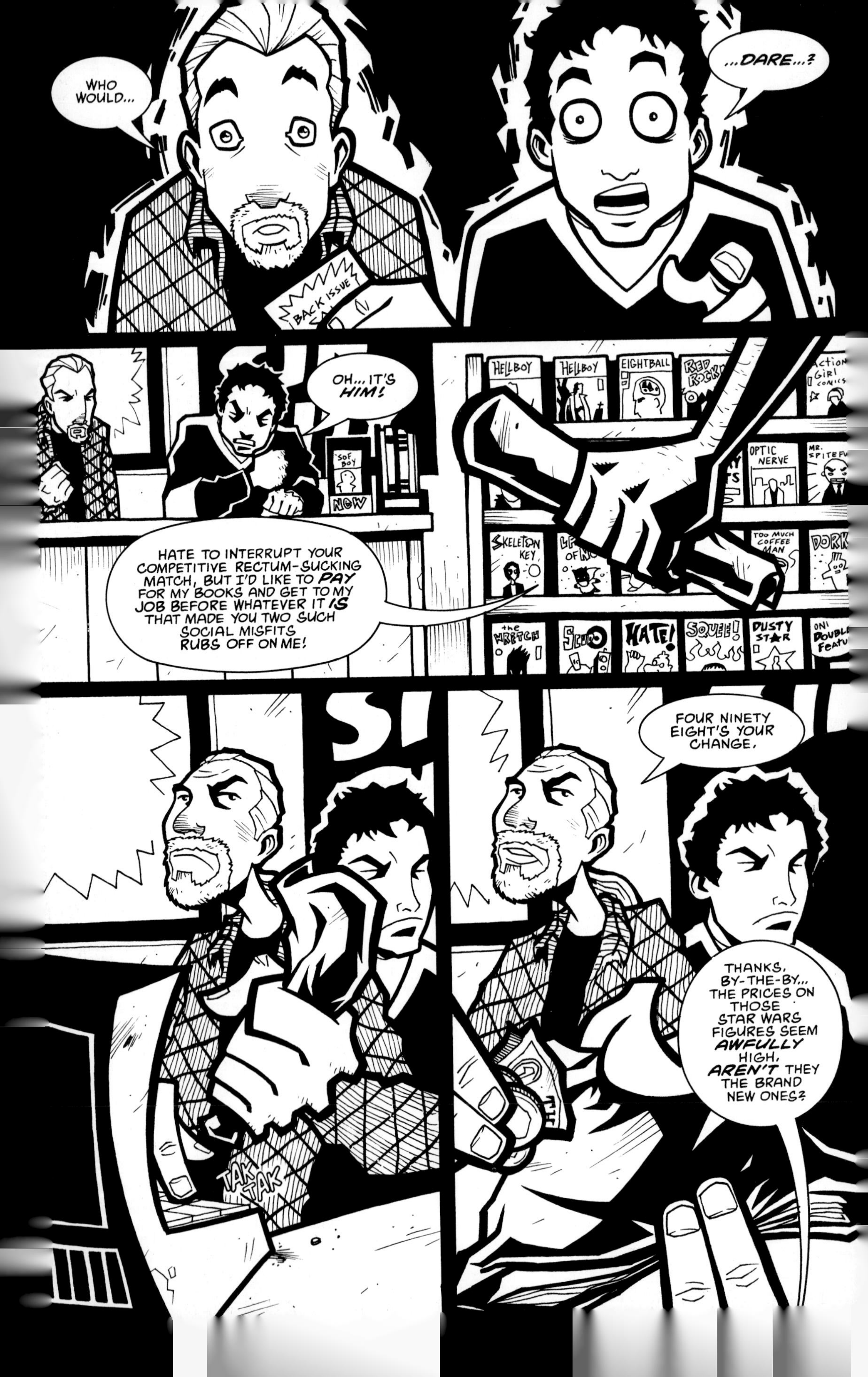
WHO WOULD...
...DARE...?
OH... IT'S HIM!
HATE TO INTERRUPT YOUR COMPETITIVE RECTUM-SUCKING MATCH, BUT I'D LIKE TO PAY FOR MY BOOKS AND GET TO MY JOB BEFORE WHATEVER IT IS THAT MADE YOU TWO SUCH SOCIAL MISFITS RUBS OFF ON ME!
HELLBOY
HELLBOY
EIGHTBALL
OPTIC NERVE
SKELETON KEY
TOO MUCH COFFEE MAN
the WRETCH
HATE!
SQUEE!
DUSTY STAR
NEW
TAK TAK
FOUR NINETY EIGHT'S YOUR CHANGE.
THANKS, BY-THE-BY... THE PRICES ON THOSE STAR WARS FIGURES SEEM AWFULLY HIGH, AREN'T THEY THE BRAND NEW ONES?

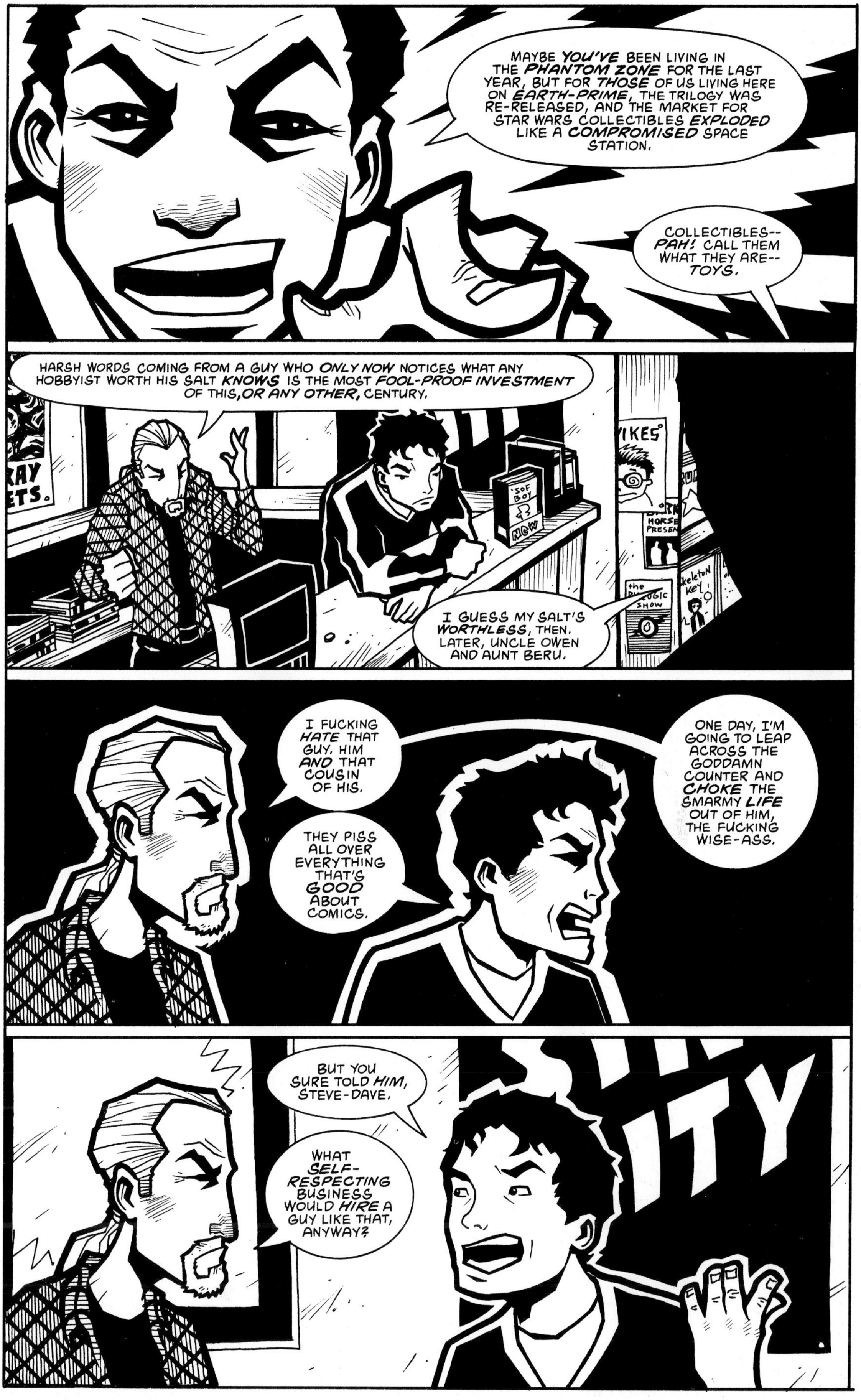
MAYBE YOU'VE BEEN LIVING IN THE PHANTOM ZONE FOR THE LAST YEAR, BUT FOR THOSE OF US LIVING HERE ON EARTH-PRIME, THE TRILOGY WAS RE-RELEASED, AND THE MARKET FOR STAR WARS COLLECTIBLES EXPLODED LIKE A COMPROMISED SPACE STATION.
COLLECTIBLES-- PAH! CALL THEM WHAT THEY ARE-- TOYS.
HARSH WORDS COMING FROM A GUY WHO ONLY NOW NOTICES WHAT ANY HOBBYIST WORTH HIS SALT KNOWS IS THE MOST FOOL-PROOF INVESTMENT OF THIS, OR ANY OTHER, CENTURY.
I GUESS MY SALT'S WORTHLESS, THEN. LATER, UNCLE OWEN AND AUNT BERU.
I FUCKING HATE THAT GUY. HIM AND THAT COUSIN OF HIS.
THEY PISS ALL OVER EVERYTHING THAT'S GOOD ABOUT COMICS.
ONE DAY, I'M GOING TO LEAP ACROSS THE GODDAMN COUNTER AND CHOKE THE SMARMY LIFE OUT OF HIM, THE FUCKING WISE-ASS.
BUT YOU SURE TOLD HIM, STEVE-DAVE.
WHAT SELF-RESPECTING BUSINESS WOULD HIRE A GUY LIKE THAT, ANYWAY?

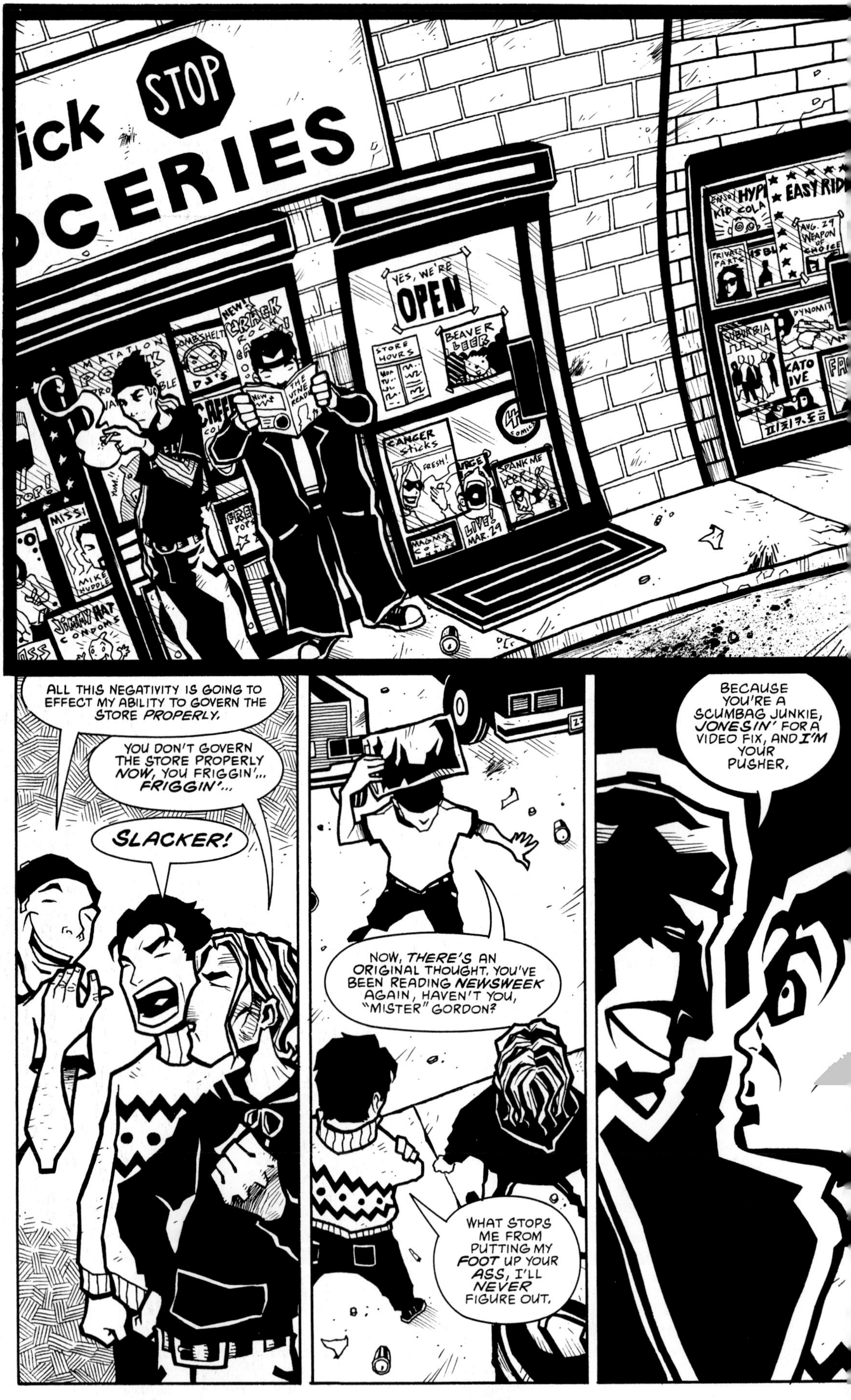

ALL THIS NEGATIVITY IS GOING TO EFFECT MY ABILITY TO GOVERN THE STORE PROPERLY.
YOU DON'T GOVERN THE STORE PROPERLY NOW, YOU FRIGGIN'... FRIGGIN'...
SLACKER!
NOW, THERE'S AN ORIGINAL THOUGHT. YOU'VE BEEN READING NEWSWEEK AGAIN, HAVEN'T YOU, "MISTER" GORDON?
WHAT STOPS ME FROM PUTTING MY FOOT UP YOUR ASS, I'LL NEVER FIGURE OUT.
BECAUSE YOU'RE A SCUMBAG JUNKIE, JONESIN' FOR A VIDEO FIX, AND I'M YOUR PUSHER.

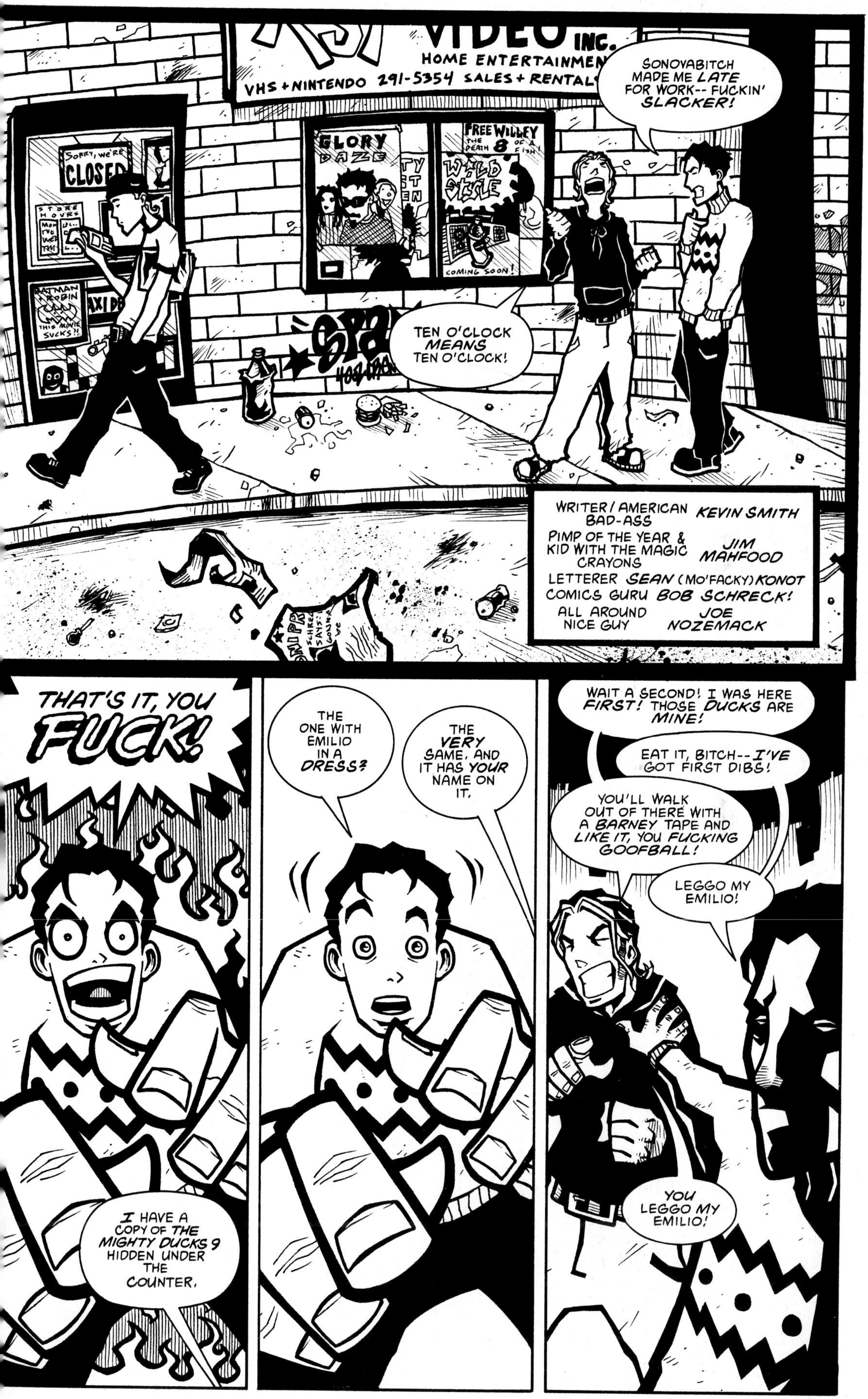
VIDEO INC.
HOME ENTERTAINMEN
VHS + NINTENDO 291-5354 SALES + RENTAL
SORRY, WE'RE CLOSED
GLORY DAZE
FREE WILLEY 8 THE DEATH OF A FISH!
WILD STYLE
COMING SOON!
BATMAN + ROBIN THIS MOVIE SUCKS!!
SONOVABITCH MADE ME *LATE* FOR WORK-- FUCKIN' *SLACKER!*
TEN O'CLOCK *MEANS* TEN O'CLOCK!
WRITER/AMERICAN BAD-ASS KEVIN SMITH
PIMP OF THE YEAR & KID WITH THE MAGIC CRAYONS JIM MAHFOOD
LETTERER SEAN (MO'FACKY) KONOT
COMICS GURU BOB SCHRECK!
ALL AROUND NICE GUY JOE NOZEMACK
THAT'S IT, YOU FUCK!
I HAVE A COPY OF *THE MIGHTY DUCKS 9* HIDDEN UNDER THE COUNTER.
THE ONE WITH EMILIO IN A *DRESS?*
THE *VERY* SAME, AND IT HAS *YOUR* NAME ON IT.
WAIT A SECOND! I WAS HERE *FIRST!* THOSE *DUCKS* ARE *MINE!*
EAT IT, BITCH-- *I'VE* GOT FIRST DIBS!
YOU'LL WALK OUT OF THERE WITH A *BARNEY* TAPE AND *LIKE IT*, YOU *FUCKING GOOFBALL!*
LEGGO MY EMILIO!
YOU LEGGO *MY* EMILIO!

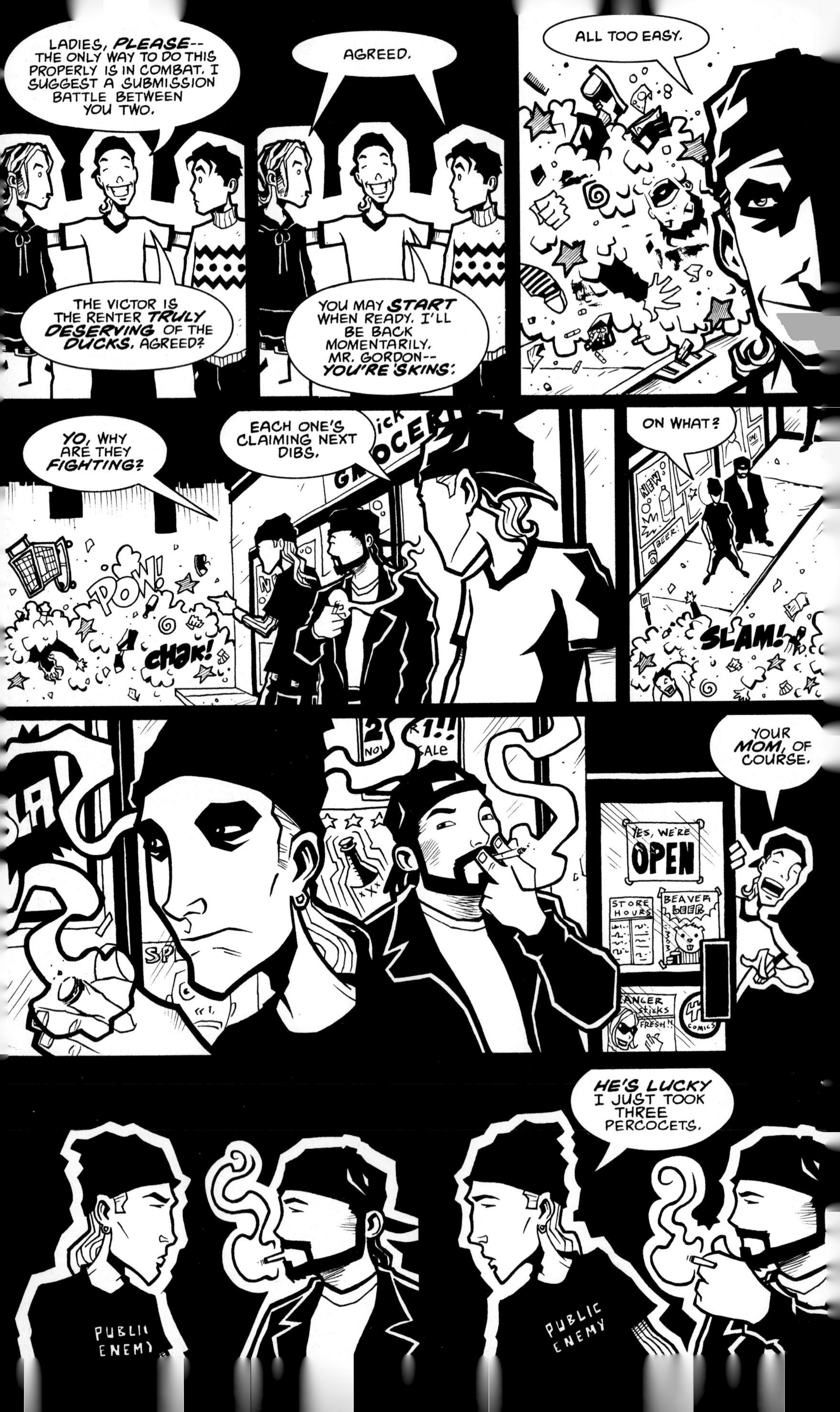
LADIES, PLEASE-- THE ONLY WAY TO DO THIS PROPERLY IS IN COMBAT. I SUGGEST A SUBMISSION BATTLE BETWEEN YOU TWO.
THE VICTOR IS THE RENTER TRULY DESERVING OF THE DUCKS. AGREED?
AGREED.
YOU MAY START WHEN READY. I'LL BE BACK MOMENTARILY. MR. GORDON-- YOU'RE 'SKINS'.
ALL TOO EASY.
YO, WHY ARE THEY FIGHTING?
EACH ONE'S CLAIMING NEXT DIBS.
POW!
CHAK!
ON WHAT?
SLAM!
YOUR MOM, OF COURSE.
YES, WE'RE OPEN
STORE HOURS
BEAVER BEER
HE'S LUCKY I JUST TOOK THREE PERCOCETS.
PUBLIC ENEMY
PUBLIC ENEMY

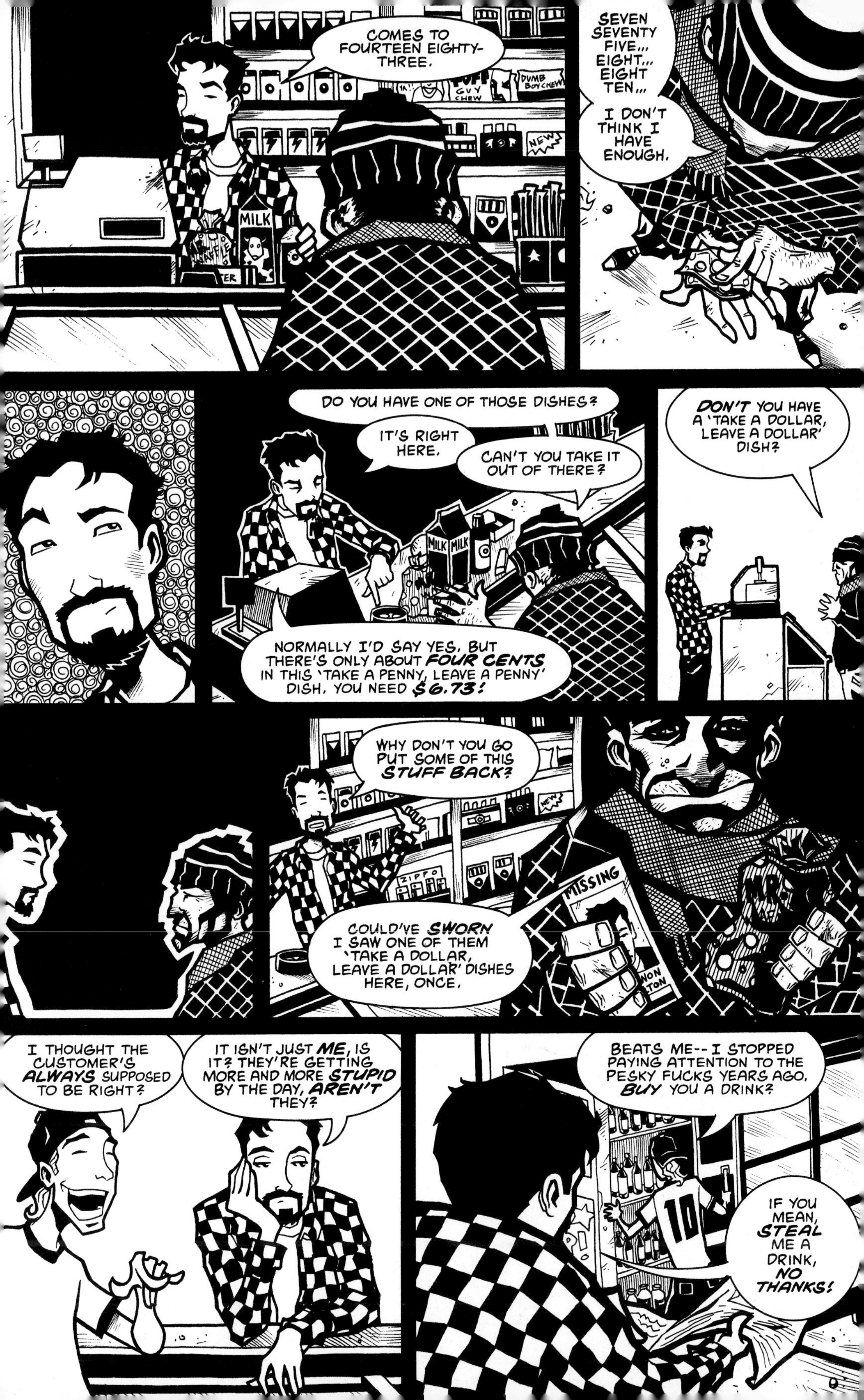
COMES TO FOURTEEN EIGHTY-THREE.
TUFF GUY CHEW
DUMB BOY CHEW
NEW
MILK
SEVEN SEVENTY FIVE... EIGHT... EIGHT TEN...
I DON'T THINK I HAVE ENOUGH.
DO YOU HAVE ONE OF THOSE DISHES?
IT'S RIGHT HERE.
CAN'T YOU TAKE IT OUT OF THERE?
MILK MILK
NORMALLY I'D SAY YES, BUT THERE'S ONLY ABOUT FOUR CENTS IN THIS 'TAKE A PENNY, LEAVE A PENNY' DISH. YOU NEED $6.73!
DON'T YOU HAVE A 'TAKE A DOLLAR, LEAVE A DOLLAR' DISH?
WHY DON'T YOU GO PUT SOME OF THIS STUFF BACK?
NEW
ZIPPO
MISSING
COULD'VE SWORN I SAW ONE OF THEM 'TAKE A DOLLAR, LEAVE A DOLLAR' DISHES HERE, ONCE.
I THOUGHT THE CUSTOMER'S ALWAYS SUPPOSED TO BE RIGHT?
IT ISN'T JUST ME, IS IT? THEY'RE GETTING MORE AND MORE STUPID BY THE DAY, AREN'T THEY?
BEATS ME-- I STOPPED PAYING ATTENTION TO THE PESKY FUCKS YEARS AGO. BUY YOU A DRINK?
IF YOU MEAN, STEAL ME A DRINK, NO THANKS!

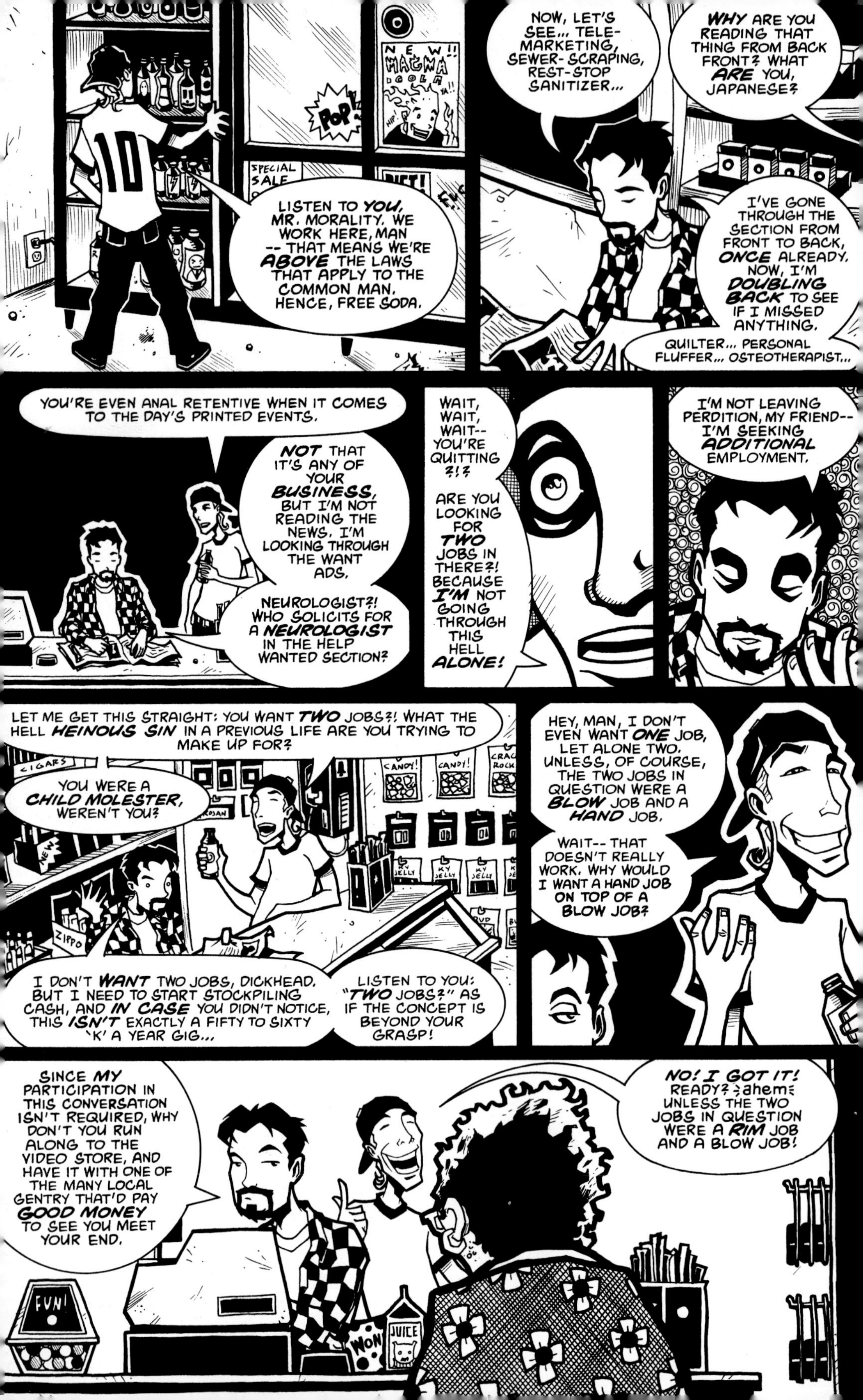
NEW!! MAGMA COLA
POP!
SPECIAL SALE
LISTEN TO YOU, MR. MORALITY. WE WORK HERE, MAN -- THAT MEANS WE'RE ABOVE THE LAWS THAT APPLY TO THE COMMON MAN. HENCE, FREE SODA.
NOW, LET'S SEE... TELE-MARKETING, SEWER-SCRAPING, REST-STOP SANITIZER...
WHY ARE YOU READING THAT THING FROM BACK FRONT? WHAT ARE YOU, JAPANESE?
I'VE GONE THROUGH THE SECTION FROM FRONT TO BACK, ONCE ALREADY. NOW, I'M DOUBLING BACK TO SEE IF I MISSED ANYTHING.
QUILTER... PERSONAL FLUFFER... OSTEOTHERAPIST...
YOU'RE EVEN ANAL RETENTIVE WHEN IT COMES TO THE DAY'S PRINTED EVENTS.
NOT THAT IT'S ANY OF YOUR BUSINESS, BUT I'M NOT READING THE NEWS. I'M LOOKING THROUGH THE WANT ADS.
NEUROLOGIST?! WHO SOLICITS FOR A NEUROLOGIST IN THE HELP WANTED SECTION?
WAIT, WAIT, WAIT-- YOU'RE QUITTING ?!?
ARE YOU LOOKING FOR TWO JOBS IN THERE?! BECAUSE I'M NOT GOING THROUGH THIS HELL ALONE!
I'M NOT LEAVING PERDITION, MY FRIEND-- I'M SEEKING ADDITIONAL EMPLOYMENT.
LET ME GET THIS STRAIGHT: YOU WANT TWO JOBS?! WHAT THE HELL HEINOUS SIN IN A PREVIOUS LIFE ARE YOU TRYING TO MAKE UP FOR?
YOU WERE A CHILD MOLESTER, WEREN'T YOU?
CIGARS
CANDY!
CANDY!
KY JELLY
ZIPPO
I DON'T WANT TWO JOBS, DICKHEAD. BUT I NEED TO START STOCKPILING CASH, AND IN CASE YOU DIDN'T NOTICE, THIS ISN'T EXACTLY A FIFTY TO SIXTY `K' A YEAR GIG...
LISTEN TO YOU: "TWO JOBS?" AS IF THE CONCEPT IS BEYOND YOUR GRASP!
HEY, MAN, I DON'T EVEN WANT ONE JOB, LET ALONE TWO. UNLESS, OF COURSE, THE TWO JOBS IN QUESTION WERE A BLOW JOB AND A HAND JOB.
WAIT-- THAT DOESN'T REALLY WORK. WHY WOULD I WANT A HAND JOB ON TOP OF A BLOW JOB?
SINCE MY PARTICIPATION IN THIS CONVERSATION ISN'T REQUIRED, WHY DON'T YOU RUN ALONG TO THE VIDEO STORE, AND HAVE IT WITH ONE OF THE MANY LOCAL GENTRY THAT'D PAY GOOD MONEY TO SEE YOU MEET YOUR END.
NO! I GOT IT! READY? ahem UNLESS THE TWO JOBS IN QUESTION WERE A RIM JOB AND A BLOW JOB!
FUN!
WON
JUICE

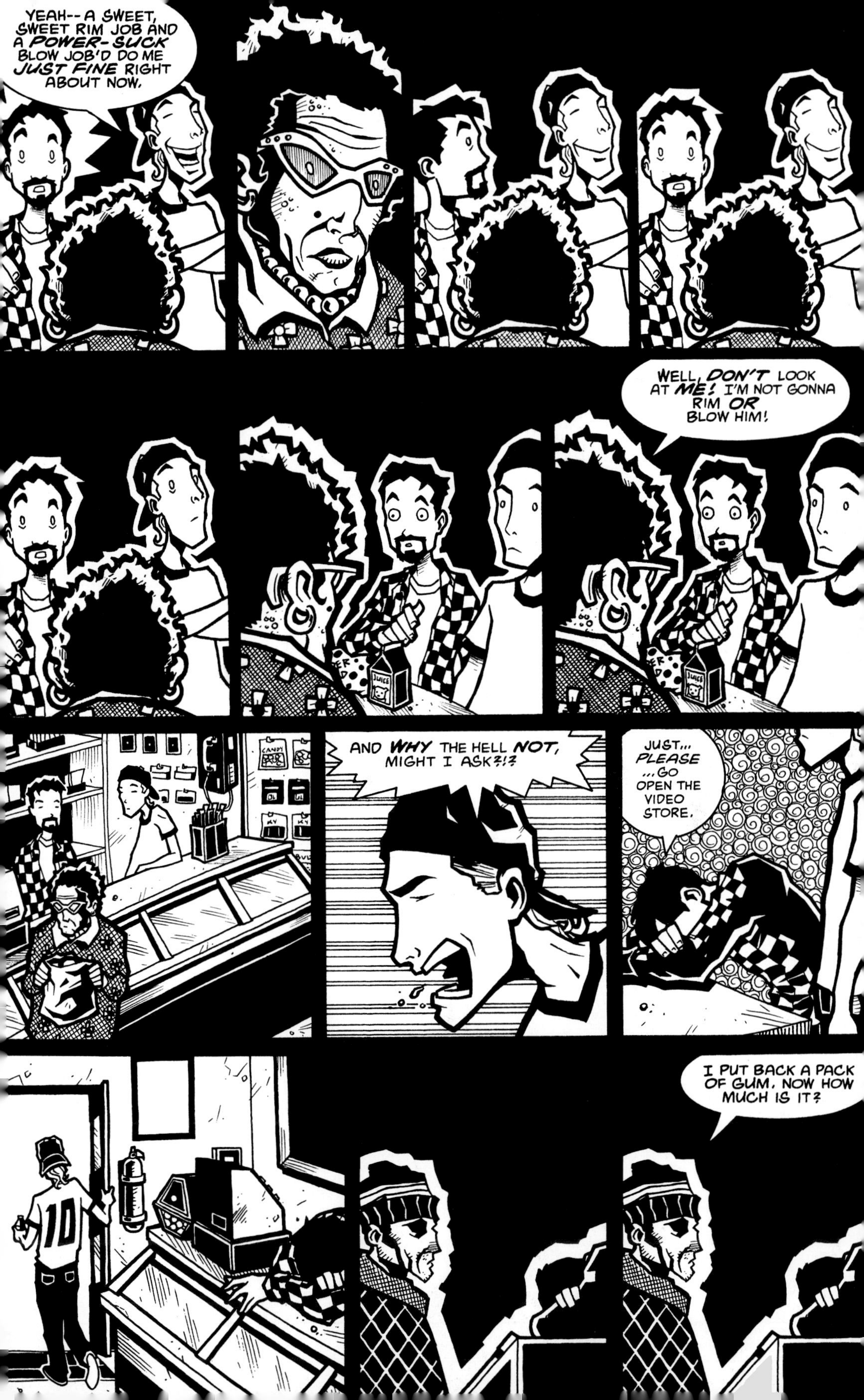
YEAH-- A SWEET, SWEET RIM JOB AND A POWER-SUCK BLOW JOB'D DO ME JUST FINE RIGHT ABOUT NOW.
WELL, DON'T LOOK AT ME! I'M NOT GONNA RIM OR BLOW HIM!
AND WHY THE HELL NOT, MIGHT I ASK?!?
JUST... PLEASE ...GO OPEN THE VIDEO STORE.
I PUT BACK A PACK OF GUM. NOW HOW MUCH IS IT?

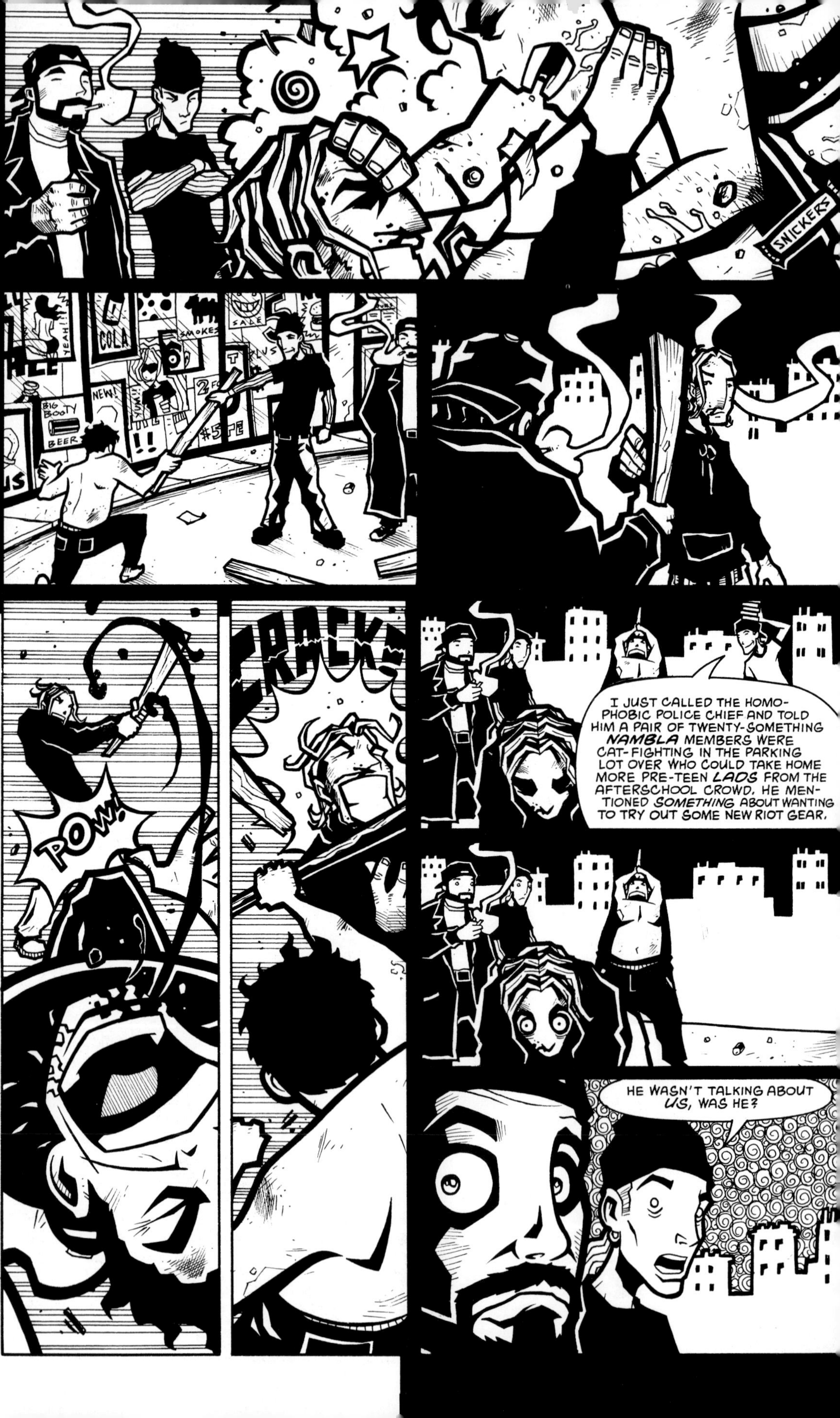
SNICKERS
COLA
SMOKES
SALE
BIG BOOTY BEER
NEW!
YEAH
POW!
CRACK!
I JUST CALLED THE HOMO-PHOBIC POLICE CHIEF AND TOLD HIM A PAIR OF TWENTY-SOMETHING NAMBLA MEMBERS WERE CAT-FIGHTING IN THE PARKING LOT OVER WHO COULD TAKE HOME MORE PRE-TEEN LADS FROM THE AFTERSCHOOL CROWD. HE MENTIONED SOMETHING ABOUT WANTING TO TRY OUT SOME NEW RIOT GEAR.
HE WASN'T TALKING ABOUT US, WAS HE?

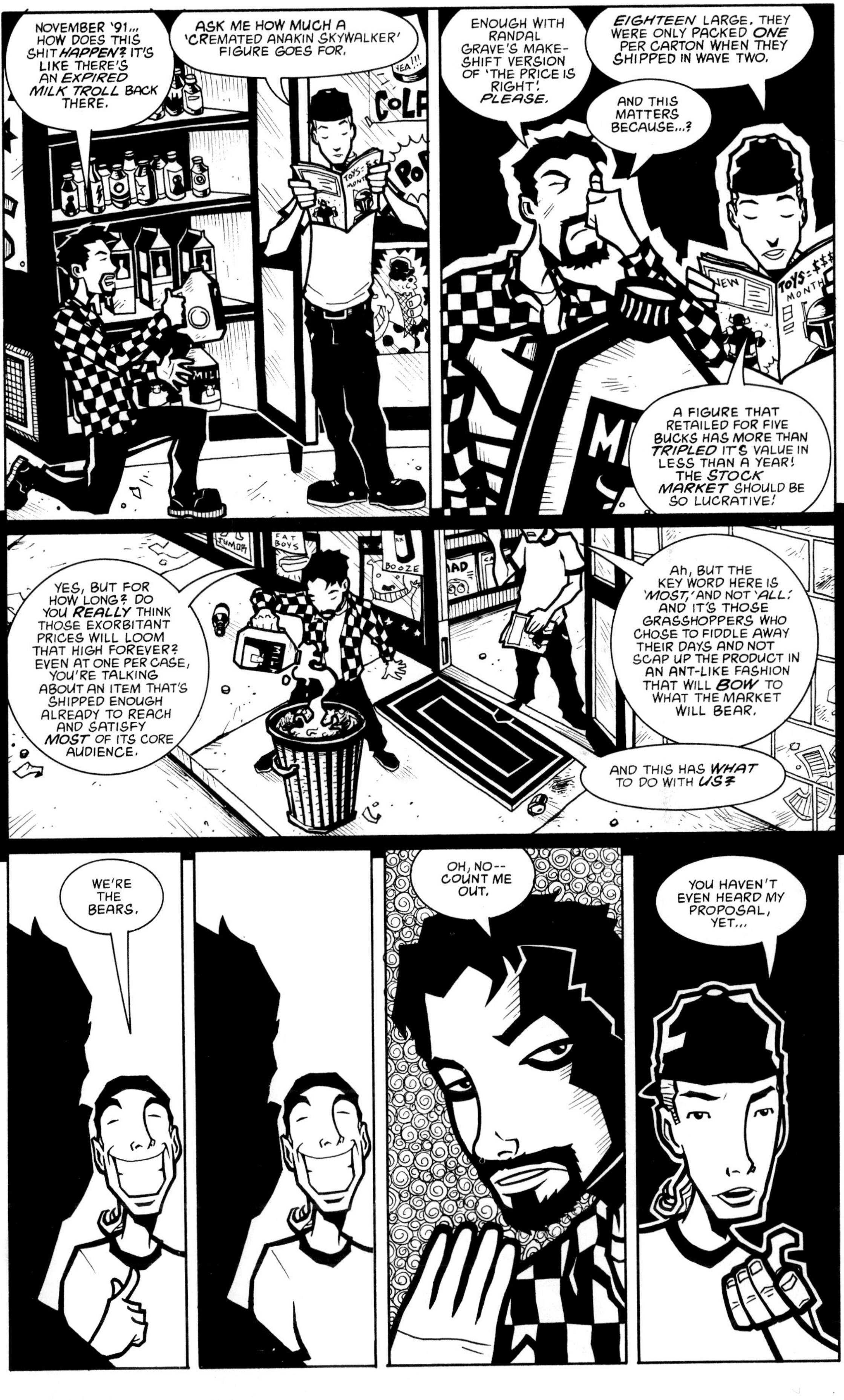
NOVEMBER '91... HOW DOES THIS SHIT HAPPEN? IT'S LIKE THERE'S AN EXPIRED MILK TROLL BACK THERE.
ASK ME HOW MUCH A 'CREMATED ANAKIN SKYWALKER' FIGURE GOES FOR.
ENOUGH WITH RANDAL GRAVE'S MAKE-SHIFT VERSION OF 'THE PRICE IS RIGHT.' PLEASE.
EIGHTEEN LARGE. THEY WERE ONLY PACKED ONE PER CARTON WHEN THEY SHIPPED IN WAVE TWO.
AND THIS MATTERS BECAUSE...?
A FIGURE THAT RETAILED FOR FIVE BUCKS HAS MORE THAN TRIPLED IT'S VALUE IN LESS THAN A YEAR! THE STOCK MARKET SHOULD BE SO LUCRATIVE!
YES, BUT FOR HOW LONG? DO YOU REALLY THINK THOSE EXORBITANT PRICES WILL LOOM THAT HIGH FOREVER? EVEN AT ONE PER CASE, YOU'RE TALKING ABOUT AN ITEM THAT'S SHIPPED ENOUGH ALREADY TO REACH AND SATISFY MOST OF ITS CORE AUDIENCE.
Ah, BUT THE KEY WORD HERE IS 'MOST,' AND NOT 'ALL.' AND IT'S THOSE GRASSHOPPERS WHO CHOSE TO FIDDLE AWAY THEIR DAYS AND NOT SCAP UP THE PRODUCT IN AN ANT-LIKE FASHION THAT WILL BOW TO WHAT THE MARKET WILL BEAR.
AND THIS HAS WHAT TO DO WITH US?
WE'RE THE BEARS.
OH, NO-- COUNT ME OUT.
YOU HAVEN'T EVEN HEARD MY PROPOSAL, YET...

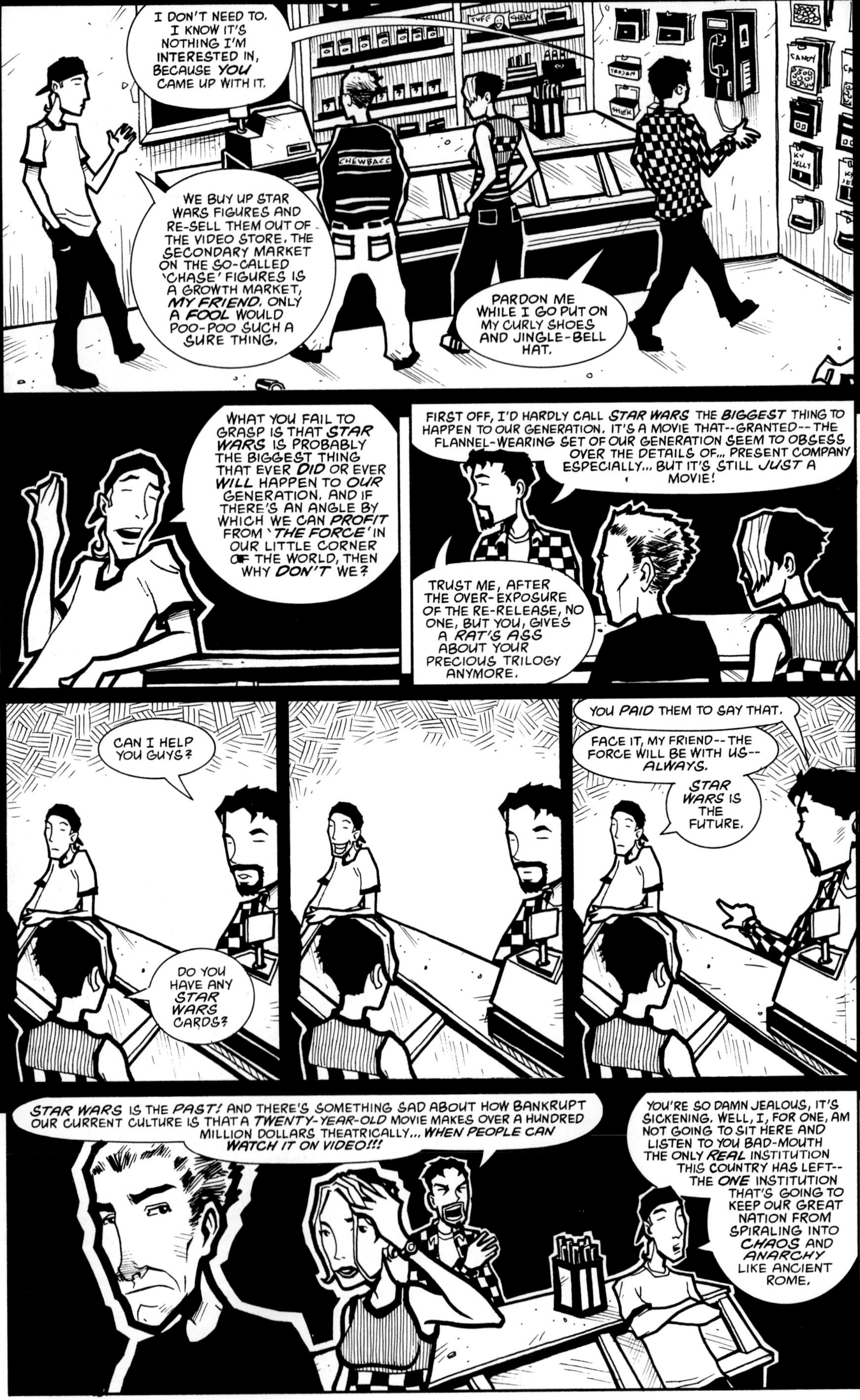

I DON'T NEED TO. I KNOW IT'S NOTHING I'M INTERESTED IN, BECAUSE YOU CAME UP WITH IT.
TUFF CHEW
WE BUY UP STAR WARS FIGURES AND RE-SELL THEM OUT OF THE VIDEO STORE. THE SECONDARY MARKET ON THE SO-CALLED 'CHASE' FIGURES IS A GROWTH MARKET, MY FRIEND. ONLY A FOOL WOULD POO-POO SUCH A SURE THING.
PARDON ME WHILE I GO PUT ON MY CURLY SHOES AND JINGLE-BELL HAT.
WHAT YOU FAIL TO GRASP IS THAT STAR WARS IS PROBABLY THE BIGGEST THING THAT EVER DID OR EVER WILL HAPPEN TO OUR GENERATION. AND IF THERE'S AN ANGLE BY WHICH WE CAN PROFIT FROM 'THE FORCE' IN OUR LITTLE CORNER OF THE WORLD, THEN WHY DON'T WE?
FIRST OFF, I'D HARDLY CALL STAR WARS THE BIGGEST THING TO HAPPEN TO OUR GENERATION. IT'S A MOVIE THAT--GRANTED--THE FLANNEL-WEARING SET OF OUR GENERATION SEEM TO OBSESS OVER THE DETAILS OF... PRESENT COMPANY ESPECIALLY... BUT IT'S STILL JUST A MOVIE!
TRUST ME, AFTER THE OVER-EXPOSURE OF THE RE-RELEASE, NO ONE, BUT YOU, GIVES A RAT'S ASS ABOUT YOUR PRECIOUS TRILOGY ANYMORE.
CAN I HELP YOU GUYS?
DO YOU HAVE ANY STAR WARS CARDS?
YOU PAID THEM TO SAY THAT.
FACE IT, MY FRIEND--THE FORCE WILL BE WITH US--ALWAYS.
STAR WARS IS THE FUTURE.
STAR WARS IS THE PAST! AND THERE'S SOMETHING SAD ABOUT HOW BANKRUPT OUR CURRENT CULTURE IS THAT A TWENTY-YEAR-OLD MOVIE MAKES OVER A HUNDRED MILLION DOLLARS THEATRICALLY... WHEN PEOPLE CAN WATCH IT ON VIDEO!!!
YOU'RE SO DAMN JEALOUS, IT'S SICKENING. WELL, I, FOR ONE, AM NOT GOING TO SIT HERE AND LISTEN TO YOU BAD-MOUTH THE ONLY REAL INSTITUTION THIS COUNTRY HAS LEFT--THE ONE INSTITUTION THAT'S GOING TO KEEP OUR GREAT NATION FROM SPIRALING INTO CHAOS AND ANARCHY LIKE ANCIENT ROME.

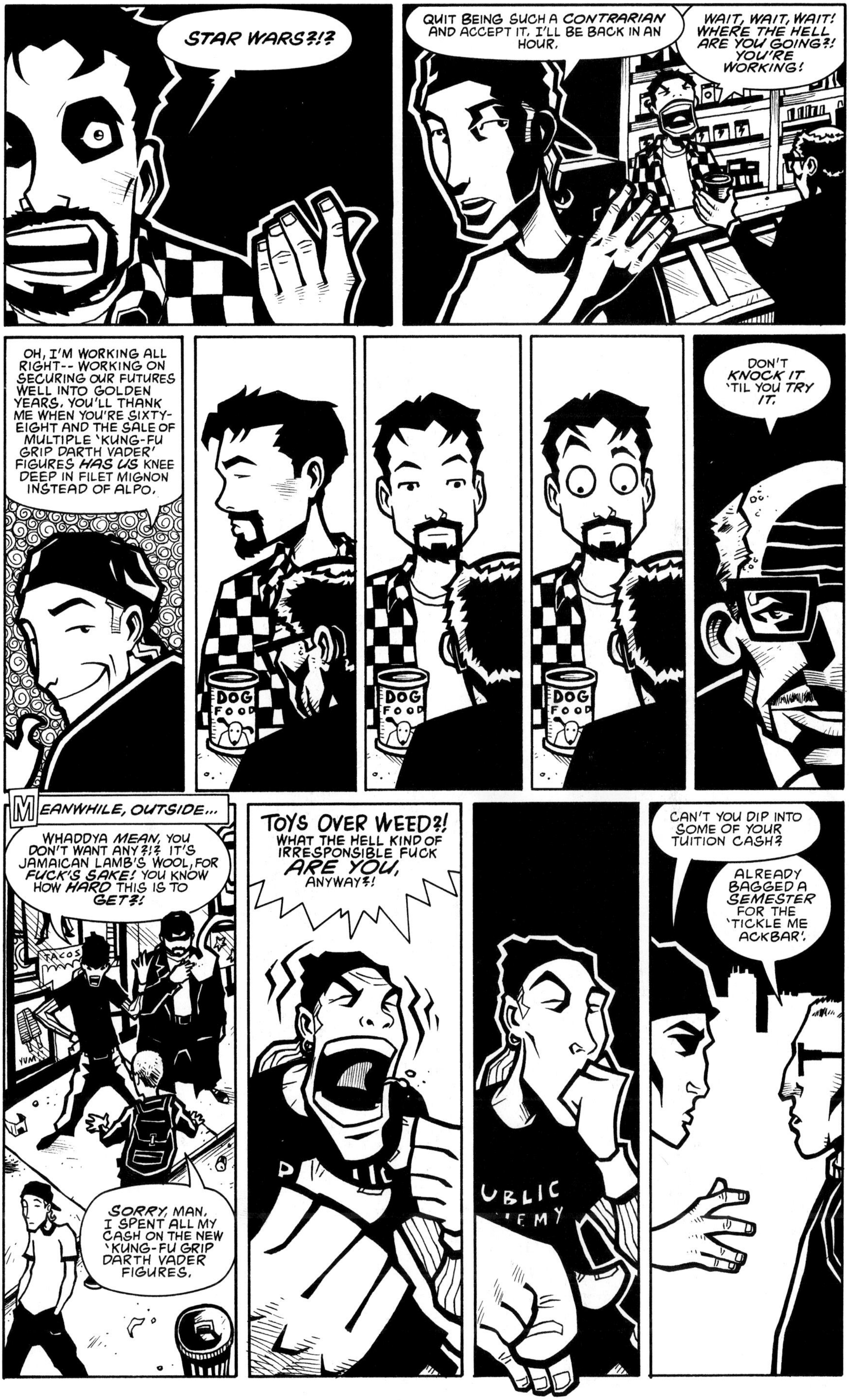

STAR WARS?!?
QUIT BEING SUCH A CONTRARIAN AND ACCEPT IT. I'LL BE BACK IN AN HOUR.
WAIT, WAIT, WAIT! WHERE THE HELL ARE YOU GOING?! YOU'RE WORKING!
OH, I'M WORKING ALL RIGHT-- WORKING ON SECURING OUR FUTURES WELL INTO GOLDEN YEARS. YOU'LL THANK ME WHEN YOU'RE SIXTY-EIGHT AND THE SALE OF MULTIPLE 'KUNG-FU GRIP DARTH VADER' FIGURES HAS US KNEE DEEP IN FILET MIGNON INSTEAD OF ALPO.
DOG FOOD
DON'T KNOCK IT 'TIL YOU TRY IT.
MEANWHILE, OUTSIDE...
WHADDYA MEAN, YOU DON'T WANT ANY?!? IT'S JAMAICAN LAMB'S WOOL, FOR FUCK'S SAKE! YOU KNOW HOW HARD THIS IS TO GET?!
TACOS
YUM
SORRY, MAN. I SPENT ALL MY CASH ON THE NEW 'KUNG-FU GRIP DARTH VADER FIGURES.
TOYS OVER WEED?! WHAT THE HELL KIND OF IRRESPONSIBLE FUCK ARE YOU, ANYWAY?!
UBLIC
CAN'T YOU DIP INTO SOME OF YOUR TUITION CASH?
ALREADY BAGGED A SEMESTER FOR THE 'TICKLE ME ACKBAR'.

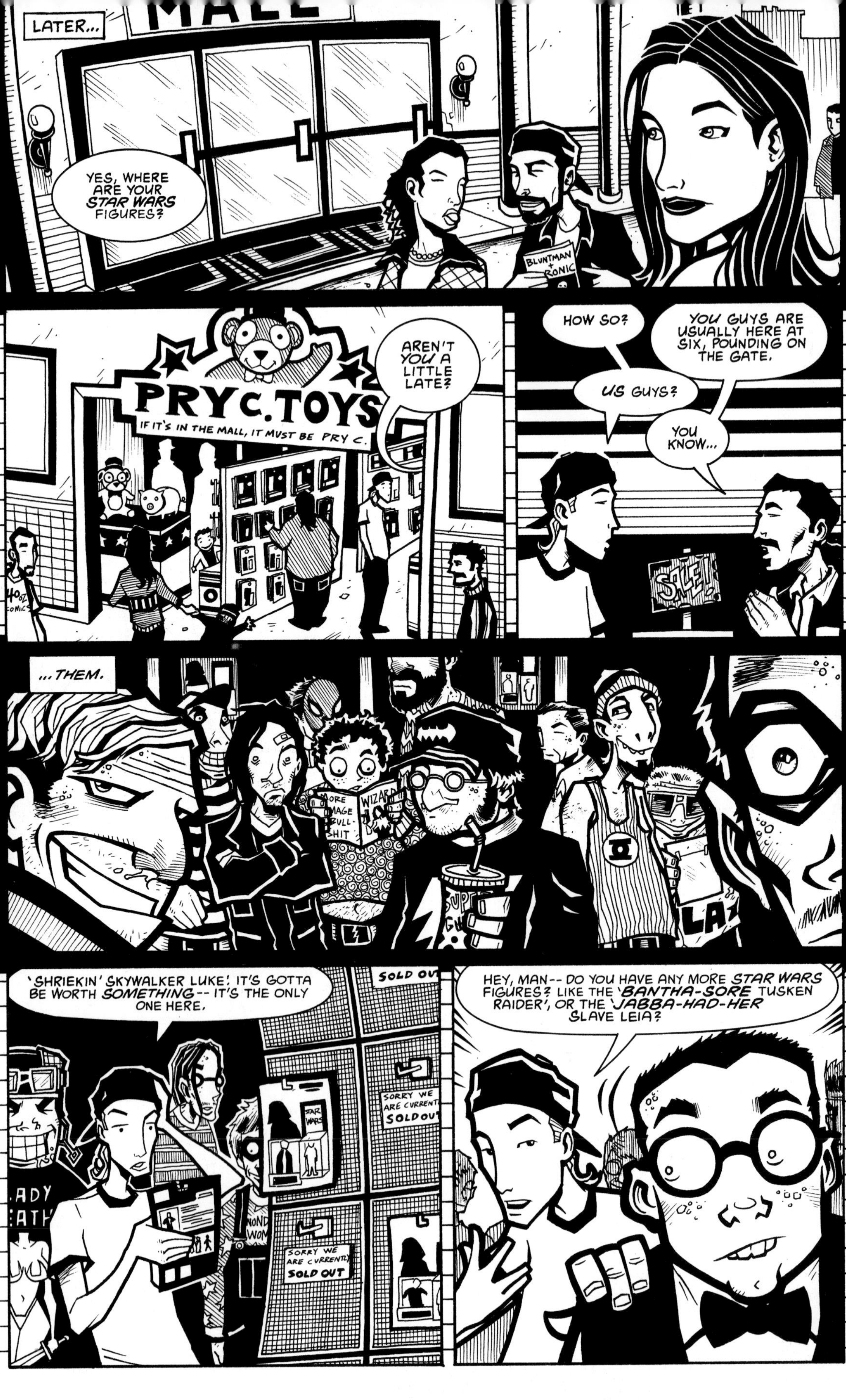
MALL
LATER...
YES, WHERE ARE YOUR *STAR WARS* FIGURES?
BLUNTMAN + CHRONIC
PRY C. TOYS
IF IT'S IN THE MALL, IT MUST BE PRY C.
AREN'T *YOU* A LITTLE LATE?
HOW SO?
YOU GUYS ARE USUALLY HERE AT SIX, POUNDING ON THE GATE.
US GUYS?
YOU KNOW...
SALE!
...THEM.
MORE IMAGE BULL-SHIT
WIZARD
'SHRIEKIN' SKYWALKER LUKE! IT'S GOTTA BE WORTH *SOMETHING* -- IT'S THE ONLY ONE HERE.
SORRY WE ARE CURRENTLY SOLD OUT
HEY, MAN-- DO YOU HAVE ANY MORE *STAR WARS* FIGURES? LIKE THE '*BANTHA-SORE* TUSKEN RAIDER', OR THE '*JABBA-HAD-HER* SLAVE LEIA'?

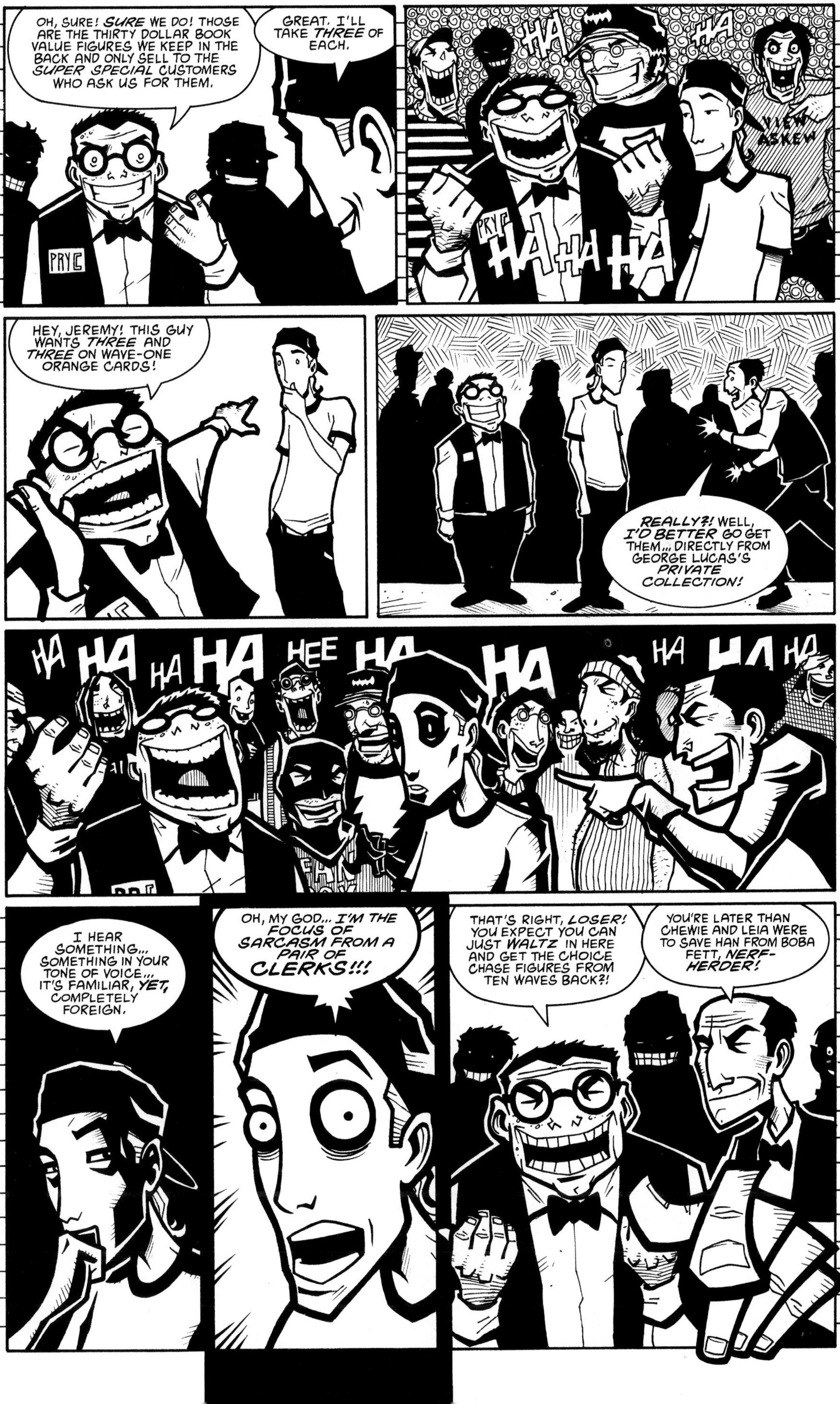
OH, SURE! SURE WE DO! THOSE ARE THE THIRTY DOLLAR BOOK VALUE FIGURES WE KEEP IN THE BACK AND ONLY SELL TO THE SUPER SPECIAL CUSTOMERS WHO ASK US FOR THEM.
GREAT. I'LL TAKE THREE OF EACH.
PRYC
HA
HA
VIEW ASKEW
PRYC
HA HA HA HA
HEY, JEREMY! THIS GUY WANTS THREE AND THREE ON WAVE-ONE ORANGE CARDS!
REALLY?! WELL, I'D BETTER GO GET THEM... DIRECTLY FROM GEORGE LUCAS'S PRIVATE COLLECTION!
HA HA HA HA HEE HA HA HA HA HA
I HEAR SOMETHING... SOMETHING IN YOUR TONE OF VOICE... IT'S FAMILIAR, YET, COMPLETELY FOREIGN.
OH, MY GOD... I'M THE FOCUS OF SARCASM FROM A PAIR OF CLERKS!!!
THAT'S RIGHT, LOSER! YOU EXPECT YOU CAN JUST WALTZ IN HERE AND GET THE CHOICE CHASE FIGURES FROM TEN WAVES BACK?!
YOU'RE LATER THAN CHEWIE AND LEIA WERE TO SAVE HAN FROM BOBA FETT, NERF-HERDER!

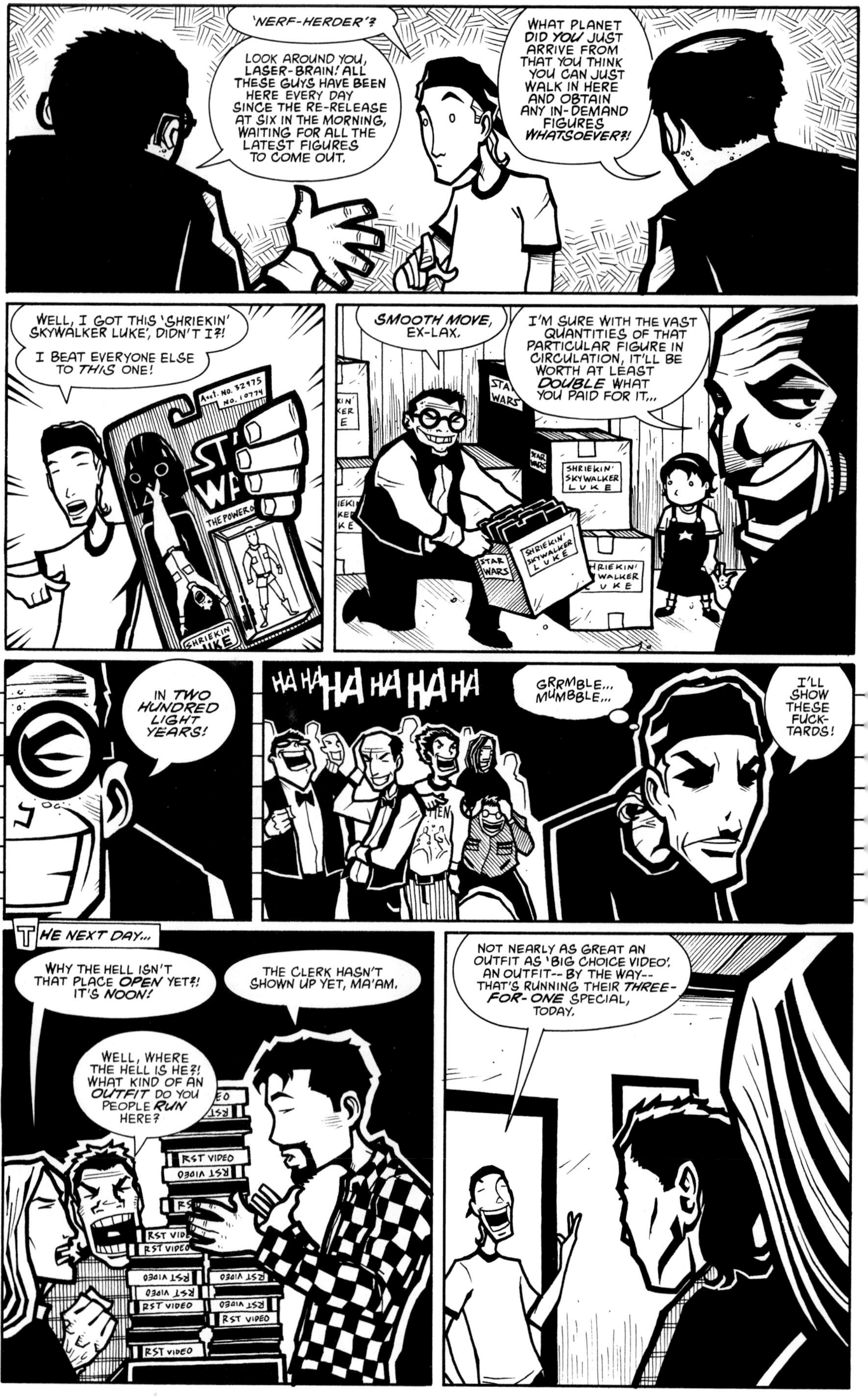
'NERF-HERDER'?
LOOK AROUND YOU, LASER-BRAIN! ALL THESE GUYS HAVE BEEN HERE EVERY DAY SINCE THE RE-RELEASE AT SIX IN THE MORNING, WAITING FOR ALL THE LATEST FIGURES TO COME OUT.
WHAT PLANET DID YOU JUST ARRIVE FROM THAT YOU THINK YOU CAN JUST WALK IN HERE AND OBTAIN ANY IN-DEMAND FIGURES WHATSOEVER?!
WELL, I GOT THIS 'SHRIEKIN' SKYWALKER LUKE', DIDN'T I?!
I BEAT EVERYONE ELSE TO THIS ONE!
Acct. No. 32975
No. 10774
STAR WARS
THE POWER O
SHRIEKIN LUKE
SMOOTH MOVE, EX-LAX.
I'M SURE WITH THE VAST QUANTITIES OF THAT PARTICULAR FIGURE IN CIRCULATION, IT'LL BE WORTH AT LEAST DOUBLE WHAT YOU PAID FOR IT...
STAR WARS
SHRIEKIN' SKYWALKER LUKE
IN TWO HUNDRED LIGHT YEARS!
HA HA HA HA HA HA
GRRMBLE... MUMBBLE...
I'LL SHOW THESE FUCK-TARDS!
THE NEXT DAY...
WHY THE HELL ISN'T THAT PLACE OPEN YET?! IT'S NOON!
THE CLERK HASN'T SHOWN UP YET, MA'AM.
WELL, WHERE THE HELL IS HE?! WHAT KIND OF AN OUTFIT DO YOU PEOPLE RUN HERE?
RST VIDEO
NOT NEARLY AS GREAT AN OUTFIT AS 'BIG CHOICE VIDEO'. AN OUTFIT-- BY THE WAY-- THAT'S RUNNING THEIR THREE-FOR-ONE SPECIAL, TODAY.

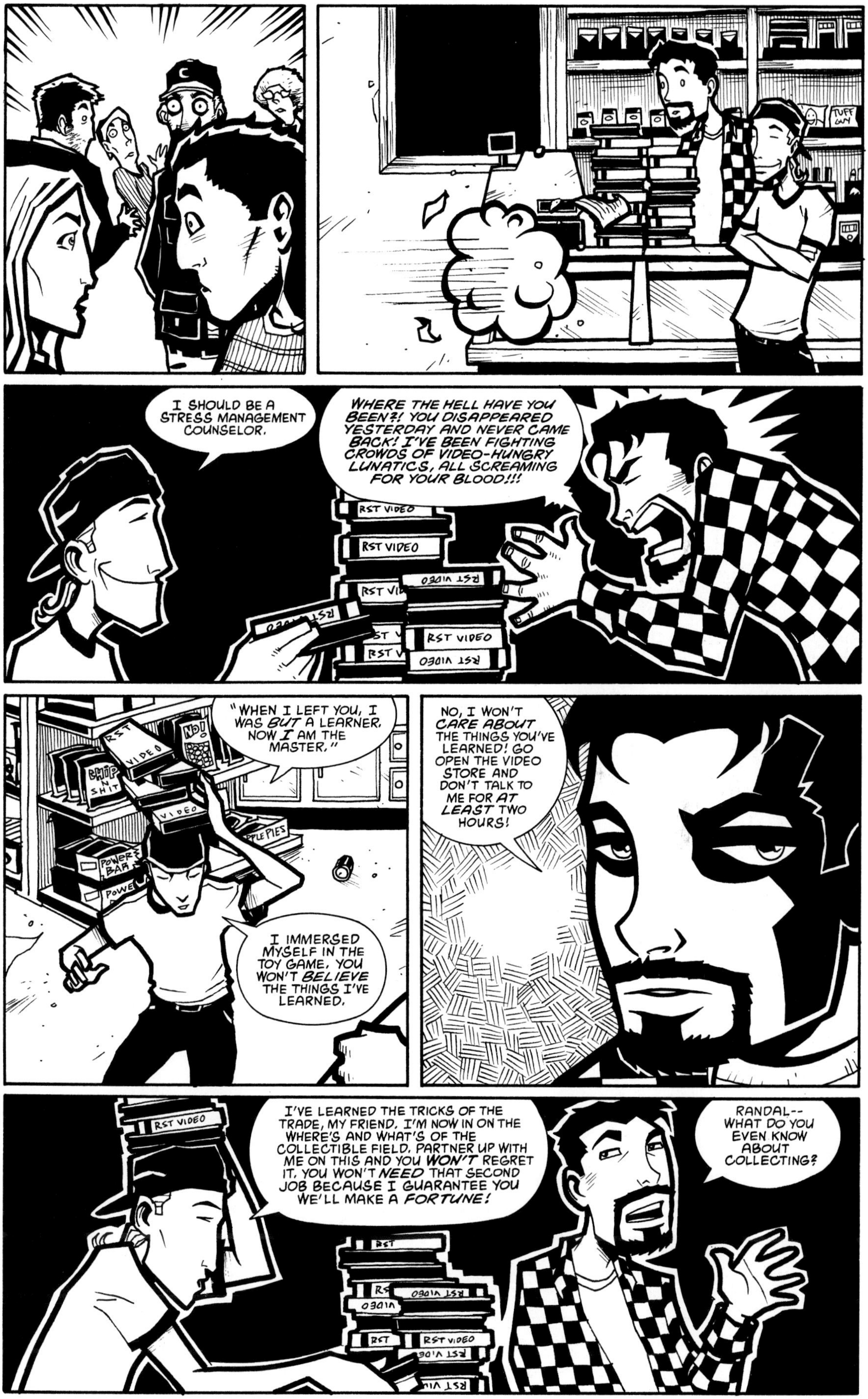
TUFF GUY
I SHOULD BE A STRESS MANAGEMENT COUNSELOR.
WHERE THE HELL HAVE YOU BEEN?! YOU DISAPPEARED YESTERDAY AND NEVER CAME BACK! I'VE BEEN FIGHTING CROWDS OF VIDEO-HUNGRY LUNATICS, ALL SCREAMING FOR YOUR BLOOD!!!
RST VIDEO
"WHEN I LEFT YOU, I WAS BUT A LEARNER. NOW I AM THE MASTER."
I IMMERSED MYSELF IN THE TOY GAME. YOU WON'T BELIEVE THE THINGS I'VE LEARNED.
NO, I WON'T CARE ABOUT THE THINGS YOU'VE LEARNED! GO OPEN THE VIDEO STORE AND DON'T TALK TO ME FOR AT LEAST TWO HOURS!
I'VE LEARNED THE TRICKS OF THE TRADE, MY FRIEND. I'M NOW IN ON THE WHERE'S AND WHAT'S OF THE COLLECTIBLE FIELD. PARTNER UP WITH ME ON THIS AND YOU WON'T REGRET IT. YOU WON'T NEED THAT SECOND JOB BECAUSE I GUARANTEE YOU WE'LL MAKE A FORTUNE!
RANDAL-- WHAT DO YOU EVEN KNOW ABOUT COLLECTING?

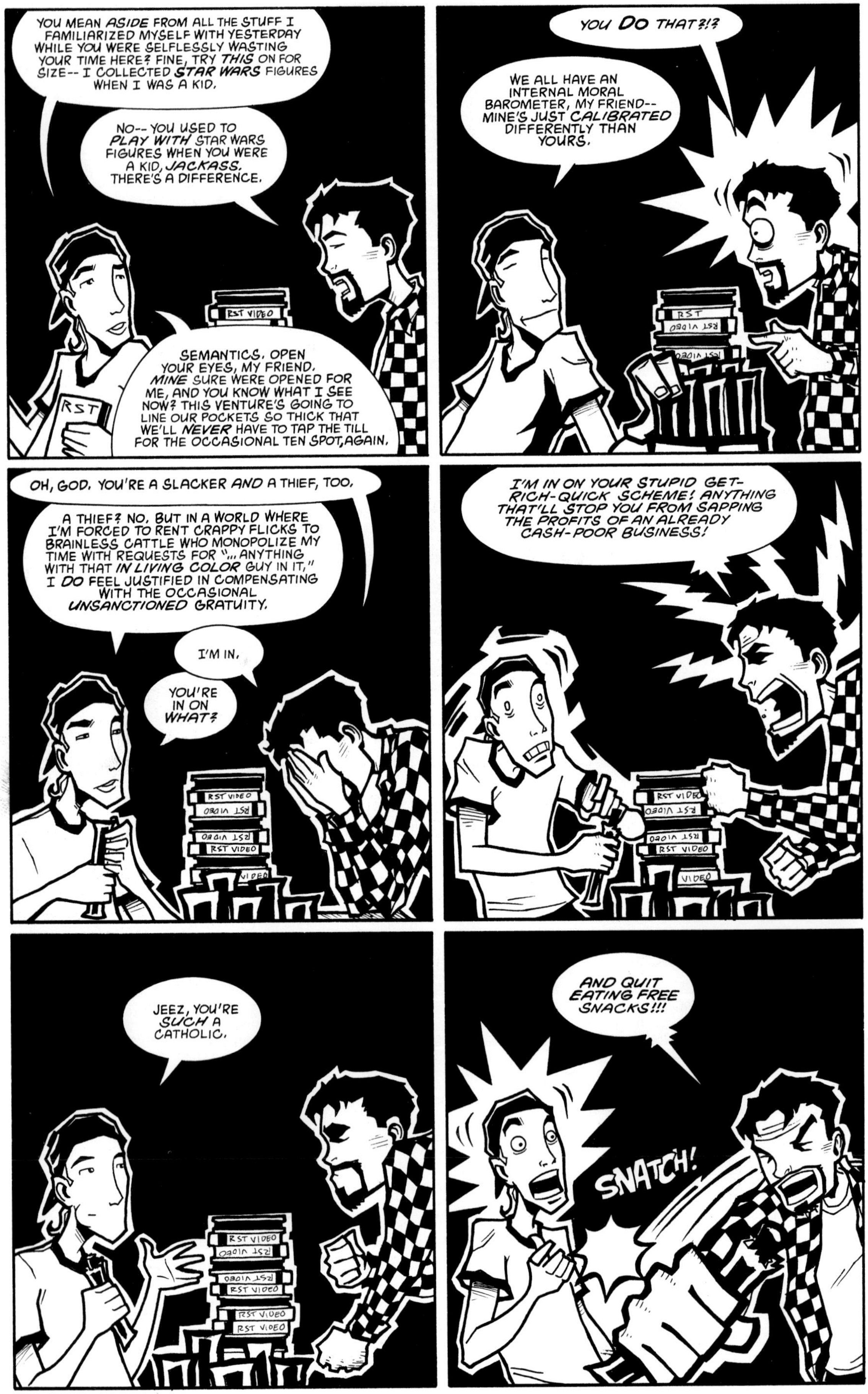
YOU MEAN ASIDE FROM ALL THE STUFF I FAMILIARIZED MYSELF WITH YESTERDAY WHILE YOU WERE SELFLESSLY WASTING YOUR TIME HERE? FINE. TRY THIS ON FOR SIZE-- I COLLECTED STAR WARS FIGURES WHEN I WAS A KID.
NO-- YOU USED TO PLAY WITH STAR WARS FIGURES WHEN YOU WERE A KID, JACKASS. THERE'S A DIFFERENCE.
RST VIDEO
RST
SEMANTICS. OPEN YOUR EYES, MY FRIEND. MINE SURE WERE OPENED FOR ME, AND YOU KNOW WHAT I SEE NOW? THIS VENTURE'S GOING TO LINE OUR POCKETS SO THICK THAT WE'LL NEVER HAVE TO TAP THE TILL FOR THE OCCASIONAL TEN SPOT, AGAIN.
YOU DO THAT?!?
WE ALL HAVE AN INTERNAL MORAL BAROMETER, MY FRIEND-- MINE'S JUST CALIBRATED DIFFERENTLY THAN YOURS.
OH, GOD. YOU'RE A SLACKER AND A THIEF, TOO.
A THIEF? NO. BUT IN A WORLD WHERE I'M FORCED TO RENT CRAPPY FLICKS TO BRAINLESS CATTLE WHO MONOPOLIZE MY TIME WITH REQUESTS FOR "...ANYTHING WITH THAT IN LIVING COLOR GUY IN IT," I DO FEEL JUSTIFIED IN COMPENSATING WITH THE OCCASIONAL UNSANCTIONED GRATUITY.
I'M IN.
YOU'RE IN ON WHAT?
I'M IN ON YOUR STUPID GET-RICH-QUICK SCHEME! ANYTHING THAT'LL STOP YOU FROM SAPPING THE PROFITS OF AN ALREADY CASH-POOR BUSINESS!
JEEZ, YOU'RE SUCH A CATHOLIC.
AND QUIT EATING FREE SNACKS!!!
SNATCH!

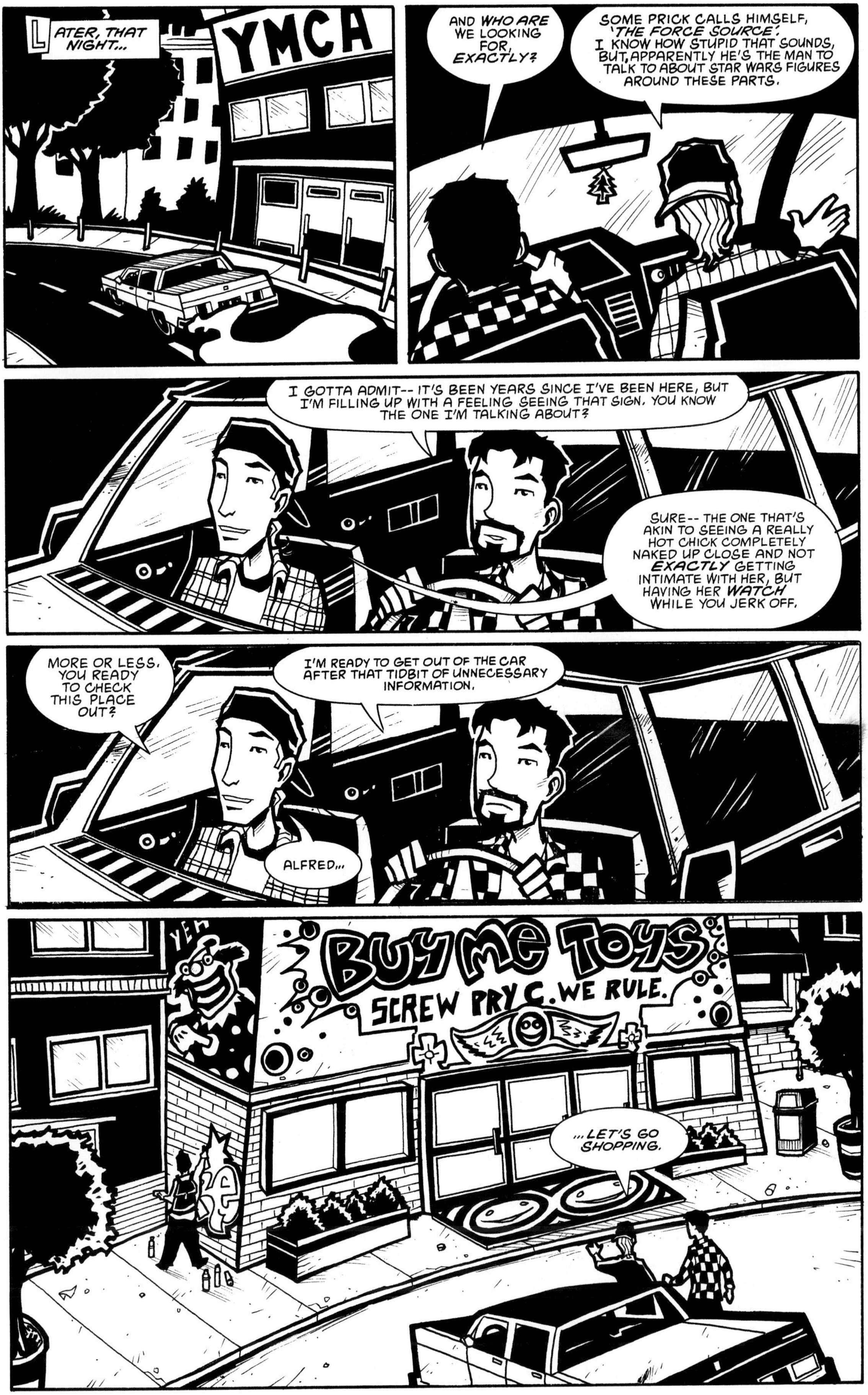
LATER, THAT NIGHT...
AND WHO ARE WE LOOKING FOR, EXACTLY?
SOME PRICK CALLS HIMSELF, 'THE FORCE SOURCE'. I KNOW HOW STUPID THAT SOUNDS, BUT, APPARENTLY HE'S THE MAN TO TALK TO ABOUT STAR WARS FIGURES AROUND THESE PARTS.
YMCA
I GOTTA ADMIT-- IT'S BEEN YEARS SINCE I'VE BEEN HERE, BUT I'M FILLING UP WITH A FEELING SEEING THAT SIGN. YOU KNOW THE ONE I'M TALKING ABOUT?
SURE-- THE ONE THAT'S AKIN TO SEEING A REALLY HOT CHICK COMPLETELY NAKED UP CLOSE AND NOT EXACTLY GETTING INTIMATE WITH HER, BUT HAVING HER WATCH WHILE YOU JERK OFF.
MORE OR LESS. YOU READY TO CHECK THIS PLACE OUT?
I'M READY TO GET OUT OF THE CAR AFTER THAT TIDBIT OF UNNECESSARY INFORMATION.
ALFRED...
BUY ME TOYS
SCREW PRY C. WE RULE.
...LET'S GO SHOPPING.

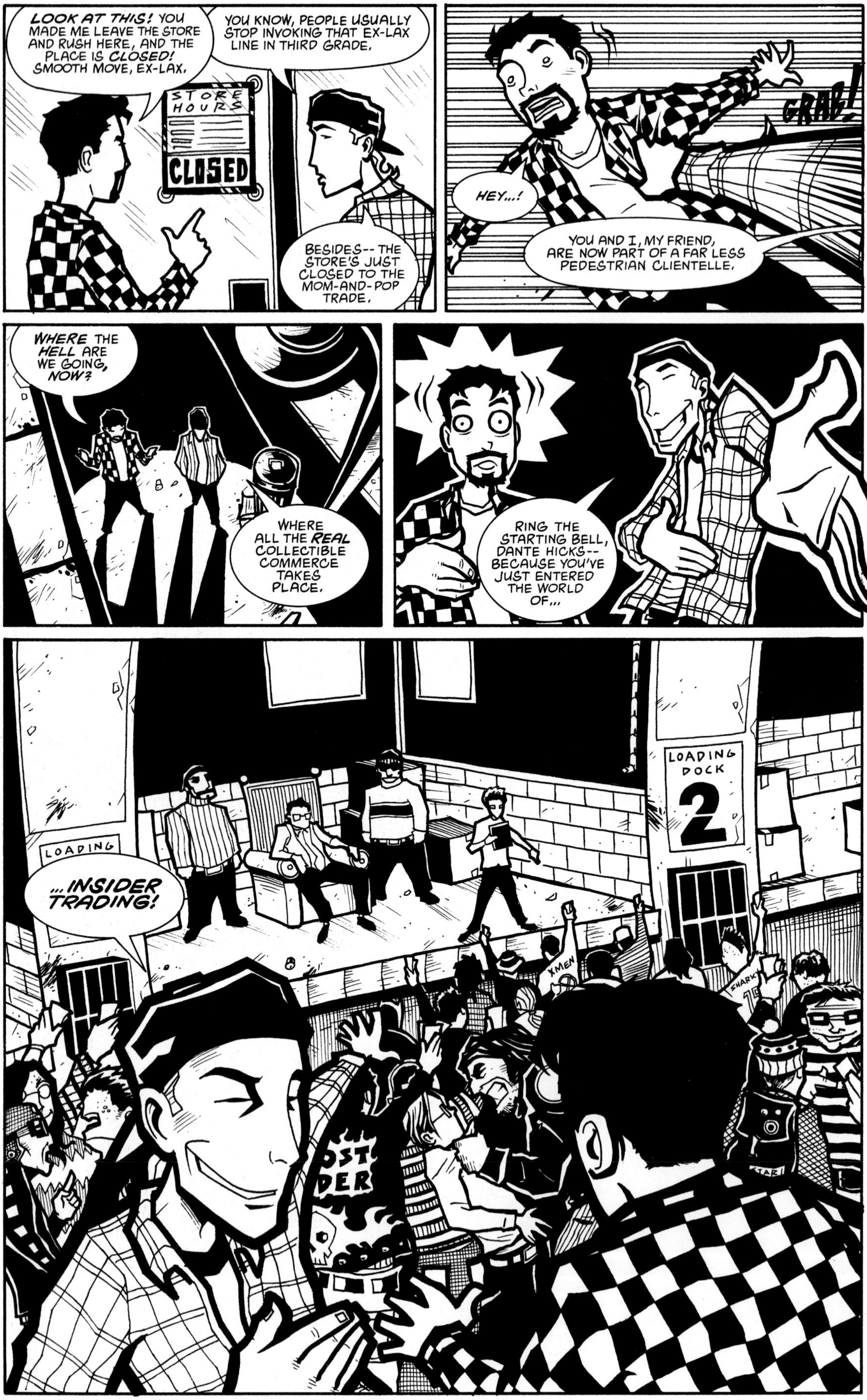
LOOK AT THIS! YOU MADE ME LEAVE THE STORE AND RUSH HERE, AND THE PLACE IS CLOSED! SMOOTH MOVE, EX-LAX.
YOU KNOW, PEOPLE USUALLY STOP INVOKING THAT EX-LAX LINE IN THIRD GRADE.
STORE HOURS
CLOSED
BESIDES-- THE STORE'S JUST CLOSED TO THE MOM-AND-POP TRADE.
GRAB!
HEY...!
YOU AND I, MY FRIEND, ARE NOW PART OF A FAR LESS PEDESTRIAN CLIENTELLE.
WHERE THE HELL ARE WE GOING, NOW?
WHERE ALL THE REAL COLLECTIBLE COMMERCE TAKES PLACE.
RING THE STARTING BELL, DANTE HICKS-- BECAUSE YOU'VE JUST ENTERED THE WORLD OF...
LOADING
LOADING DOCK 2
...INSIDER TRADING!
XMEN
SHARK

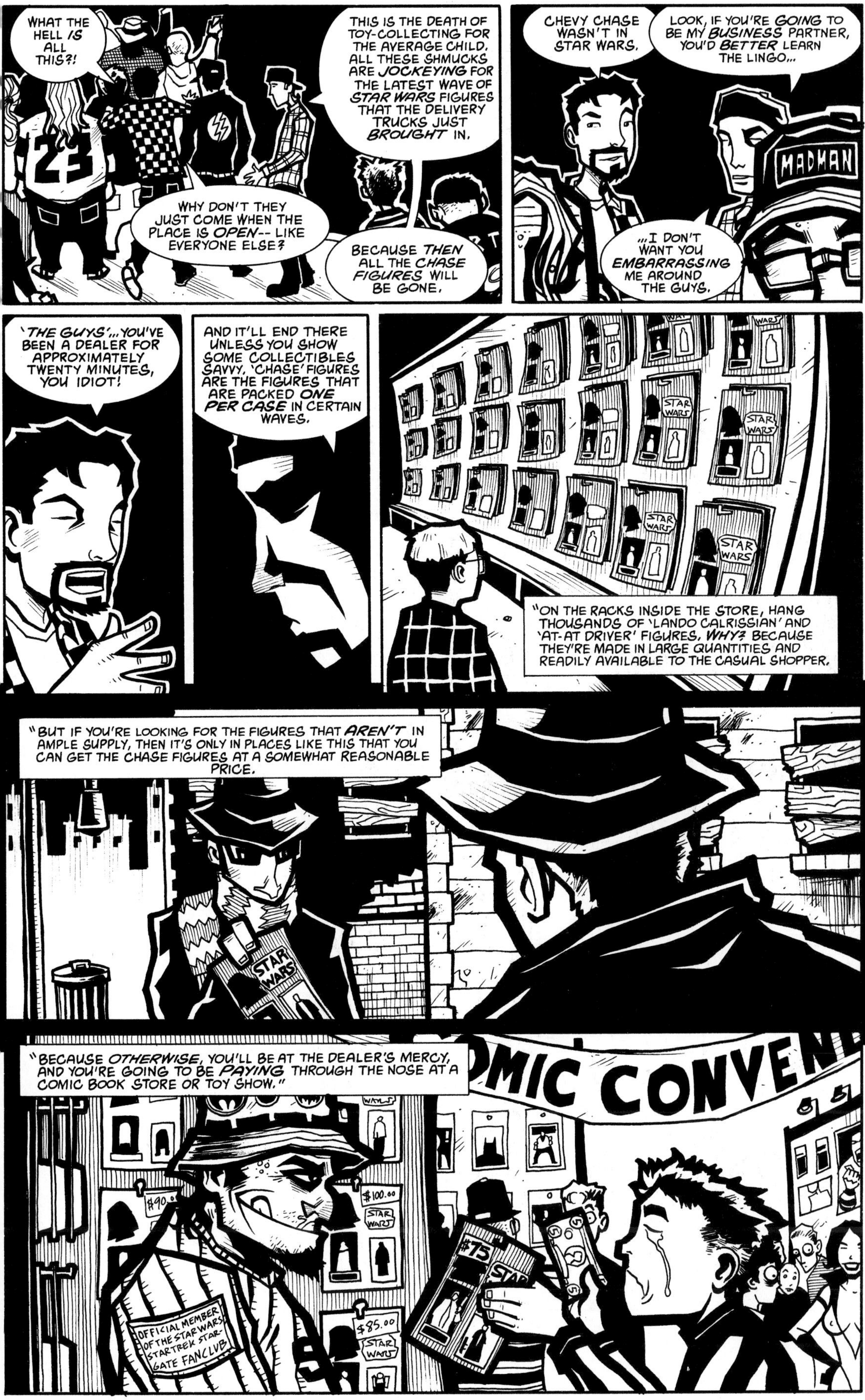
WHAT THE HELL *IS* ALL THIS?!
THIS IS THE DEATH OF TOY-COLLECTING FOR THE AVERAGE CHILD. ALL THESE SHMUCKS ARE *JOCKEYING* FOR THE LATEST WAVE OF *STAR WARS* FIGURES THAT THE DELIVERY TRUCKS JUST *BROUGHT* IN.
WHY DON'T THEY JUST COME WHEN THE PLACE IS *OPEN*-- LIKE EVERYONE ELSE?
BECAUSE *THEN* ALL THE *CHASE FIGURES* WILL BE GONE.
CHEVY CHASE WASN'T IN STAR WARS.
LOOK, IF YOU'RE *GOING* TO BE MY *BUSINESS* PARTNER, YOU'D *BETTER* LEARN THE LINGO...
MADMAN
...I DON'T WANT YOU *EMBARRASSING* ME AROUND THE GUYS.
'*THE GUYS*'... YOU'VE BEEN A DEALER FOR APPROXIMATELY TWENTY MINUTES, YOU IDIOT!
AND IT'LL END THERE UNLESS YOU SHOW SOME COLLECTIBLES SAVVY. 'CHASE' FIGURES ARE THE FIGURES THAT ARE PACKED *ONE PER CASE* IN CERTAIN WAVES.
STAR WARS
"ON THE RACKS INSIDE THE STORE, HANG THOUSANDS OF 'LANDO CALRISSIAN' AND 'AT-AT DRIVER' FIGURES. *WHY?* BECAUSE THEY'RE MADE IN LARGE QUANTITIES AND READILY AVAILABLE TO THE CASUAL SHOPPER.
"BUT IF YOU'RE LOOKING FOR THE FIGURES THAT *AREN'T* IN AMPLE SUPPLY, THEN IT'S ONLY IN PLACES LIKE THIS THAT YOU CAN GET THE CHASE FIGURES AT A SOMEWHAT REASONABLE PRICE.
STAR WARS
"BECAUSE *OTHERWISE*, YOU'LL BE AT THE DEALER'S MERCY, AND YOU'RE GOING TO BE *PAYING* THROUGH THE NOSE AT A COMIC BOOK STORE OR TOY SHOW."
OMIC CONVEN
$90.00
$100.00
STAR WARS
$85.00
STAR WARS
$75
OFFICIAL MEMBER OF THE STAR WARS STARTREK STARGATE FANCLUB

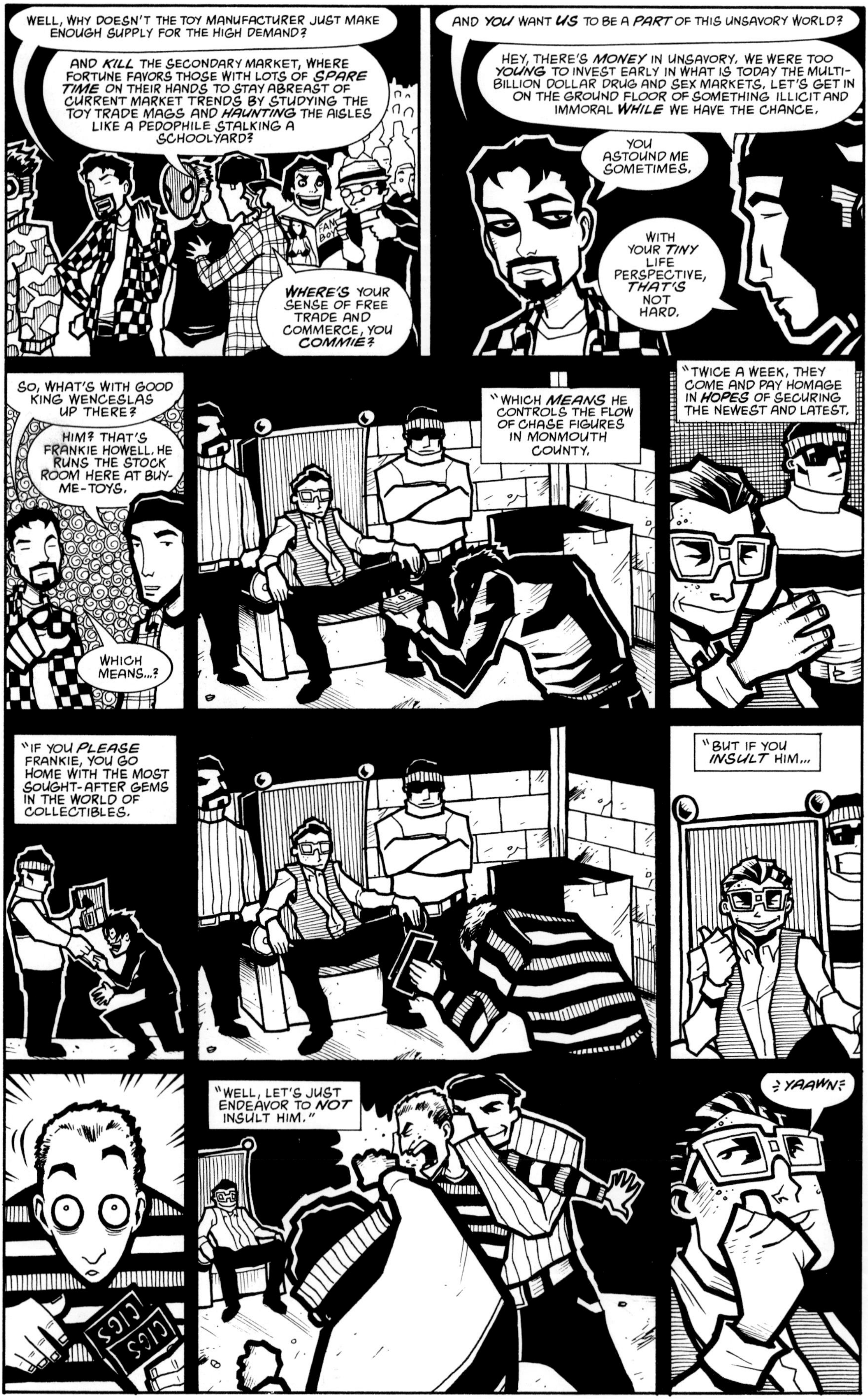
WELL, WHY DOESN'T THE TOY MANUFACTURER JUST MAKE ENOUGH SUPPLY FOR THE HIGH DEMAND?
AND KILL THE SECONDARY MARKET, WHERE FORTUNE FAVORS THOSE WITH LOTS OF SPARE TIME ON THEIR HANDS TO STAY ABREAST OF CURRENT MARKET TRENDS BY STUDYING THE TOY TRADE MAGS AND HAUNTING THE AISLES LIKE A PEDOPHILE STALKING A SCHOOLYARD?
FAN BOY
WHERE'S YOUR SENSE OF FREE TRADE AND COMMERCE, YOU COMMIE?
AND YOU WANT US TO BE A PART OF THIS UNSAVORY WORLD?
HEY, THERE'S MONEY IN UNSAVORY. WE WERE TOO YOUNG TO INVEST EARLY IN WHAT IS TODAY THE MULTI-BILLION DOLLAR DRUG AND SEX MARKETS. LET'S GET IN ON THE GROUND FLOOR OF SOMETHING ILLICIT AND IMMORAL WHILE WE HAVE THE CHANCE.
YOU ASTOUND ME SOMETIMES.
WITH YOUR TINY LIFE PERSPECTIVE, THAT'S NOT HARD.
SO, WHAT'S WITH GOOD KING WENCESLAS UP THERE?
HIM? THAT'S FRANKIE HOWELL. HE RUNS THE STOCK ROOM HERE AT BUY-ME-TOYS.
WHICH MEANS...?
"WHICH MEANS HE CONTROLS THE FLOW OF CHASE FIGURES IN MONMOUTH COUNTY.
"TWICE A WEEK, THEY COME AND PAY HOMAGE IN HOPES OF SECURING THE NEWEST AND LATEST.
"IF YOU PLEASE FRANKIE, YOU GO HOME WITH THE MOST SOUGHT-AFTER GEMS IN THE WORLD OF COLLECTIBLES.
"BUT IF YOU INSULT HIM...
CIGS
CIGS
"WELL, LET'S JUST ENDEAVOR TO NOT INSULT HIM."
YAAWN

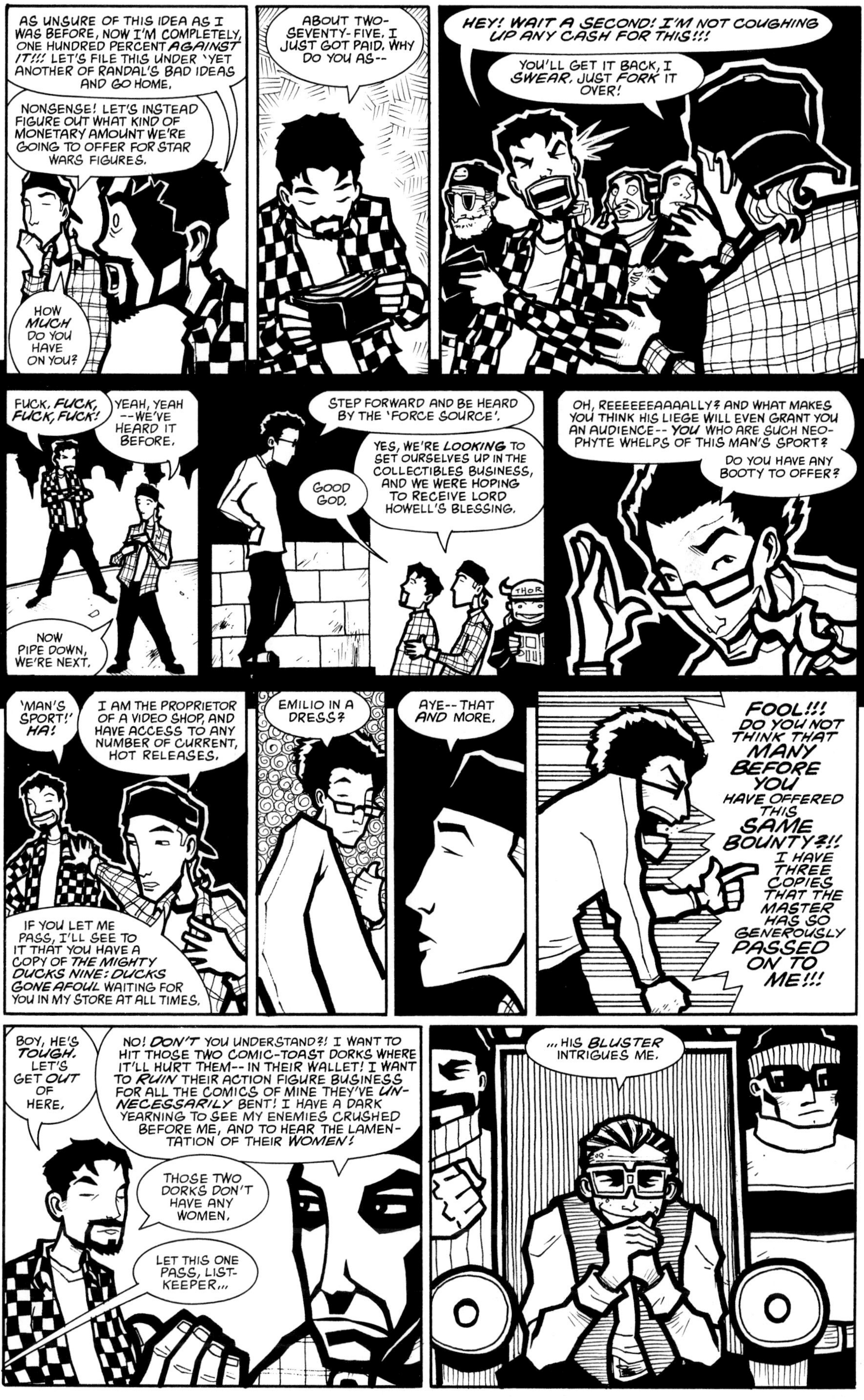
AS UNSURE OF THIS IDEA AS I WAS BEFORE, NOW I'M COMPLETELY, ONE HUNDRED PERCENT AGAINST IT!!! LET'S FILE THIS UNDER 'YET ANOTHER OF RANDAL'S BAD IDEAS AND GO HOME.
NONSENSE! LET'S INSTEAD FIGURE OUT WHAT KIND OF MONETARY AMOUNT WE'RE GOING TO OFFER FOR STAR WARS FIGURES.
HOW MUCH DO YOU HAVE ON YOU?
ABOUT TWO-SEVENTY-FIVE. I JUST GOT PAID. WHY DO YOU AS--
HEY! WAIT A SECOND! I'M NOT COUGHING UP ANY CASH FOR THIS!!!
YOU'LL GET IT BACK, I SWEAR. JUST FORK IT OVER!
FUCK, FUCK, FUCK, FUCK!
YEAH, YEAH --WE'VE HEARD IT BEFORE.
NOW PIPE DOWN, WE'RE NEXT.
STEP FORWARD AND BE HEARD BY THE 'FORCE SOURCE'.
YES, WE'RE LOOKING TO SET OURSELVES UP IN THE COLLECTIBLES BUSINESS, AND WE WERE HOPING TO RECEIVE LORD HOWELL'S BLESSING.
GOOD GOD.
THOR
OH, REEEEEEAAAALLY? AND WHAT MAKES YOU THINK HIS LIEGE WILL EVEN GRANT YOU AN AUDIENCE-- YOU WHO ARE SUCH NEOPHYTE WHELPS OF THIS MAN'S SPORT?
DO YOU HAVE ANY BOOTY TO OFFER?
'MAN'S SPORT!' HA!
I AM THE PROPRIETOR OF A VIDEO SHOP, AND HAVE ACCESS TO ANY NUMBER OF CURRENT, HOT RELEASES.
IF YOU LET ME PASS, I'LL SEE TO IT THAT YOU HAVE A COPY OF THE MIGHTY DUCKS NINE: DUCKS GONE AFOUL WAITING FOR YOU IN MY STORE AT ALL TIMES.
EMILIO IN A DRESS?
AYE--THAT AND MORE.
FOOL!!! DO YOU NOT THINK THAT MANY BEFORE YOU HAVE OFFERED THIS SAME BOUNTY?!! I HAVE THREE COPIES THAT THE MASTER HAS SO GENEROUSLY PASSED ON TO ME!!!
BOY, HE'S TOUGH. LET'S GET OUT OF HERE.
NO! DON'T YOU UNDERSTAND?! I WANT TO HIT THOSE TWO COMIC-TOAST DORKS WHERE IT'LL HURT THEM-- IN THEIR WALLET! I WANT TO RUIN THEIR ACTION FIGURE BUSINESS FOR ALL THE COMICS OF MINE THEY'VE UNNECESSARILY BENT! I HAVE A DARK YEARNING TO SEE MY ENEMIES CRUSHED BEFORE ME, AND TO HEAR THE LAMENTATION OF THEIR WOMEN!
THOSE TWO DORKS DON'T HAVE ANY WOMEN.
LET THIS ONE PASS, LIST-KEEPER...
...HIS BLUSTER INTRIGUES ME.

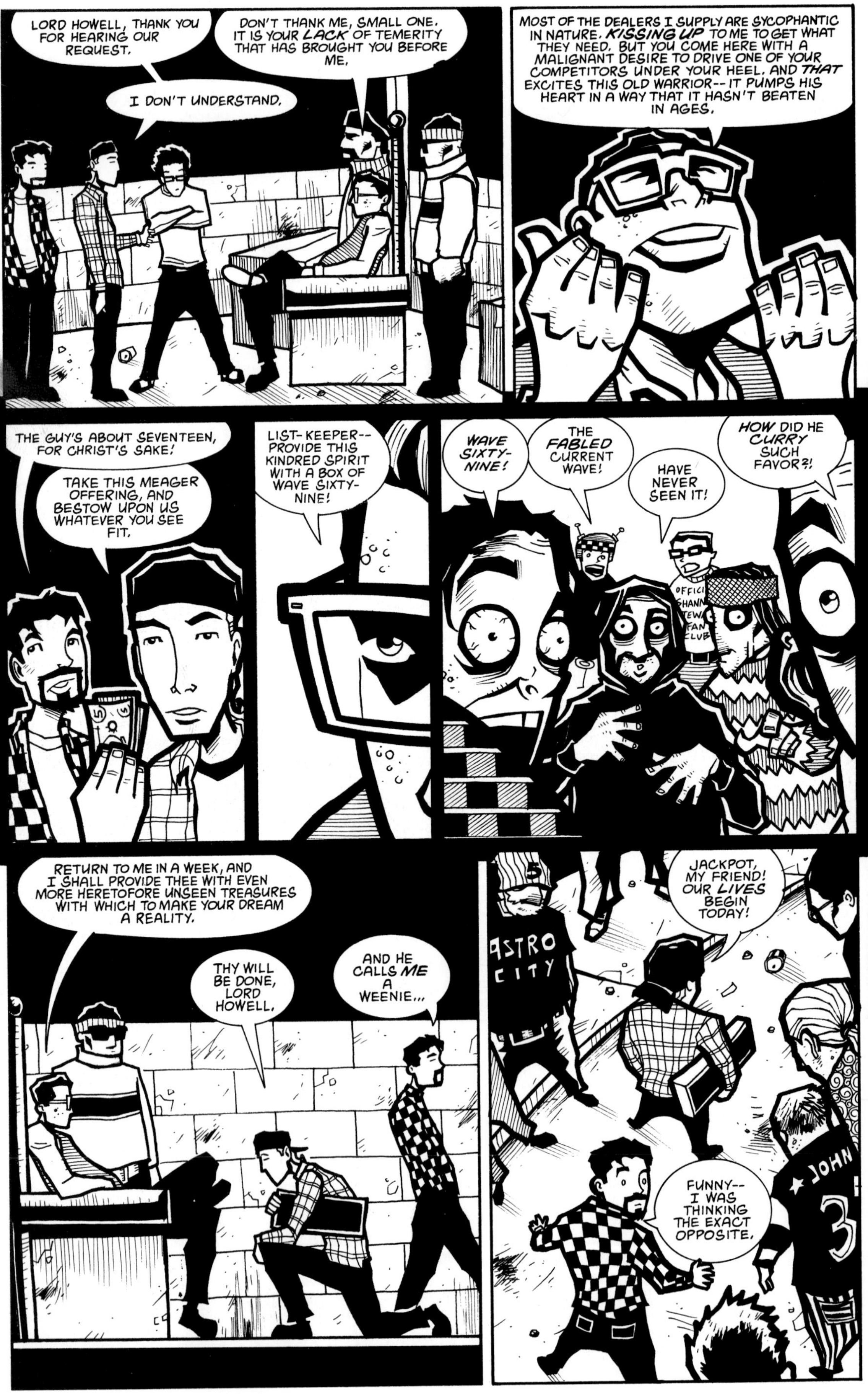
LORD HOWELL, THANK YOU FOR HEARING OUR REQUEST.
I DON'T UNDERSTAND.
DON'T THANK ME, SMALL ONE. IT IS YOUR LACK OF TEMERITY THAT HAS BROUGHT YOU BEFORE ME.
MOST OF THE DEALERS I SUPPLY ARE SYCOPHANTIC IN NATURE. KISSING UP TO ME TO GET WHAT THEY NEED. BUT YOU COME HERE WITH A MALIGNANT DESIRE TO DRIVE ONE OF YOUR COMPETITORS UNDER YOUR HEEL. AND THAT EXCITES THIS OLD WARRIOR-- IT PUMPS HIS HEART IN A WAY THAT IT HASN'T BEATEN IN AGES.
THE GUY'S ABOUT SEVENTEEN, FOR CHRIST'S SAKE!
TAKE THIS MEAGER OFFERING, AND BESTOW UPON US WHATEVER YOU SEE FIT.
LIST-KEEPER-- PROVIDE THIS KINDRED SPIRIT WITH A BOX OF WAVE SIXTY-NINE!
WAVE SIXTY-NINE!
THE FABLED CURRENT WAVE!
HAVE NEVER SEEN IT!
HOW DID HE CURRY SUCH FAVOR?!
RETURN TO ME IN A WEEK, AND I SHALL PROVIDE THEE WITH EVEN MORE HERETOFORE UNSEEN TREASURES WITH WHICH TO MAKE YOUR DREAM A REALITY.
THY WILL BE DONE, LORD HOWELL.
AND HE CALLS ME A WEENIE...
JACKPOT, MY FRIEND! OUR LIVES BEGIN TODAY!
FUNNY-- I WAS THINKING THE EXACT OPPOSITE.
ASTRO CITY
JOHN 3

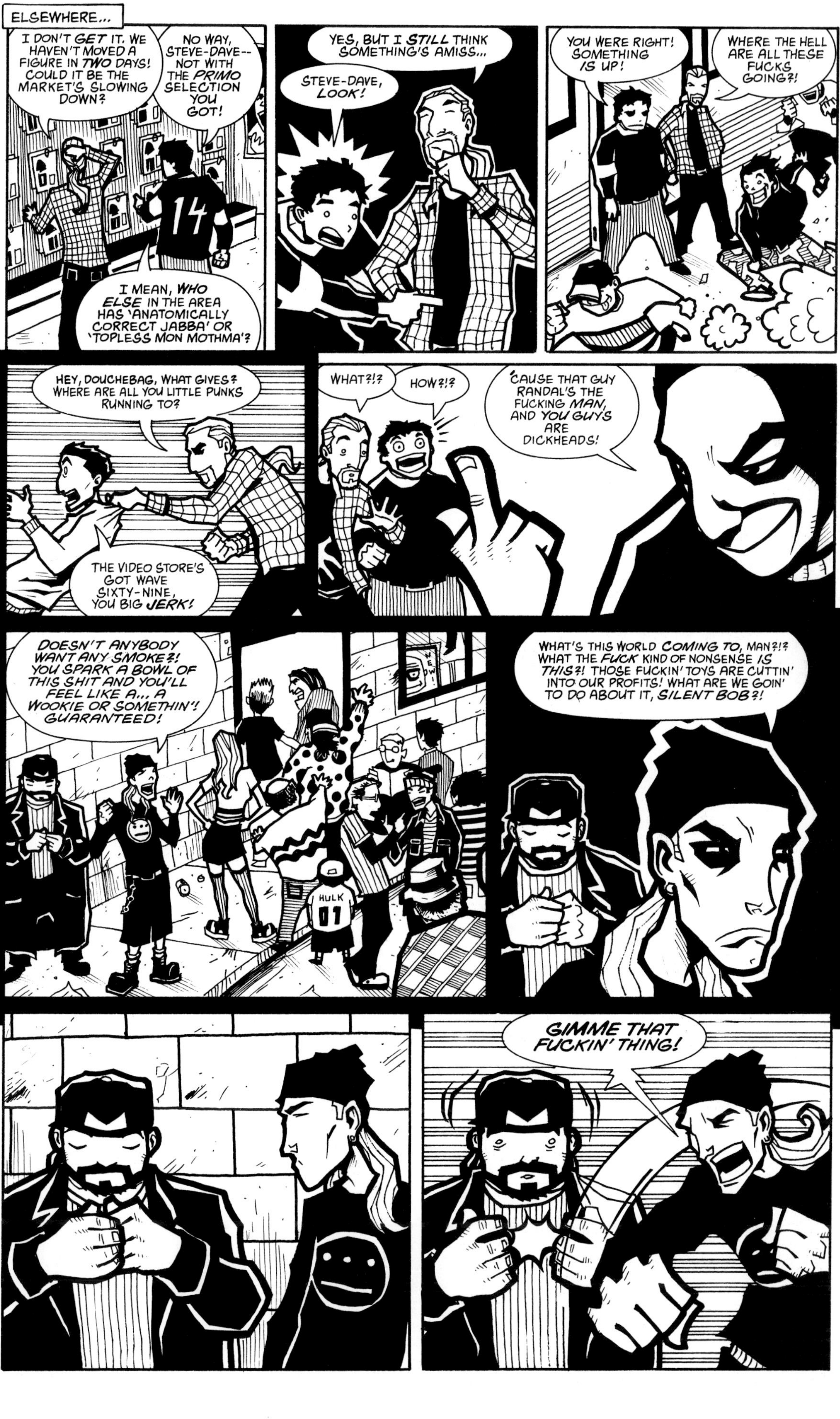
ELSEWHERE...
I DON'T GET IT. WE HAVEN'T MOVED A FIGURE IN TWO DAYS! COULD IT BE THE MARKET'S SLOWING DOWN?
NO WAY, STEVE-DAVE--NOT WITH THE PRIMO SELECTION YOU GOT!
I MEAN, WHO ELSE IN THE AREA HAS 'ANATOMICALLY CORRECT JABBA' OR 'TOPLESS MON MOTHMA'?
YES, BUT I STILL THINK SOMETHING'S AMISS...
STEVE-DAVE, LOOK!
YOU WERE RIGHT! SOMETHING IS UP!
WHERE THE HELL ARE ALL THESE FUCKS GOING?!
HEY, DOUCHEBAG, WHAT GIVES? WHERE ARE ALL YOU LITTLE PUNKS RUNNING TO?
THE VIDEO STORE'S GOT WAVE SIXTY-NINE, YOU BIG JERK!
WHAT?!?
HOW?!?
'CAUSE THAT GUY RANDAL'S THE FUCKING MAN, AND YOU GUYS ARE DICKHEADS!
DOESN'T ANYBODY WANT ANY SMOKE?! YOU SPARK A BOWL OF THIS SHIT AND YOU'LL FEEL LIKE A... A WOOKIE OR SOMETHIN'! GUARANTEED!
HULK 01
WHAT'S THIS WORLD COMING TO, MAN?!? WHAT THE FUCK KIND OF NONSENSE IS THIS?! THOSE FUCKIN' TOYS ARE CUTTIN' INTO OUR PROFITS! WHAT ARE WE GOIN' TO DO ABOUT IT, SILENT BOB?!
GIMME THAT FUCKIN' THING!

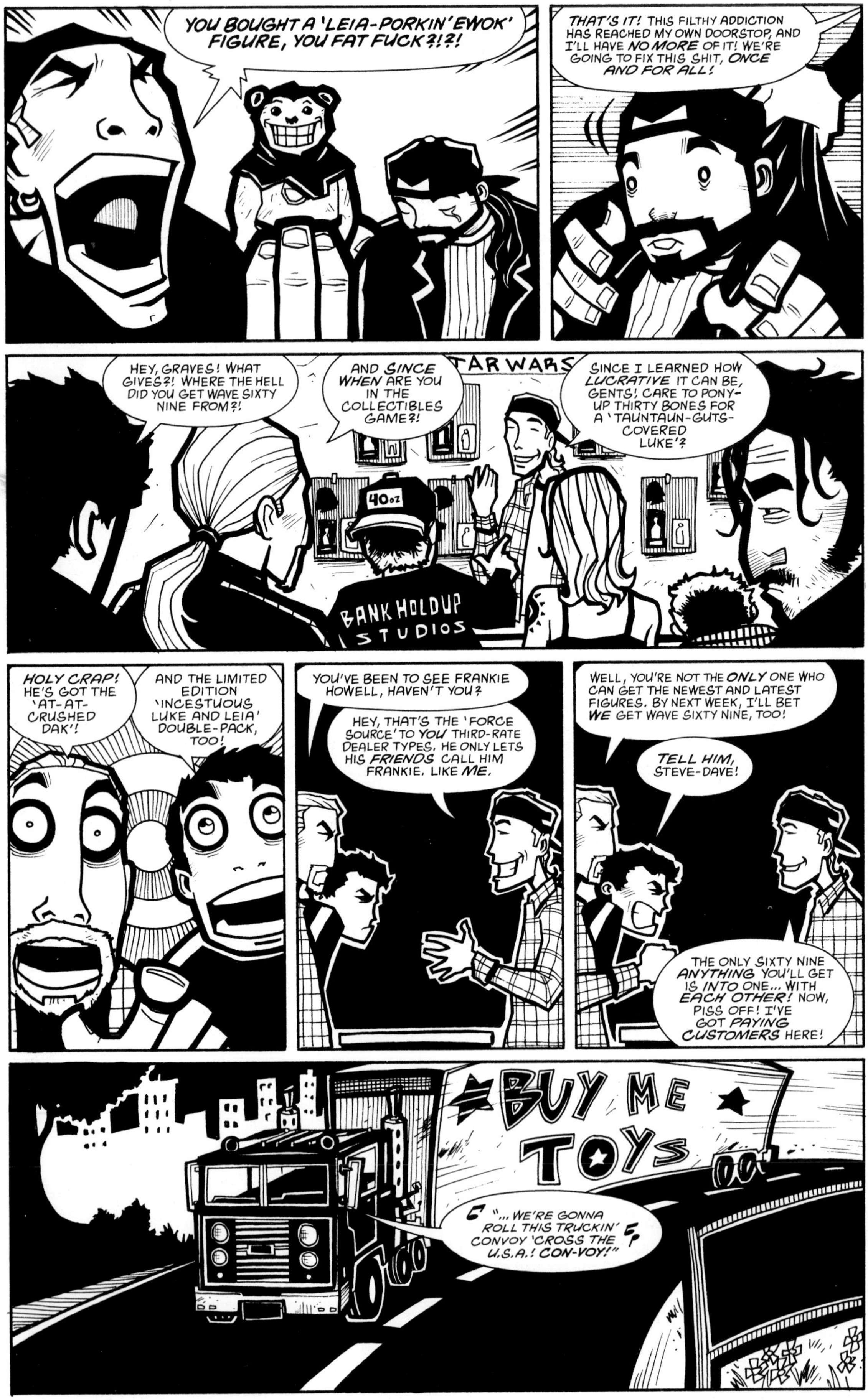

YOU BOUGHT A 'LEIA-PORKIN' EWOK' FIGURE, YOU FAT FUCK?!?!
THAT'S IT! THIS FILTHY ADDICTION HAS REACHED MY OWN DOORSTOP, AND I'LL HAVE NO MORE OF IT! WE'RE GOING TO FIX THIS SHIT, ONCE AND FOR ALL!
STAR WARS
HEY, GRAVES! WHAT GIVES?! WHERE THE HELL DID YOU GET WAVE SIXTY NINE FROM?!
AND SINCE WHEN ARE YOU IN THE COLLECTIBLES GAME?!
SINCE I LEARNED HOW LUCRATIVE IT CAN BE, GENTS! CARE TO PONY-UP THIRTY BONES FOR A 'TAUNTAUN-GUTS-COVERED LUKE'?
40oz
BANK HOLDUP STUDIOS
HOLY CRAP! HE'S GOT THE 'AT-AT-CRUSHED DAK'!
AND THE LIMITED EDITION 'INCESTUOUS LUKE AND LEIA' DOUBLE-PACK, TOO!
YOU'VE BEEN TO SEE FRANKIE HOWELL, HAVEN'T YOU?
HEY, THAT'S THE 'FORCE SOURCE' TO YOU THIRD-RATE DEALER TYPES. HE ONLY LETS HIS FRIENDS CALL HIM FRANKIE. LIKE ME.
WELL, YOU'RE NOT THE ONLY ONE WHO CAN GET THE NEWEST AND LATEST FIGURES. BY NEXT WEEK, I'LL BET WE GET WAVE SIXTY NINE, TOO!
TELL HIM, STEVE-DAVE!
THE ONLY SIXTY NINE ANYTHING YOU'LL GET IS INTO ONE... WITH EACH OTHER! NOW, PISS OFF! I'VE GOT PAYING CUSTOMERS HERE!
BUY ME TOYS
"...WE'RE GONNA ROLL THIS TRUCKIN' CONVOY 'CROSS THE U.S.A.! CON-VOY!"

SAY... THAT LOOKS LIKE SOME GOOD OL' BOYS IN NEED OF SOME ASSISTANCE. I'D *BETTER* PULL OVER.

HEY, THERE! CAN I *HELP* YOU BOYS?

DEPENDS ON WHAT YOU'RE HAULING. *SNOOGANS!*

THE NEXT NIGHT...

FELT LIKE THIS FUCKIN' DAY WOULD *NEVER* COME.

I'VE GOTTA ADMIT-- THIS COLLECTIBLES THING IS A *PRETTY SWEET DEAL.*

YOU WANNA SEE *HOW* SWEET? HERE'S YOUR INITIAL TWO HUNDRED AND SEVENTY FIVE DOLLAR INVESTMENT BACK, *AND* WE'VE GOT *THREE HUNDRED BUCKS* IN PROFIT WITH WHICH TO BUY MORE FIGURES!

IF I *EVER* DOUBT YOUR SAVVY AGAIN, BELT ME IN THE MOUTH.

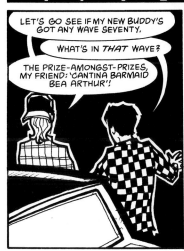

LET'S GO SEE IF MY NEW BUDDY'S GOT ANY WAVE SEVENTY.

WHAT'S IN *THAT* WAVE?

THE PRIZE-AMONGST-PRIZES, MY FRIEND: 'CANTINA BARMAID BEA ARTHUR'!

RISE, OH, MOST FAVOURED SUBJECTS, NO COURTSHIP, NO CEREMONIES HERE-- NOT AMONGST *FRIENDS.*

LORD HOWELL, ON BENDED KNEE WE COME TO THEE, REQUESTING FURTHER ASSISTANCE.

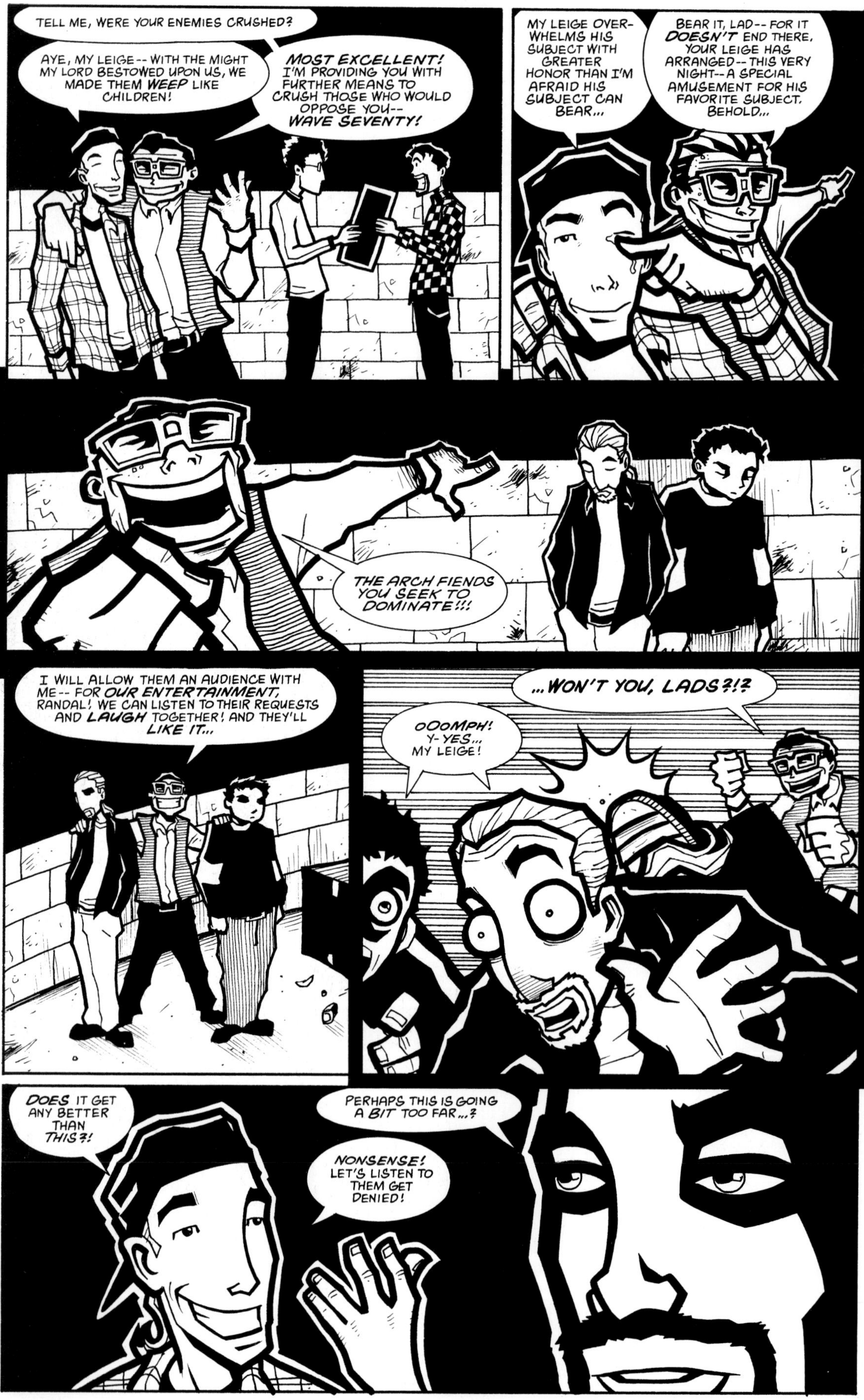

TELL ME, WERE YOUR ENEMIES CRUSHED?
AYE, MY LEIGE -- WITH THE MIGHT MY LORD BESTOWED UPON US, WE MADE THEM WEEP LIKE CHILDREN!
MOST EXCELLENT! I'M PROVIDING YOU WITH FURTHER MEANS TO CRUSH THOSE WHO WOULD OPPOSE YOU-- WAVE SEVENTY!
MY LEIGE OVER-WHELMS HIS SUBJECT WITH GREATER HONOR THAN I'M AFRAID HIS SUBJECT CAN BEAR...
BEAR IT, LAD -- FOR IT DOESN'T END THERE. YOUR LEIGE HAS ARRANGED -- THIS VERY NIGHT -- A SPECIAL AMUSEMENT FOR HIS FAVORITE SUBJECT. BEHOLD...
THE ARCH FIENDS YOU SEEK TO DOMINATE!!!
I WILL ALLOW THEM AN AUDIENCE WITH ME -- FOR OUR ENTERTAINMENT, RANDAL! WE CAN LISTEN TO THEIR REQUESTS AND LAUGH TOGETHER! AND THEY'LL LIKE IT...
...WON'T YOU, LADS?!?
OOOMPH! Y-YES... MY LEIGE!
DOES IT GET ANY BETTER THAN THIS?!
PERHAPS THIS IS GOING A BIT TOO FAR...?
NONSENSE! LET'S LISTEN TO THEM GET DENIED!

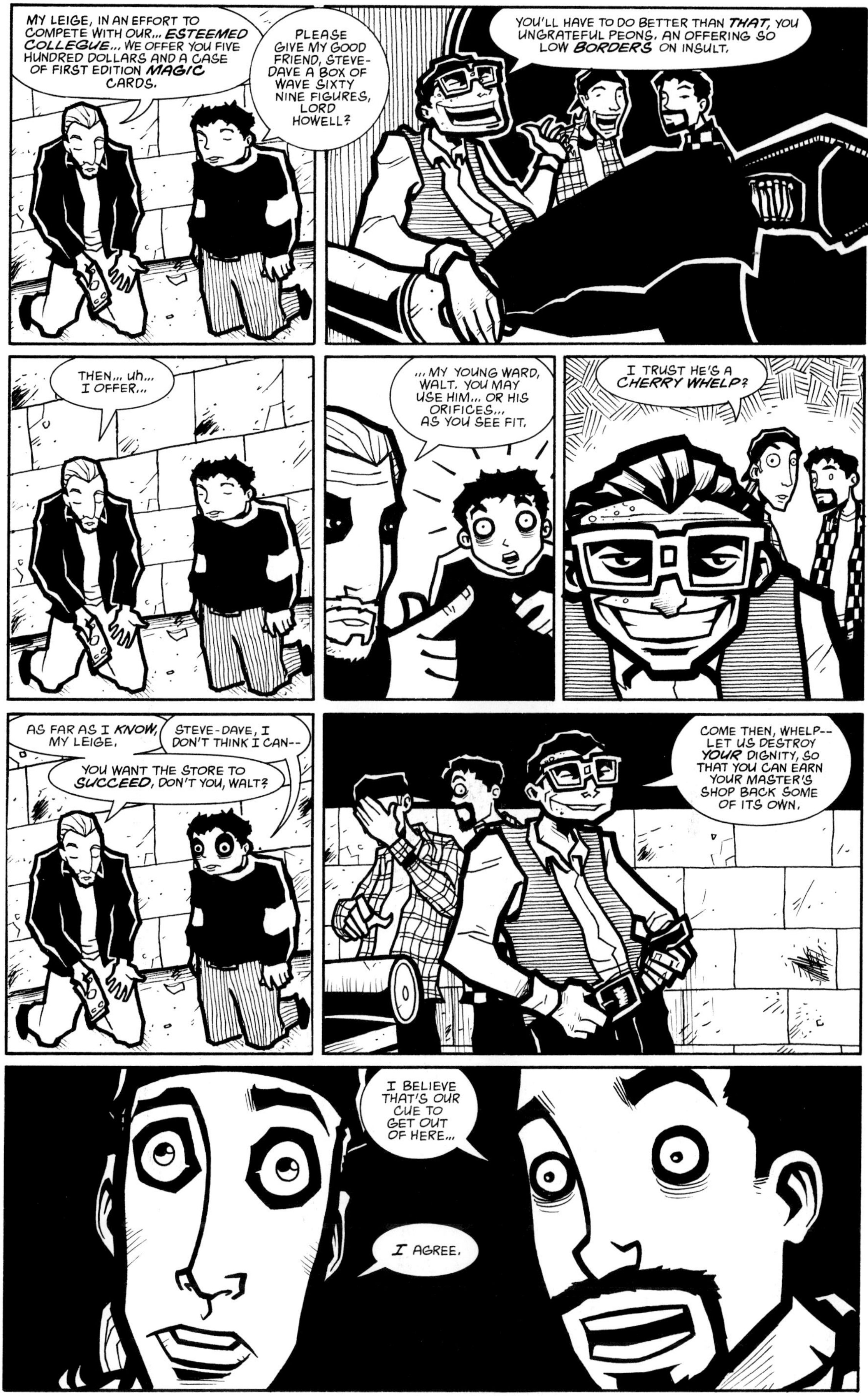
MY LEIGE, IN AN EFFORT TO COMPETE WITH OUR... ESTEEMED COLLEGUE... WE OFFER YOU FIVE HUNDRED DOLLARS AND A CASE OF FIRST EDITION MAGIC CARDS.
PLEASE GIVE MY GOOD FRIEND, STEVE-DAVE A BOX OF WAVE SIXTY NINE FIGURES, LORD HOWELL?
YOU'LL HAVE TO DO BETTER THAN THAT, YOU UNGRATEFUL PEONS. AN OFFERING SO LOW BORDERS ON INSULT.
THEN... uh... I OFFER...
...MY YOUNG WARD, WALT. YOU MAY USE HIM... OR HIS ORIFICES... AS YOU SEE FIT.
I TRUST HE'S A CHERRY WHELP?
AS FAR AS I KNOW, MY LEIGE.
STEVE-DAVE, I DON'T THINK I CAN--
YOU WANT THE STORE TO SUCCEED, DON'T YOU, WALT?
COME THEN, WHELP-- LET US DESTROY YOUR DIGNITY, SO THAT YOU CAN EARN YOUR MASTER'S SHOP BACK SOME OF ITS OWN.
I BELIEVE THAT'S OUR CUE TO GET OUT OF HERE...
I AGREE.

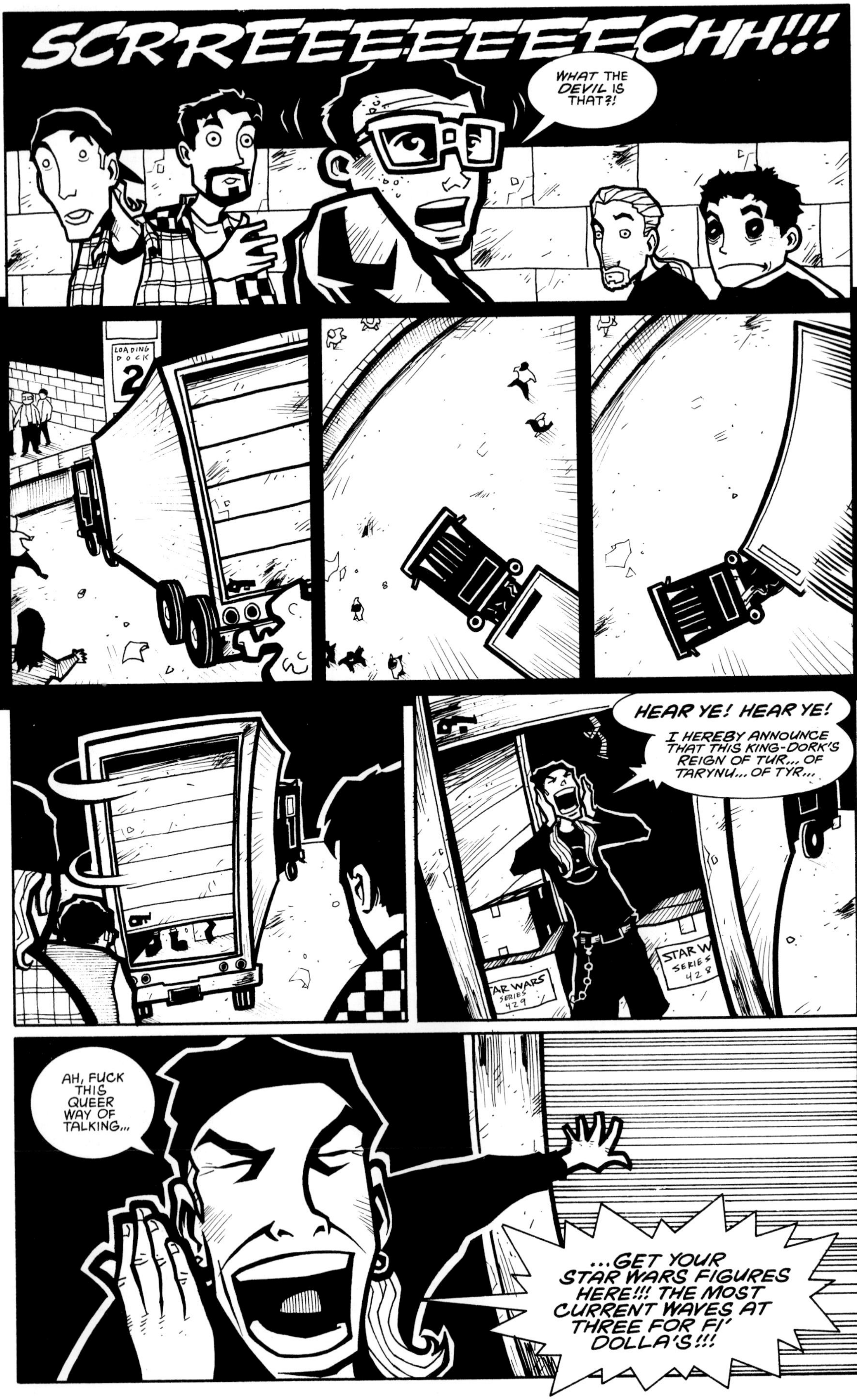
SCRREEEEEEEEEECHH!!!
WHAT THE DEVIL IS THAT?!
LOADING DOCK 2
HEAR YE! HEAR YE!
I HEREBY ANNOUNCE THAT THIS KING-DORK'S REIGN OF TUR... OF TARYNU... OF TYR...
STAR WARS SERIES 429
STAR W SERIES 428
AH, FUCK THIS QUEER WAY OF TALKING...
...GET YOUR STAR WARS FIGURES HERE!!! THE MOST CURRENT WAVES AT THREE FOR FI' DOLLA'S!!!

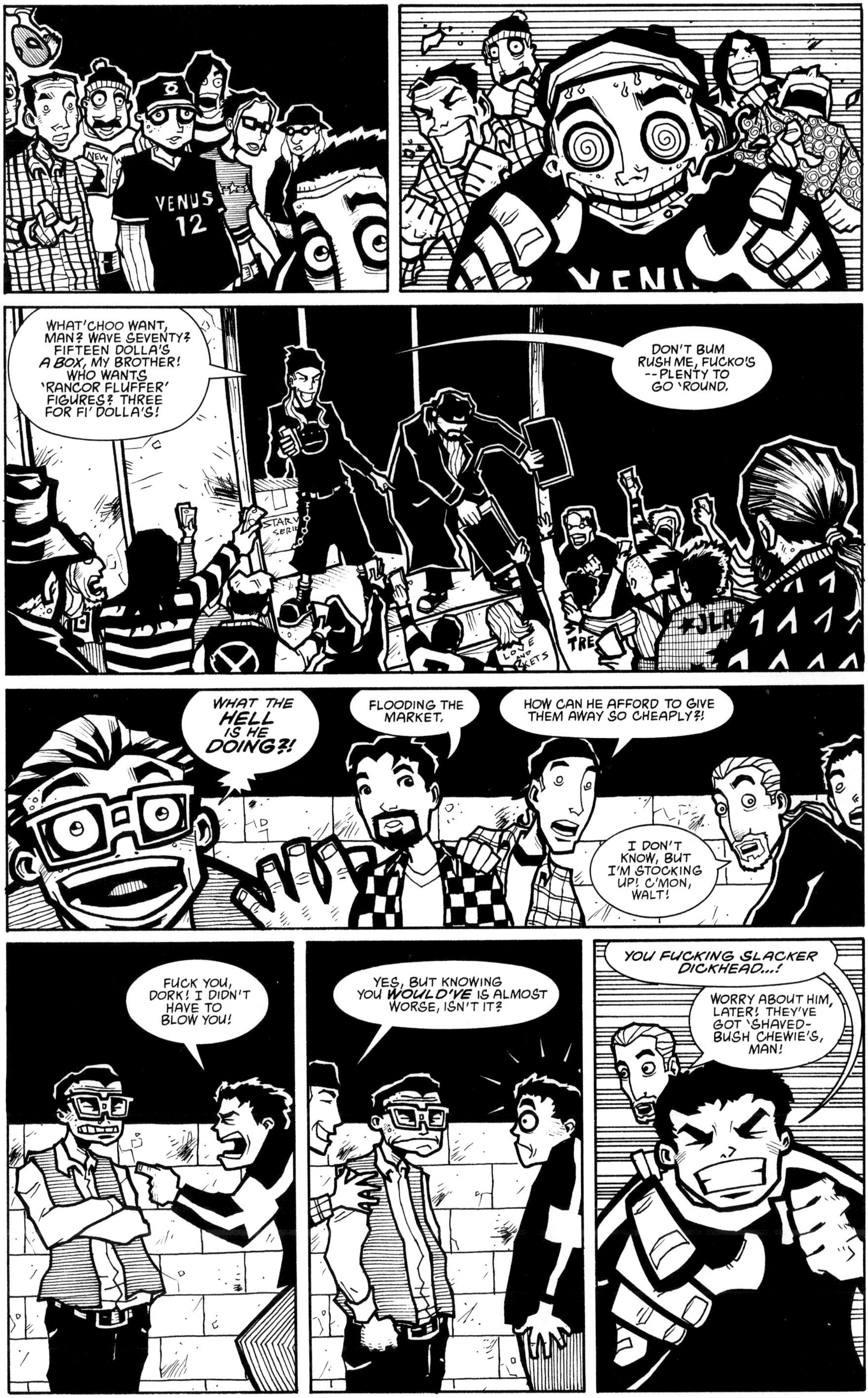
VENUS
12
WHAT'CHOO WANT, MAN? WAVE SEVENTY? FIFTEEN DOLLA'S A BOX, MY BROTHER! WHO WANTS 'RANCOR FLUFFER' FIGURES? THREE FOR FI' DOLLA'S!
DON'T BUM RUSH ME, FUCKO'S --PLENTY TO GO 'ROUND.
WHAT THE HELL IS HE DOING?!
FLOODING THE MARKET.
HOW CAN HE AFFORD TO GIVE THEM AWAY SO CHEAPLY?!
I DON'T KNOW, BUT I'M STOCKING UP! C'MON, WALT!
FUCK YOU, DORK! I DIDN'T HAVE TO BLOW YOU!
YES, BUT KNOWING YOU WOULD'VE IS ALMOST WORSE, ISN'T IT?
YOU FUCKING SLACKER DICKHEAD...!
WORRY ABOUT HIM, LATER! THEY'VE GOT 'SHAVED-BUSH CHEWIE'S, MAN!

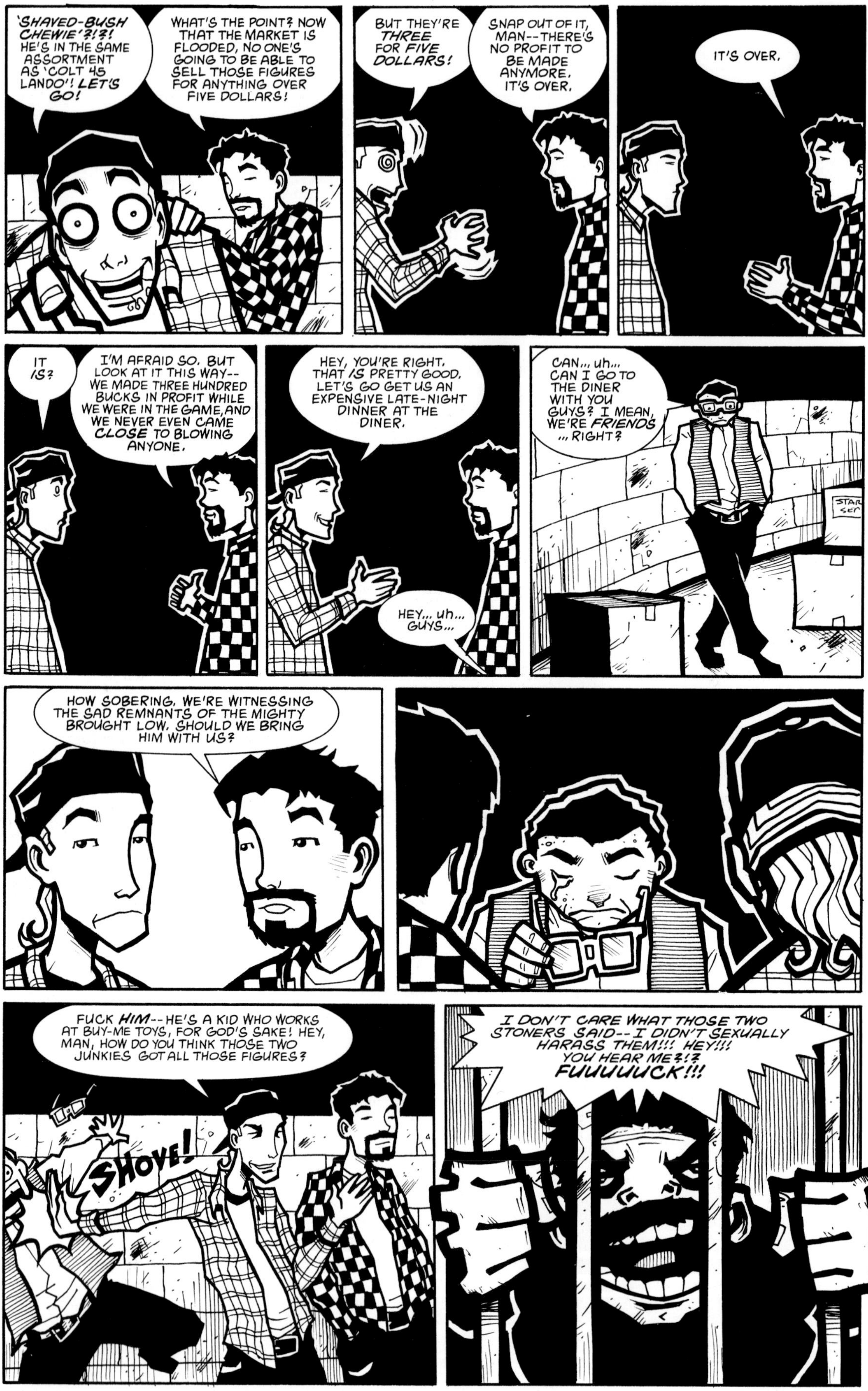

'SHAVED-BUSH CHEWIE'?!?! HE'S IN THE SAME ASSORTMENT AS 'COLT 45 LANDO'! LET'S GO!
WHAT'S THE POINT? NOW THAT THE MARKET IS FLOODED, NO ONE'S GOING TO BE ABLE TO SELL THOSE FIGURES FOR ANYTHING OVER FIVE DOLLARS!
BUT THEY'RE THREE FOR FIVE DOLLARS!
SNAP OUT OF IT, MAN--THERE'S NO PROFIT TO BE MADE ANYMORE. IT'S OVER.
IT'S OVER.
IT IS?
I'M AFRAID SO. BUT LOOK AT IT THIS WAY-- WE MADE THREE HUNDRED BUCKS IN PROFIT WHILE WE WERE IN THE GAME, AND WE NEVER EVEN CAME CLOSE TO BLOWING ANYONE.
HEY, YOU'RE RIGHT. THAT IS PRETTY GOOD. LET'S GO GET US AN EXPENSIVE LATE-NIGHT DINNER AT THE DINER.
HEY... uh... GUYS...
CAN... uh... CAN I GO TO THE DINER WITH YOU GUYS? I MEAN, WE'RE FRIENDS ...RIGHT?
HOW SOBERING. WE'RE WITNESSING THE SAD REMNANTS OF THE MIGHTY BROUGHT LOW. SHOULD WE BRING HIM WITH US?
FUCK HIM--HE'S A KID WHO WORKS AT BUY-ME TOYS, FOR GOD'S SAKE! HEY, MAN, HOW DO YOU THINK THOSE TWO JUNKIES GOT ALL THOSE FIGURES?
SHOVE!
I DON'T CARE WHAT THOSE TWO STONERS SAID--I DIDN'T SEXUALLY HARASS THEM!!! HEY!!! YOU HEAR ME?!? FUUUUUCK!!!

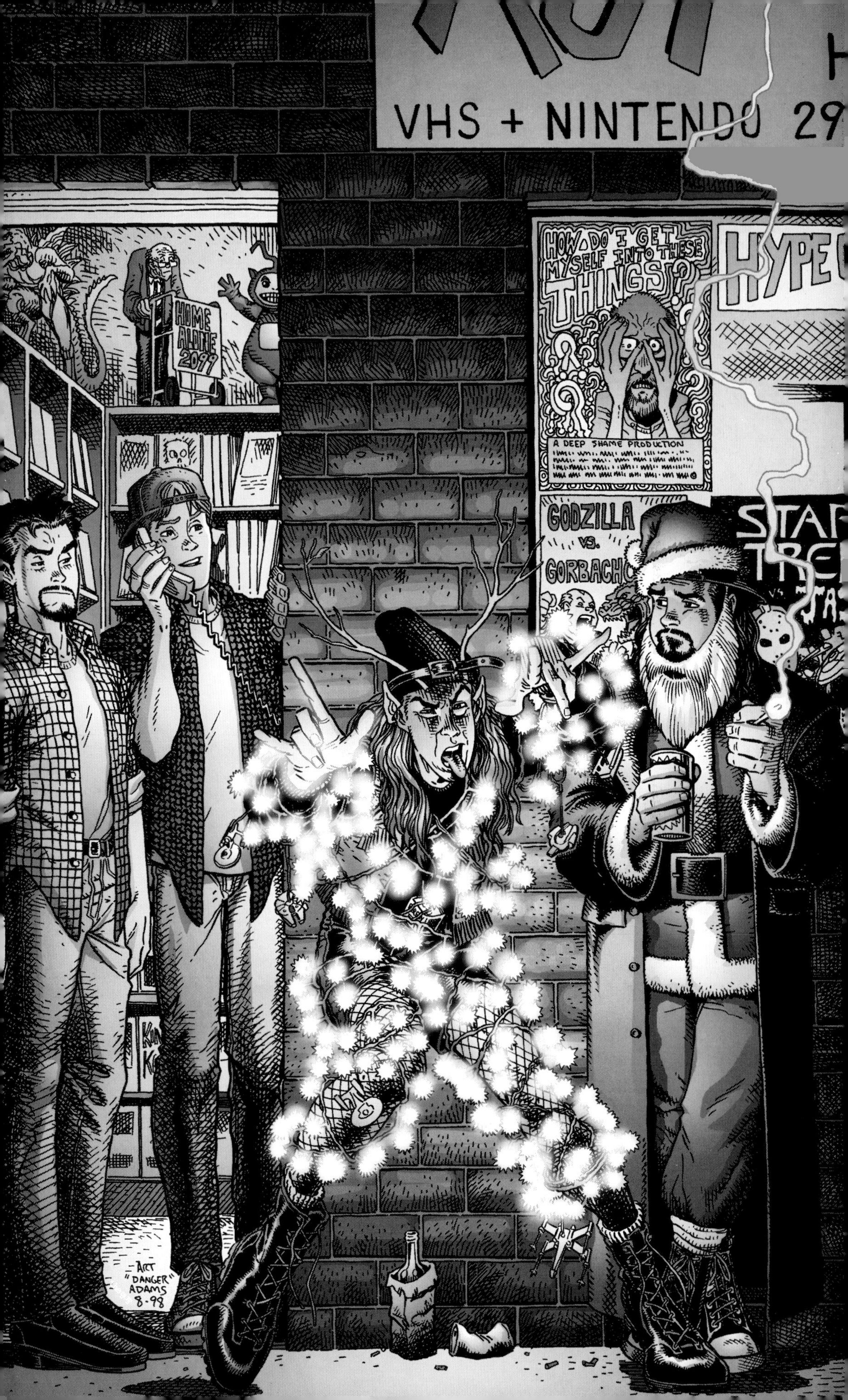
VHS + NINTENDO 29
HOME ALONE 2099
HOW DO I GET MYSELF INTO THESE THINGS!?
A DEEP SHAME PRODUCTION
HYPE
GODZILLA vs. GORBACH
STAR TRE
ART "DANGER" ADAMS 8-98

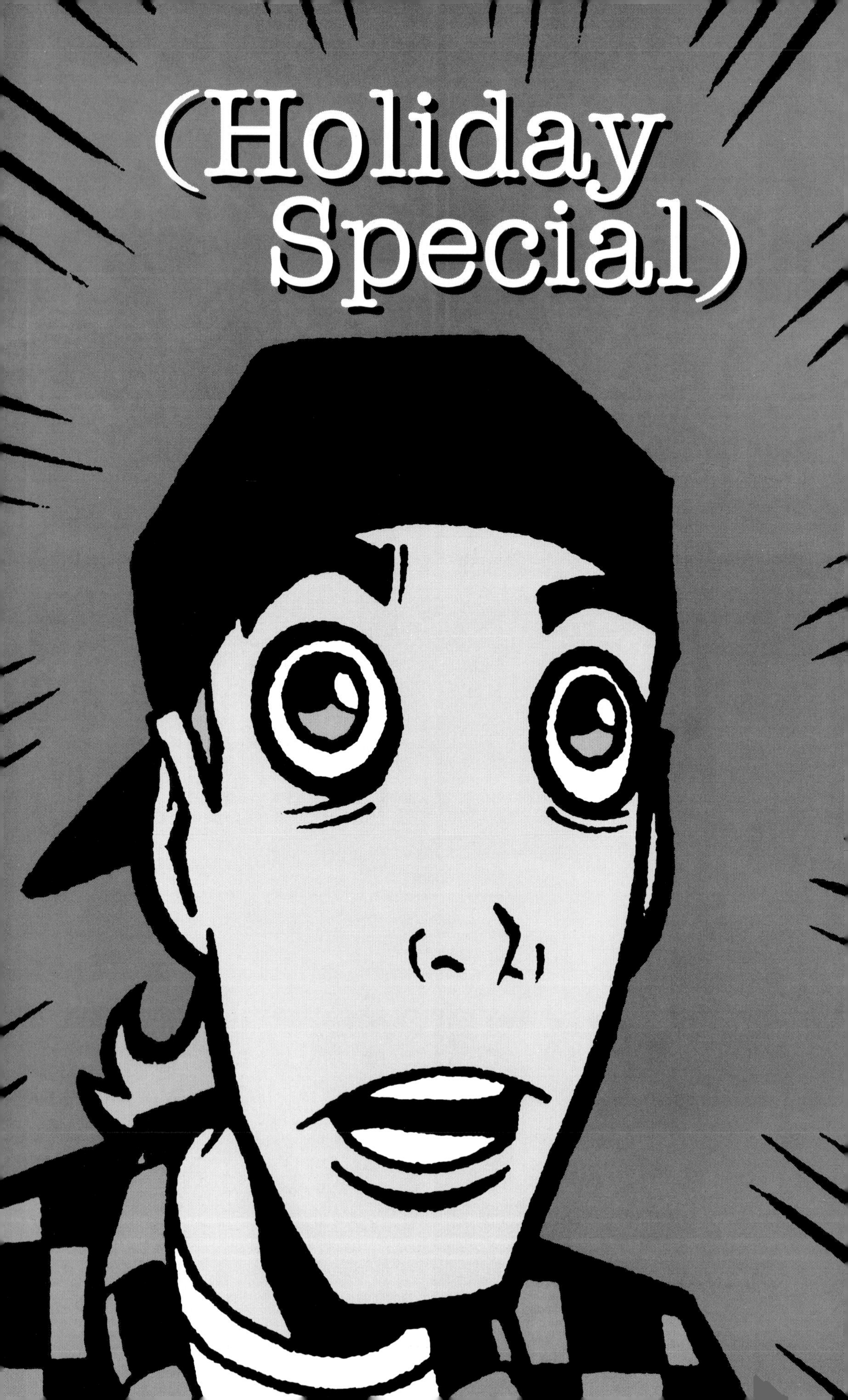
(Holiday Special)

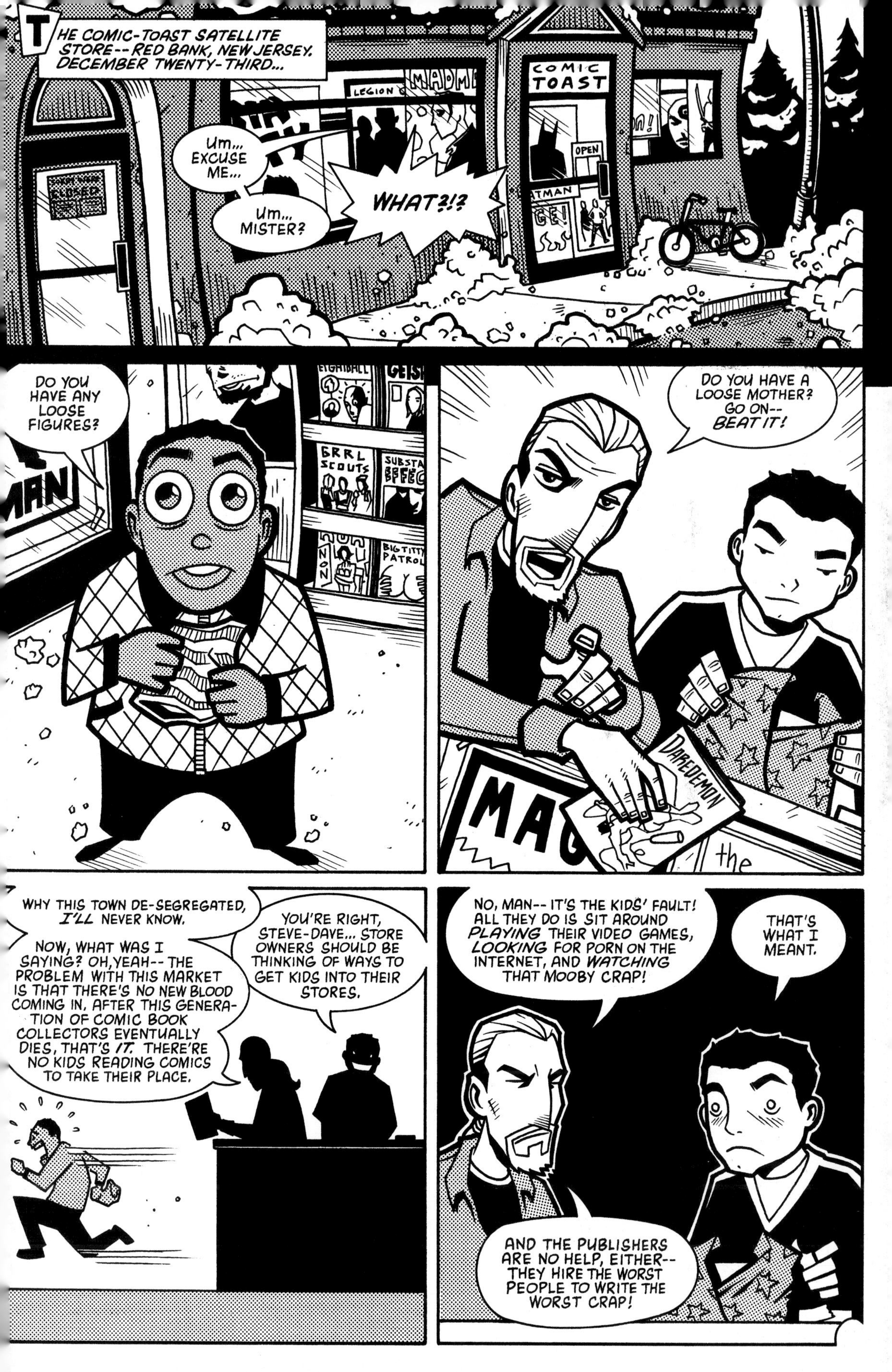
THE COMIC-TOAST SATELLITE STORE--RED BANK, NEW JERSEY. DECEMBER TWENTY-THIRD...
Um... EXCUSE ME...
Um... MISTER?
WHAT?!?
DO YOU HAVE ANY LOOSE FIGURES?
DO YOU HAVE A LOOSE MOTHER? GO ON-- BEAT IT!
WHY THIS TOWN DE-SEGREGATED, I'LL NEVER KNOW.
NOW, WHAT WAS I SAYING? OH, YEAH-- THE PROBLEM WITH THIS MARKET IS THAT THERE'S NO NEW BLOOD COMING IN. AFTER THIS GENERATION OF COMIC BOOK COLLECTORS EVENTUALLY DIES, THAT'S IT. THERE'RE NO KIDS READING COMICS TO TAKE THEIR PLACE.
YOU'RE RIGHT, STEVE-DAVE... STORE OWNERS SHOULD BE THINKING OF WAYS TO GET KIDS INTO THEIR STORES.
NO, MAN-- IT'S THE KIDS' FAULT! ALL THEY DO IS SIT AROUND PLAYING THEIR VIDEO GAMES, LOOKING FOR PORN ON THE INTERNET, AND WATCHING THAT MOOBY CRAP!
THAT'S WHAT I MEANT.
AND THE PUBLISHERS ARE NO HELP, EITHER-- THEY HIRE THE WORST PEOPLE TO WRITE THE WORST CRAP!

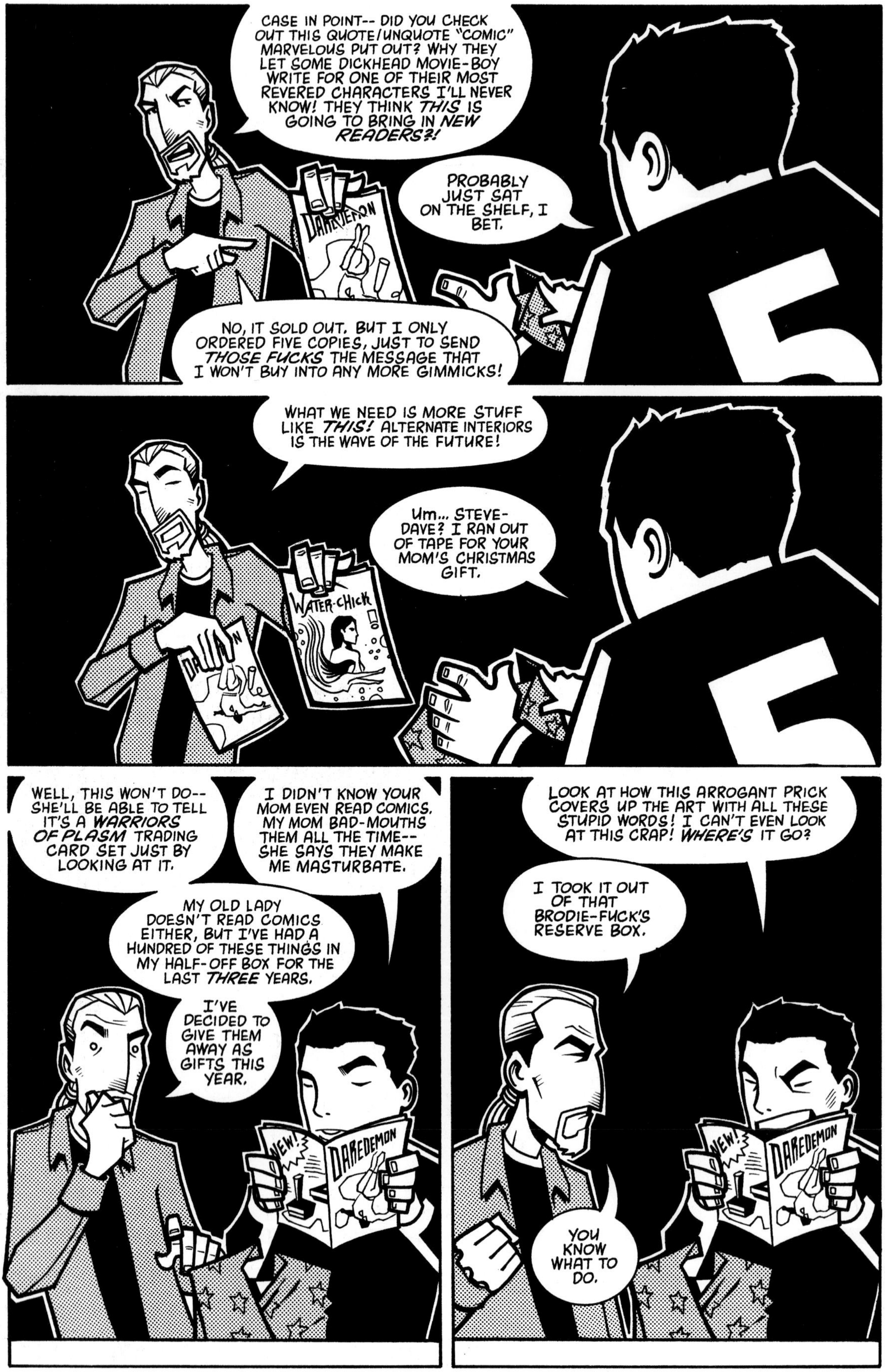
CASE IN POINT-- DID YOU CHECK OUT THIS QUOTE/UNQUOTE "COMIC" MARVELOUS PUT OUT? WHY THEY LET SOME DICKHEAD MOVIE-BOY WRITE FOR ONE OF THEIR MOST REVERED CHARACTERS I'LL NEVER KNOW! THEY THINK *THIS* IS GOING TO BRING IN *NEW READERS?!*
PROBABLY JUST SAT ON THE SHELF, I BET.
NO, IT SOLD OUT. BUT I ONLY ORDERED FIVE COPIES, JUST TO SEND *THOSE FUCKS* THE MESSAGE THAT I WON'T BUY INTO ANY MORE GIMMICKS!
WHAT WE NEED IS MORE STUFF LIKE *THIS!* ALTERNATE INTERIORS IS THE WAVE OF THE FUTURE!
WATER-CHICK
Um... STEVE-DAVE? I RAN OUT OF TAPE FOR YOUR MOM'S CHRISTMAS GIFT.
WELL, THIS WON'T DO-- SHE'LL BE ABLE TO TELL IT'S A *WARRIORS OF PLASM* TRADING CARD SET JUST BY LOOKING AT IT.
I DIDN'T KNOW YOUR MOM EVEN READ COMICS. MY MOM BAD-MOUTHS THEM ALL THE TIME-- SHE SAYS THEY MAKE ME MASTURBATE.
MY OLD LADY DOESN'T READ COMICS EITHER, BUT I'VE HAD A HUNDRED OF THESE THINGS IN MY HALF-OFF BOX FOR THE LAST *THREE* YEARS.
I'VE DECIDED TO GIVE THEM AWAY AS GIFTS THIS YEAR.
NEW!
DAREDEMON
LOOK AT HOW THIS ARROGANT PRICK COVERS UP THE ART WITH ALL THESE STUPID WORDS! I CAN'T EVEN LOOK AT THIS CRAP! *WHERE'S* IT GO?
I TOOK IT OUT OF THAT BRODIE-FUCK'S RESERVE BOX.
YOU KNOW WHAT TO DO.

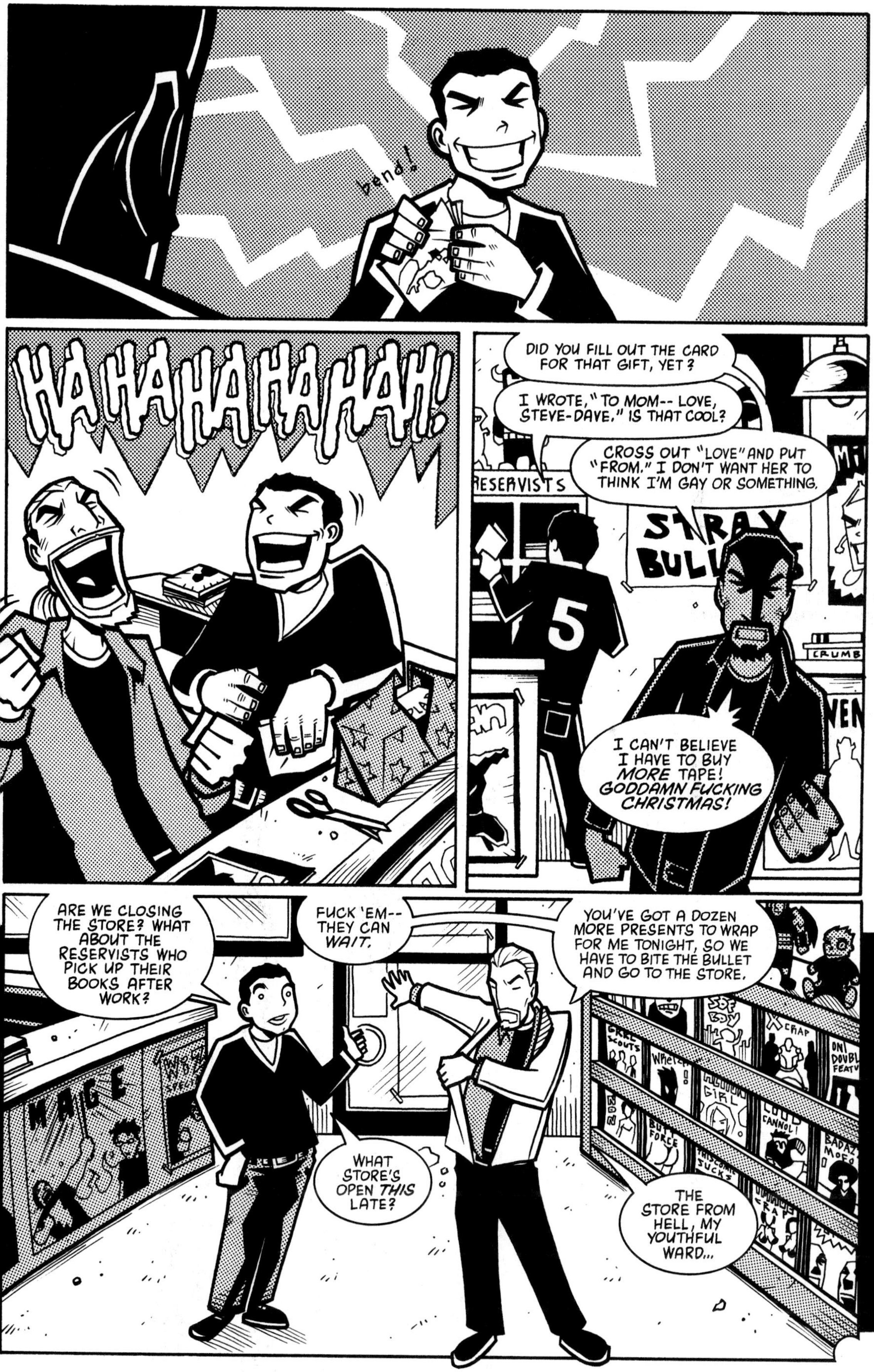
bend!
HAHAHAHAHAHAH!
DID YOU FILL OUT THE CARD FOR THAT GIFT, YET?
I WROTE, "TO MOM-- LOVE, STEVE-DAVE." IS THAT COOL?
CROSS OUT "LOVE" AND PUT "FROM." I DON'T WANT HER TO THINK I'M GAY OR SOMETHING.
RESERVISTS
STRAY BULL
CRUMB
I CAN'T BELIEVE I HAVE TO BUY *MORE* TAPE! *GODDAMN FUCKING CHRISTMAS!*
ARE WE CLOSING THE STORE? WHAT ABOUT THE RESERVISTS WHO PICK UP THEIR BOOKS AFTER WORK?
FUCK 'EM-- THEY CAN *WAIT.*
YOU'VE GOT A DOZEN MORE PRESENTS TO WRAP FOR ME TONIGHT, SO WE HAVE TO BITE THE BULLET AND GO TO THE STORE.
WHAT STORE'S OPEN *THIS* LATE?
THE STORE FROM HELL, MY YOUTHFUL WARD...

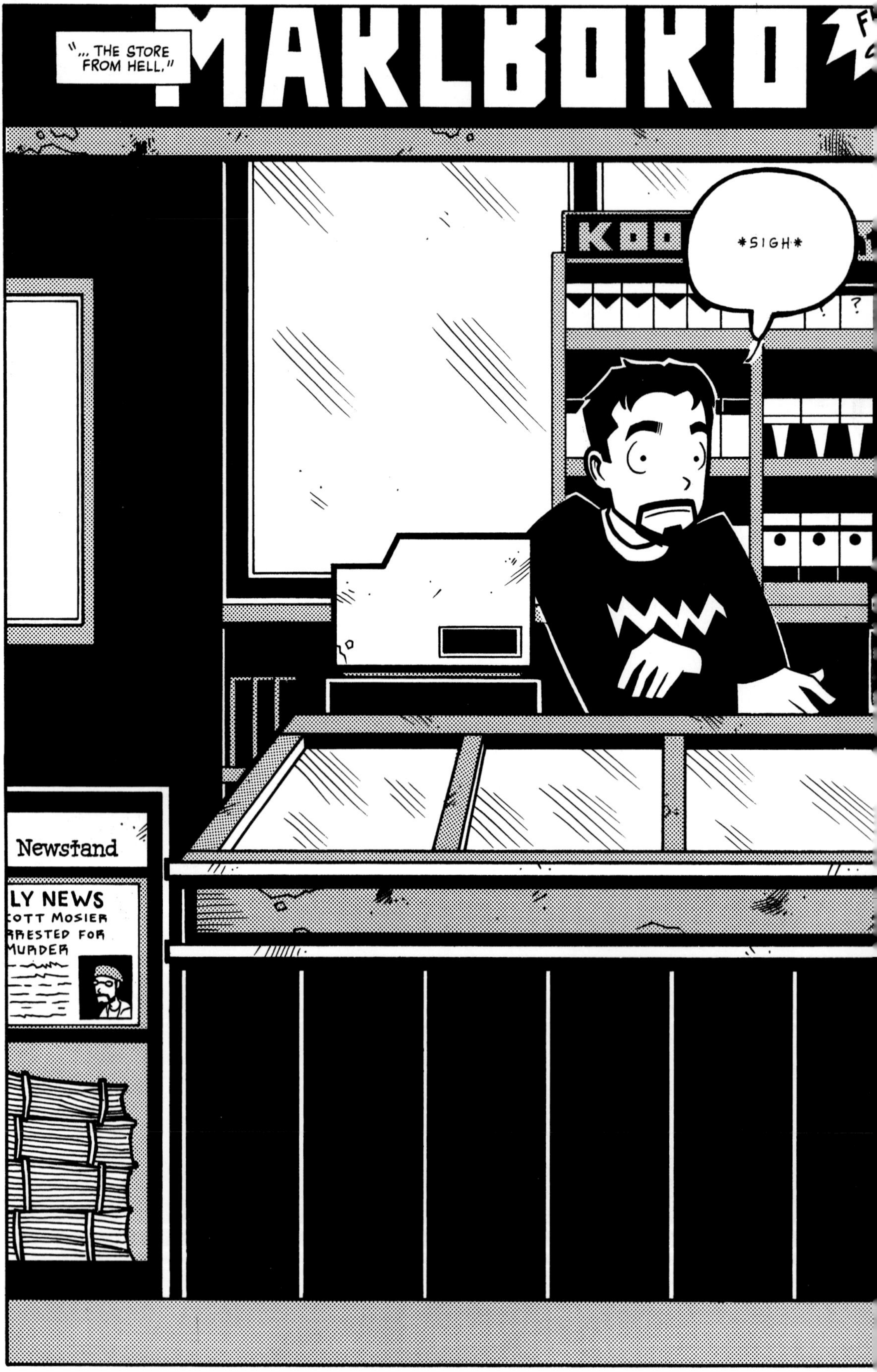
"... THE STORE FROM HELL."
MARLBORO
SIGH
Newsstand
LY NEWS
COTT MOSIER
RRESTED FOR
MURDER

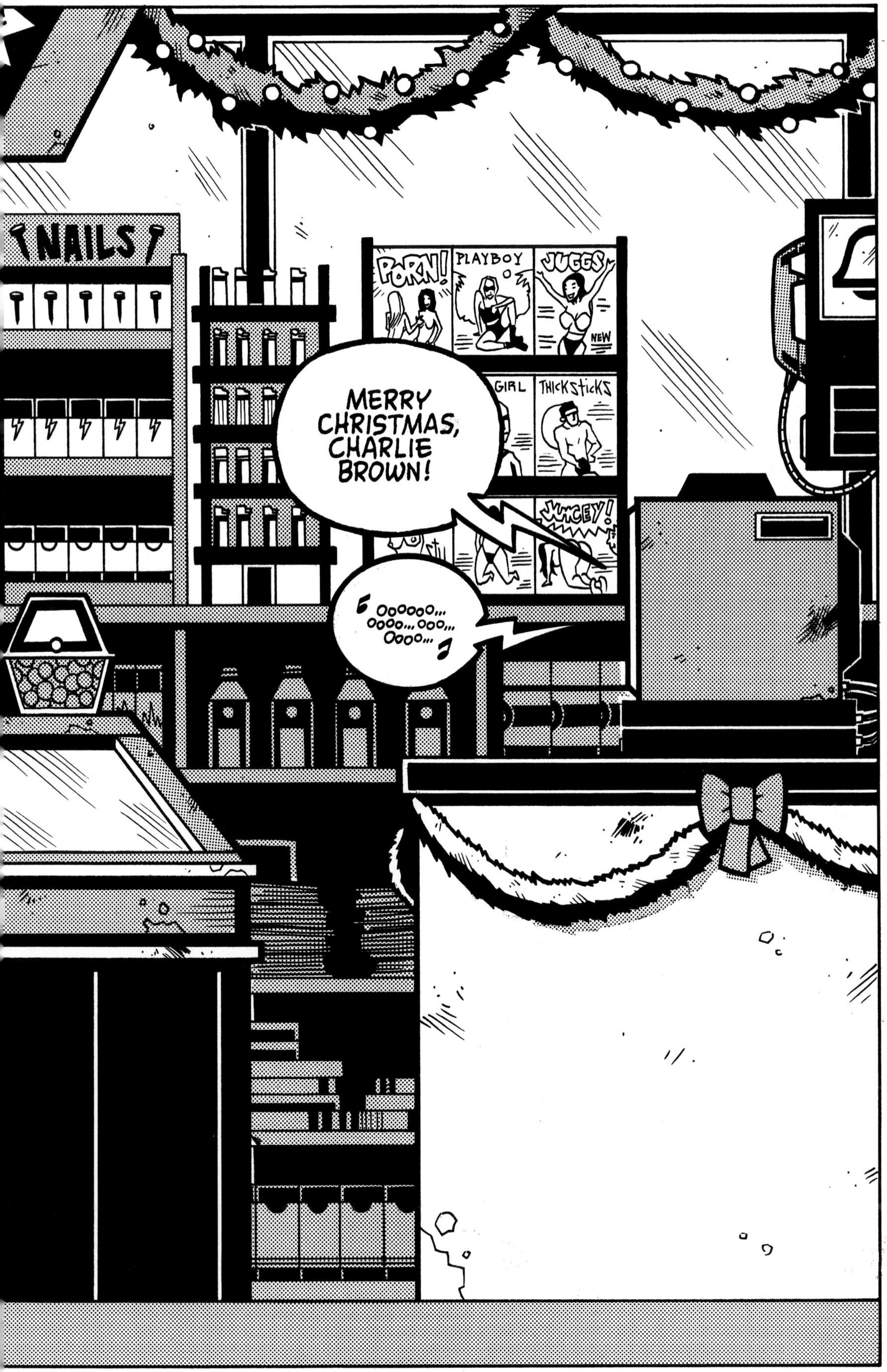

NAILS
PORN!
PLAYBOY
JUGGS
NEW
GIRL
THICKSTICKS
JUICEY!
MERRY CHRISTMAS, CHARLIE BROWN!
Oooooo... oooo... ooo... Oooo...

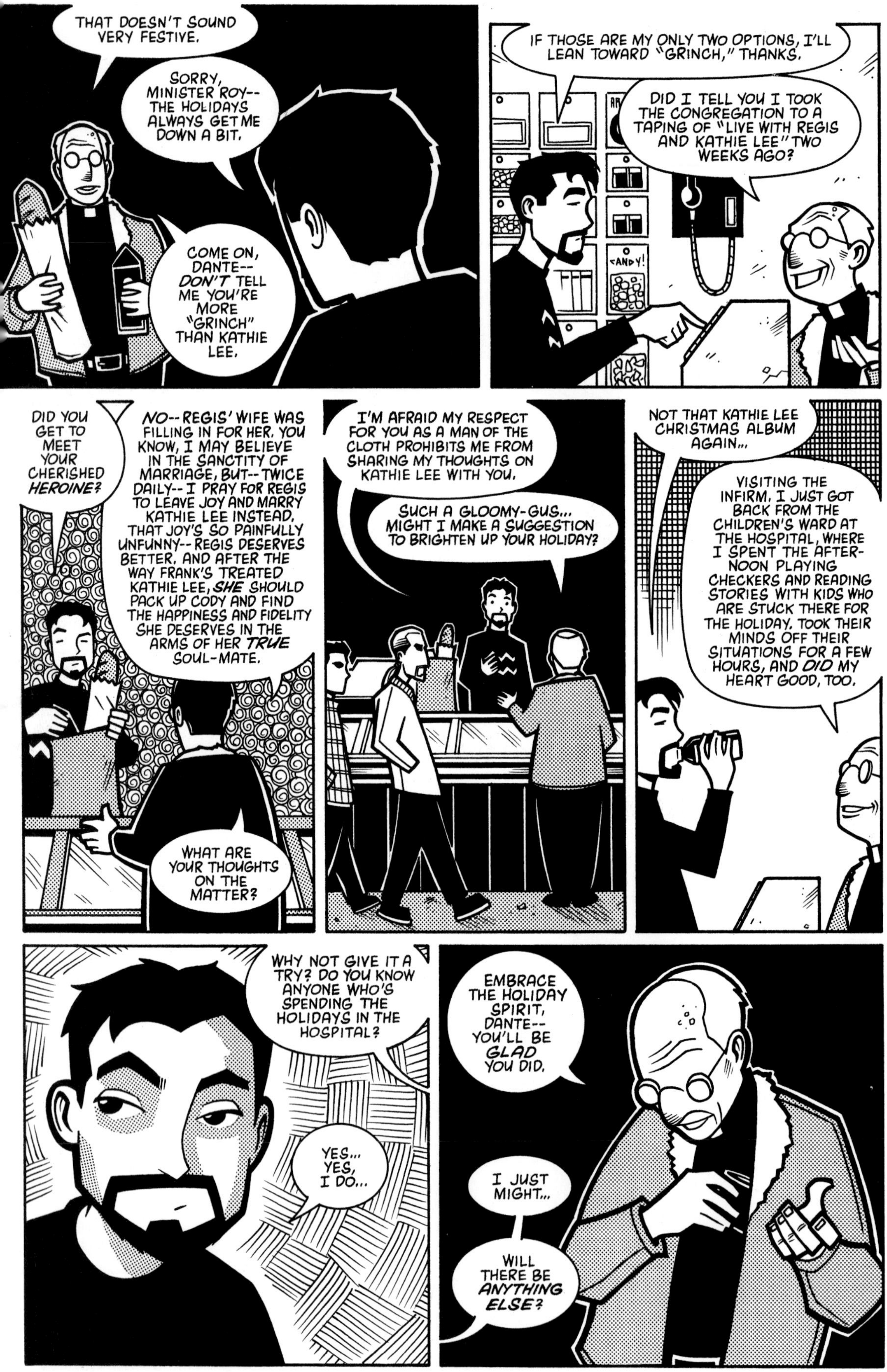
THAT DOESN'T SOUND VERY FESTIVE.
SORRY, MINISTER ROY-- THE HOLIDAYS ALWAYS GET ME DOWN A BIT.
COME ON, DANTE-- *DON'T* TELL ME YOU'RE MORE "GRINCH" THAN KATHIE LEE.
IF THOSE ARE MY ONLY TWO OPTIONS, I'LL LEAN TOWARD "GRINCH," THANKS.
DID I TELL YOU I TOOK THE CONGREGATION TO A TAPING OF "LIVE WITH REGIS AND KATHIE LEE" TWO WEEKS AGO?
CANDY!
DID YOU GET TO MEET YOUR CHERISHED *HEROINE*?
NO-- REGIS' WIFE WAS FILLING IN FOR HER. YOU KNOW, I MAY BELIEVE IN THE SANCTITY OF MARRIAGE, BUT-- TWICE DAILY-- I PRAY FOR REGIS TO LEAVE JOY AND MARRY KATHIE LEE INSTEAD. THAT JOY'S SO PAINFULLY UNFUNNY-- REGIS DESERVES BETTER. AND AFTER THE WAY FRANK'S TREATED KATHIE LEE, *SHE* SHOULD PACK UP CODY AND FIND THE HAPPINESS AND FIDELITY SHE DESERVES IN THE ARMS OF HER *TRUE* SOUL-MATE.
WHAT ARE YOUR THOUGHTS ON THE MATTER?
I'M AFRAID MY RESPECT FOR YOU AS A MAN OF THE CLOTH PROHIBITS ME FROM SHARING MY THOUGHTS ON KATHIE LEE WITH YOU.
SUCH A GLOOMY-GUS... MIGHT I MAKE A SUGGESTION TO BRIGHTEN UP YOUR HOLIDAY?
NOT THAT KATHIE LEE CHRISTMAS ALBUM AGAIN...
VISITING THE INFIRM. I JUST GOT BACK FROM THE CHILDREN'S WARD AT THE HOSPITAL, WHERE I SPENT THE AFTER-NOON PLAYING CHECKERS AND READING STORIES WITH KIDS WHO ARE STUCK THERE FOR THE HOLIDAY. TOOK THEIR MINDS OFF THEIR SITUATIONS FOR A FEW HOURS, AND *DID* MY HEART GOOD, TOO.
WHY NOT GIVE IT A TRY? DO YOU KNOW ANYONE WHO'S SPENDING THE HOLIDAYS IN THE HOSPITAL?
YES... YES, I DO...
EMBRACE THE HOLIDAY SPIRIT, DANTE-- YOU'LL BE *GLAD* YOU DID.
I JUST MIGHT...
WILL THERE BE *ANYTHING ELSE*?

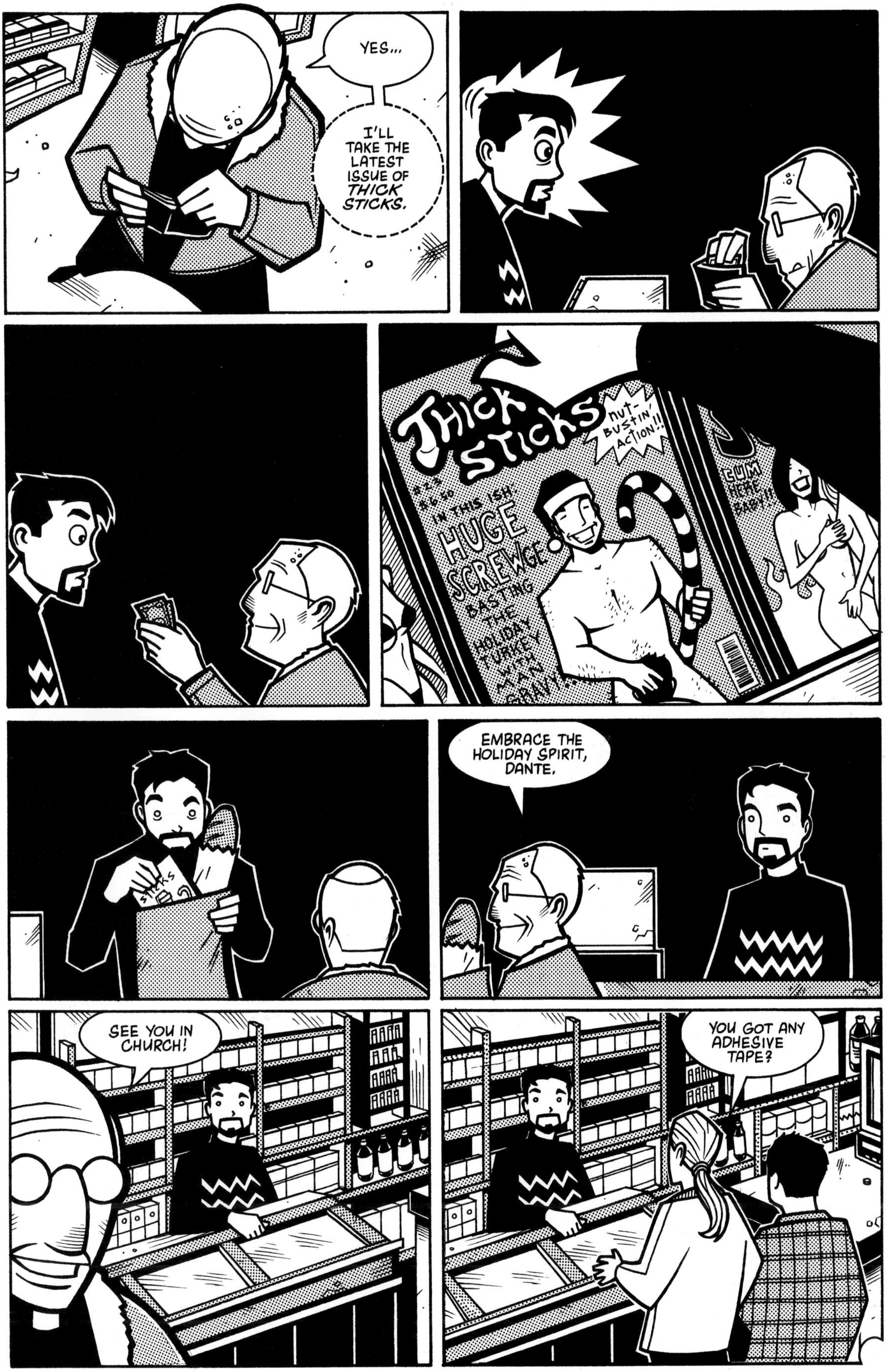
YES...
I'LL TAKE THE LATEST ISSUE OF THICK STICKS.
THICK STICKS
NUT-BUSTIN' ACTION!!
$6.50
IN THIS ISH, HUGE SCREWGE BASTING THE HOLIDAY TURKEY WITH MAN GRAVY...
CUM HERE BABY!!
EMBRACE THE HOLIDAY SPIRIT, DANTE.
SEE YOU IN CHURCH!
YOU GOT ANY ADHESIVE TAPE?

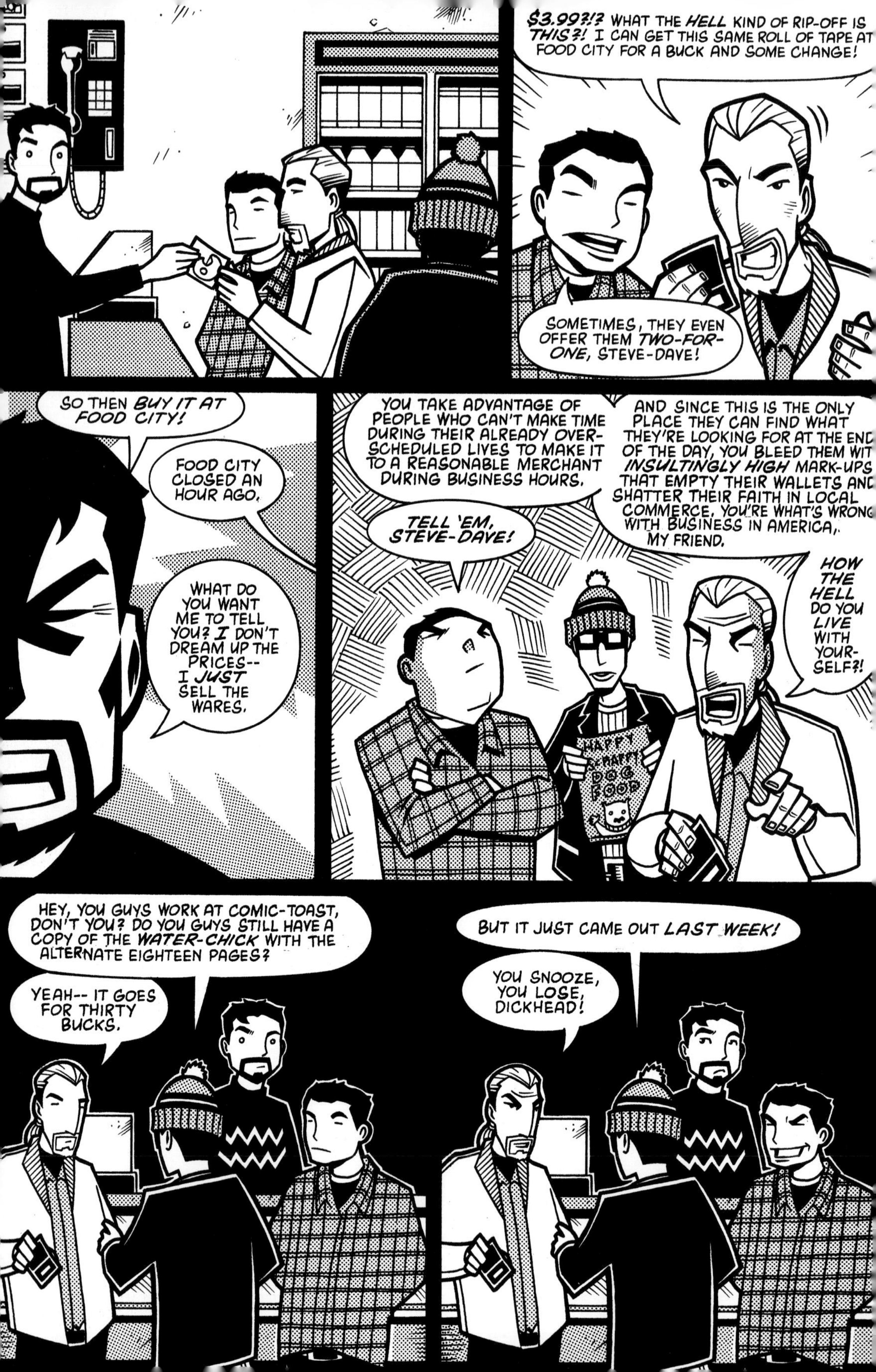
$3.99?!? WHAT THE HELL KIND OF RIP-OFF IS THIS?! I CAN GET THIS SAME ROLL OF TAPE AT FOOD CITY FOR A BUCK AND SOME CHANGE!
SOMETIMES, THEY EVEN OFFER THEM TWO-FOR-ONE, STEVE-DAVE!
SO THEN BUY IT AT FOOD CITY!
FOOD CITY CLOSED AN HOUR AGO.
WHAT DO YOU WANT ME TO TELL YOU? I DON'T DREAM UP THE PRICES-- I JUST SELL THE WARES.
YOU TAKE ADVANTAGE OF PEOPLE WHO CAN'T MAKE TIME DURING THEIR ALREADY OVER-SCHEDULED LIVES TO MAKE IT TO A REASONABLE MERCHANT DURING BUSINESS HOURS.
AND SINCE THIS IS THE ONLY PLACE THEY CAN FIND WHAT THEY'RE LOOKING FOR AT THE END OF THE DAY, YOU BLEED THEM WITH INSULTINGLY HIGH MARK-UPS THAT EMPTY THEIR WALLETS AND SHATTER THEIR FAITH IN LOCAL COMMERCE. YOU'RE WHAT'S WRONG WITH BUSINESS IN AMERICA, MY FRIEND.
TELL 'EM, STEVE-DAVE!
HOW THE HELL DO YOU LIVE WITH YOUR-SELF?!
HAPPY SCRAPPY DOG FOOD
HEY, YOU GUYS WORK AT COMIC-TOAST, DON'T YOU? DO YOU GUYS STILL HAVE A COPY OF THE WATER-CHICK WITH THE ALTERNATE EIGHTEEN PAGES?
YEAH-- IT GOES FOR THIRTY BUCKS.
BUT IT JUST CAME OUT LAST WEEK!
YOU SNOOZE, YOU LOSE, DICKHEAD!

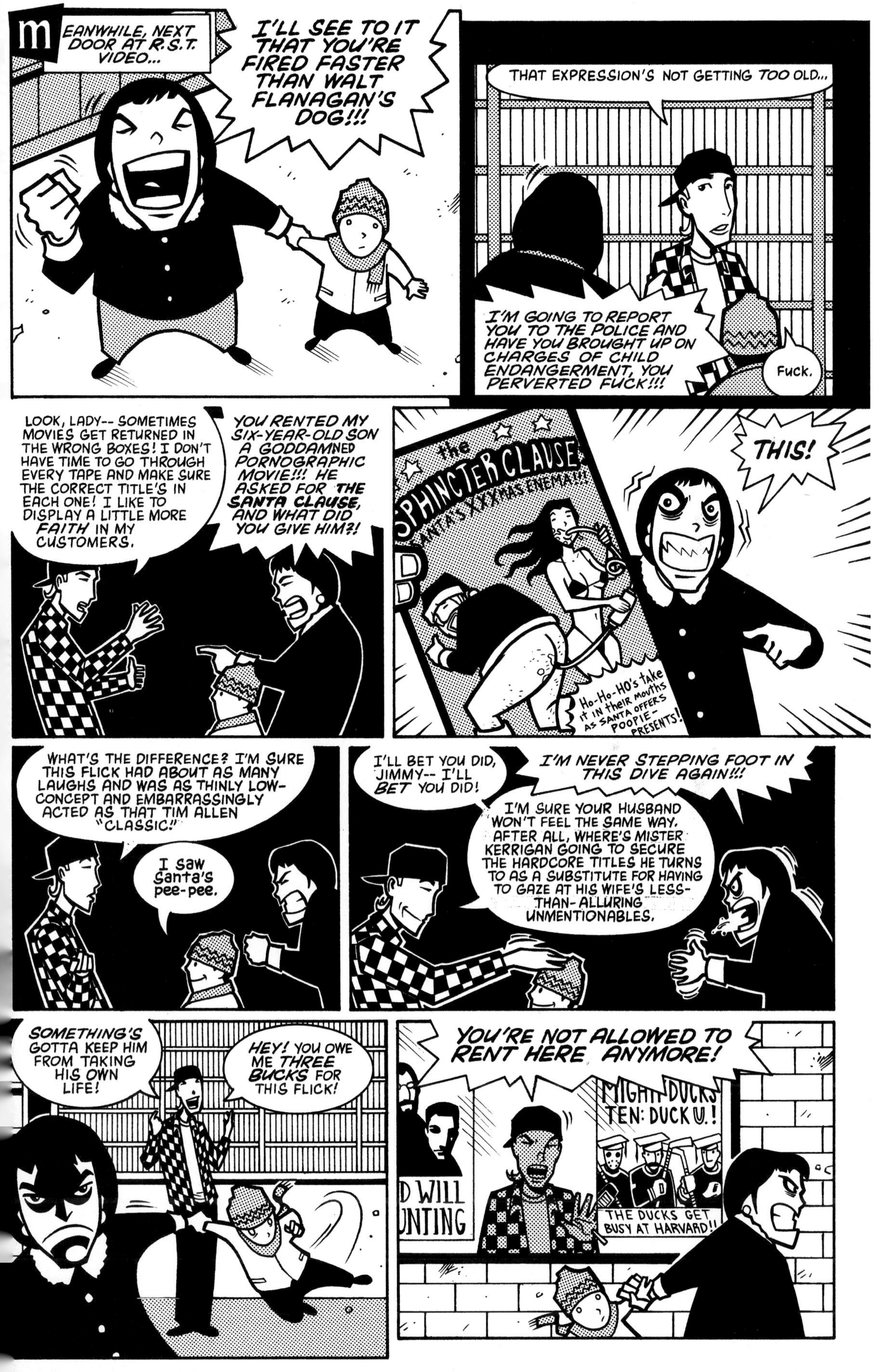
MEANWHILE, NEXT DOOR AT R.S.T. VIDEO...
I'LL SEE TO IT THAT YOU'RE FIRED FASTER THAN WALT FLANAGAN'S DOG!!!
THAT EXPRESSION'S NOT GETTING TOO OLD...
I'M GOING TO REPORT YOU TO THE POLICE AND HAVE YOU BROUGHT UP ON CHARGES OF CHILD ENDANGERMENT, YOU PERVERTED FUCK!!!
Fuck.
LOOK, LADY-- SOMETIMES MOVIES GET RETURNED IN THE WRONG BOXES! I DON'T HAVE TIME TO GO THROUGH EVERY TAPE AND MAKE SURE THE CORRECT TITLE'S IN EACH ONE! I LIKE TO DISPLAY A LITTLE MORE FAITH IN MY CUSTOMERS.
YOU RENTED MY SIX-YEAR-OLD SON A GODDAMNED PORNOGRAPHIC MOVIE!!! HE ASKED FOR THE SANTA CLAUSE, AND WHAT DID YOU GIVE HIM?!
the SPHINCTER CLAUSE
SANTA'S XXXMAS ENEMA!!!
Ho-Ho-HO's take it in their mouths as Santa offers Poopie-Presents!
THIS!
WHAT'S THE DIFFERENCE? I'M SURE THIS FLICK HAD ABOUT AS MANY LAUGHS AND WAS AS THINLY LOW-CONCEPT AND EMBARRASSINGLY ACTED AS THAT TIM ALLEN "CLASSIC!"
I saw Santa's pee-pee.
I'LL BET YOU DID, JIMMY-- I'LL BET YOU DID!
I'M NEVER STEPPING FOOT IN THIS DIVE AGAIN!!!
I'M SURE YOUR HUSBAND WON'T FEEL THE SAME WAY. AFTER ALL, WHERE'S MISTER KERRIGAN GOING TO SECURE THE HARDCORE TITLES HE TURNS TO AS A SUBSTITUTE FOR HAVING TO GAZE AT HIS WIFE'S LESS-THAN-ALLURING UNMENTIONABLES.
SOMETHING'S GOTTA KEEP HIM FROM TAKING HIS OWN LIFE!
HEY! YOU OWE ME THREE BUCKS FOR THIS FLICK!
YOU'RE NOT ALLOWED TO RENT HERE ANYMORE!
MIGHTY DUCKS TEN: DUCK U.!
THE DUCKS GET BUSY AT HARVARD!!
D WILL
UNTING

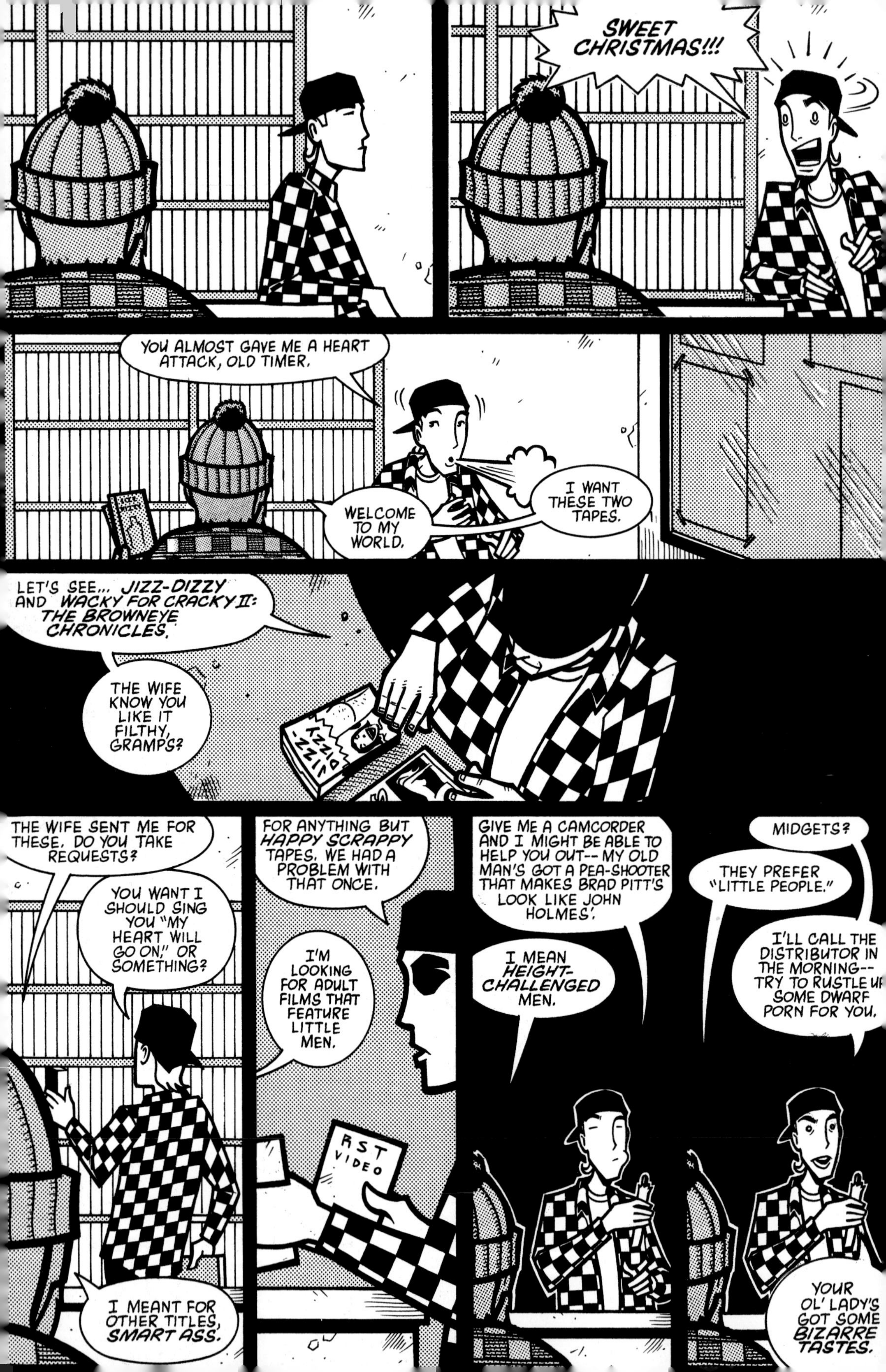
SWEET CHRISTMAS!!!
YOU ALMOST GAVE ME A HEART ATTACK, OLD TIMER.
WELCOME TO MY WORLD.
I WANT THESE TWO TAPES.
LET'S SEE... JIZZ-DIZZY AND WACKY FOR CRACKY II: THE BROWNEYE CHRONICLES.
THE WIFE KNOW YOU LIKE IT FILTHY, GRAMPS?
JIZZ-DIZZY
THE WIFE SENT ME FOR THESE. DO YOU TAKE REQUESTS?
YOU WANT I SHOULD SING YOU "MY HEART WILL GO ON," OR SOMETHING?
I MEANT FOR OTHER TITLES, SMART ASS.
FOR ANYTHING BUT HAPPY SCRAPPY TAPES. WE HAD A PROBLEM WITH THAT ONCE.
I'M LOOKING FOR ADULT FILMS THAT FEATURE LITTLE MEN.
RST VIDEO
GIVE ME A CAMCORDER AND I MIGHT BE ABLE TO HELP YOU OUT-- MY OLD MAN'S GOT A PEA-SHOOTER THAT MAKES BRAD PITT'S LOOK LIKE JOHN HOLMES'.
I MEAN HEIGHT-CHALLENGED MEN.
MIDGETS?
THEY PREFER "LITTLE PEOPLE."
I'LL CALL THE DISTRIBUTOR IN THE MORNING-- TRY TO RUSTLE UP SOME DWARF PORN FOR YOU.
YOUR OL' LADY'S GOT SOME BIZARRE TASTES.

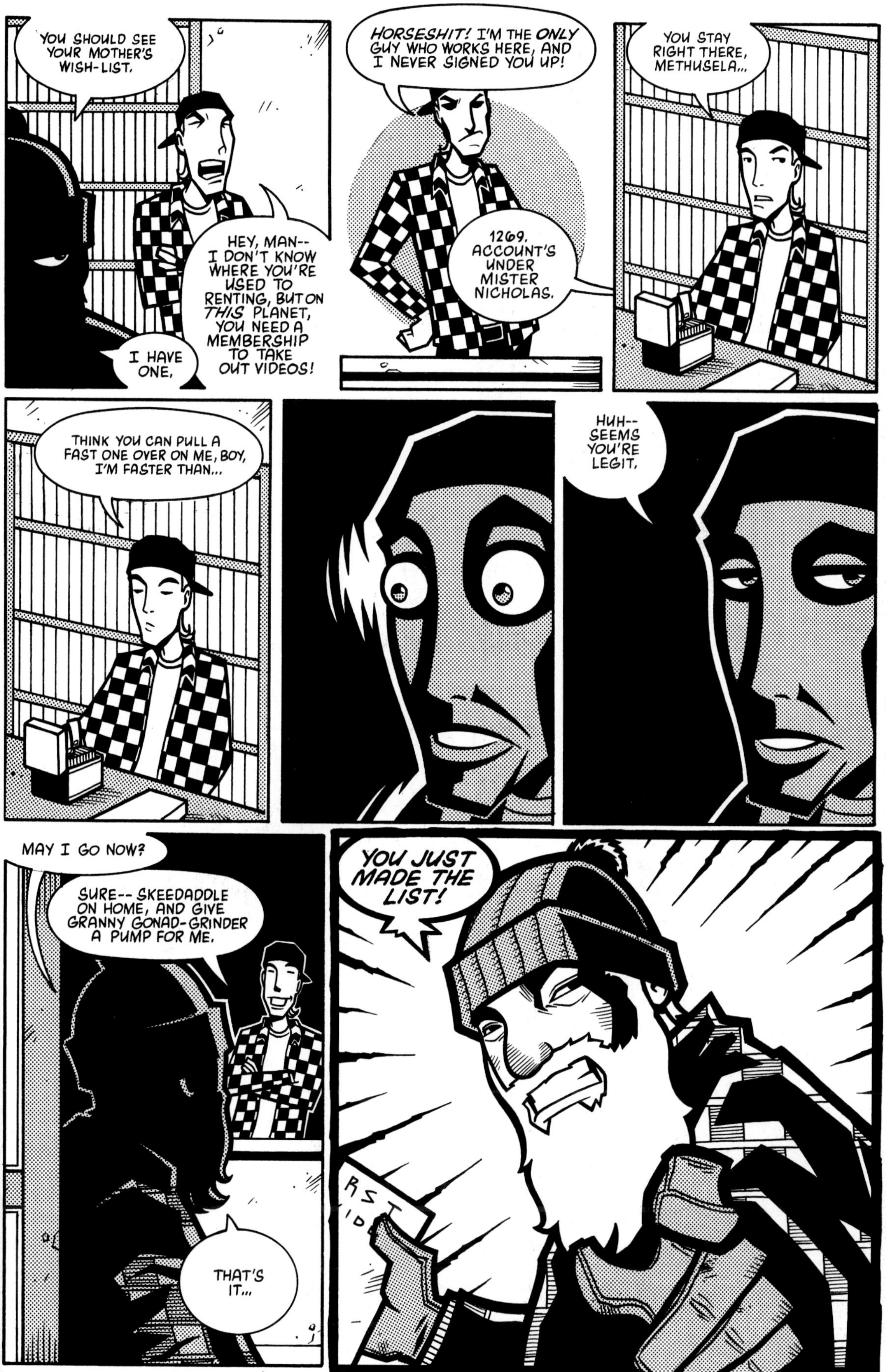
YOU SHOULD SEE YOUR MOTHER'S WISH-LIST.
HEY, MAN-- I DON'T KNOW WHERE YOU'RE USED TO RENTING, BUT ON *THIS* PLANET, YOU NEED A MEMBERSHIP TO TAKE OUT VIDEOS!
I HAVE ONE.
HORSESHIT! I'M THE *ONLY* GUY WHO WORKS HERE, AND I NEVER SIGNED YOU UP!
1269. ACCOUNT'S UNDER MISTER NICHOLAS.
YOU STAY RIGHT THERE, METHUSELA...
THINK YOU CAN PULL A FAST ONE OVER ON ME, BOY, I'M FASTER THAN...
HUH-- SEEMS YOU'RE LEGIT.
MAY I GO NOW?
SURE-- SKEEDADDLE ON HOME, AND GIVE GRANNY GONAD-GRINDER A PUMP FOR ME.
THAT'S IT...
YOU JUST MADE THE LIST!

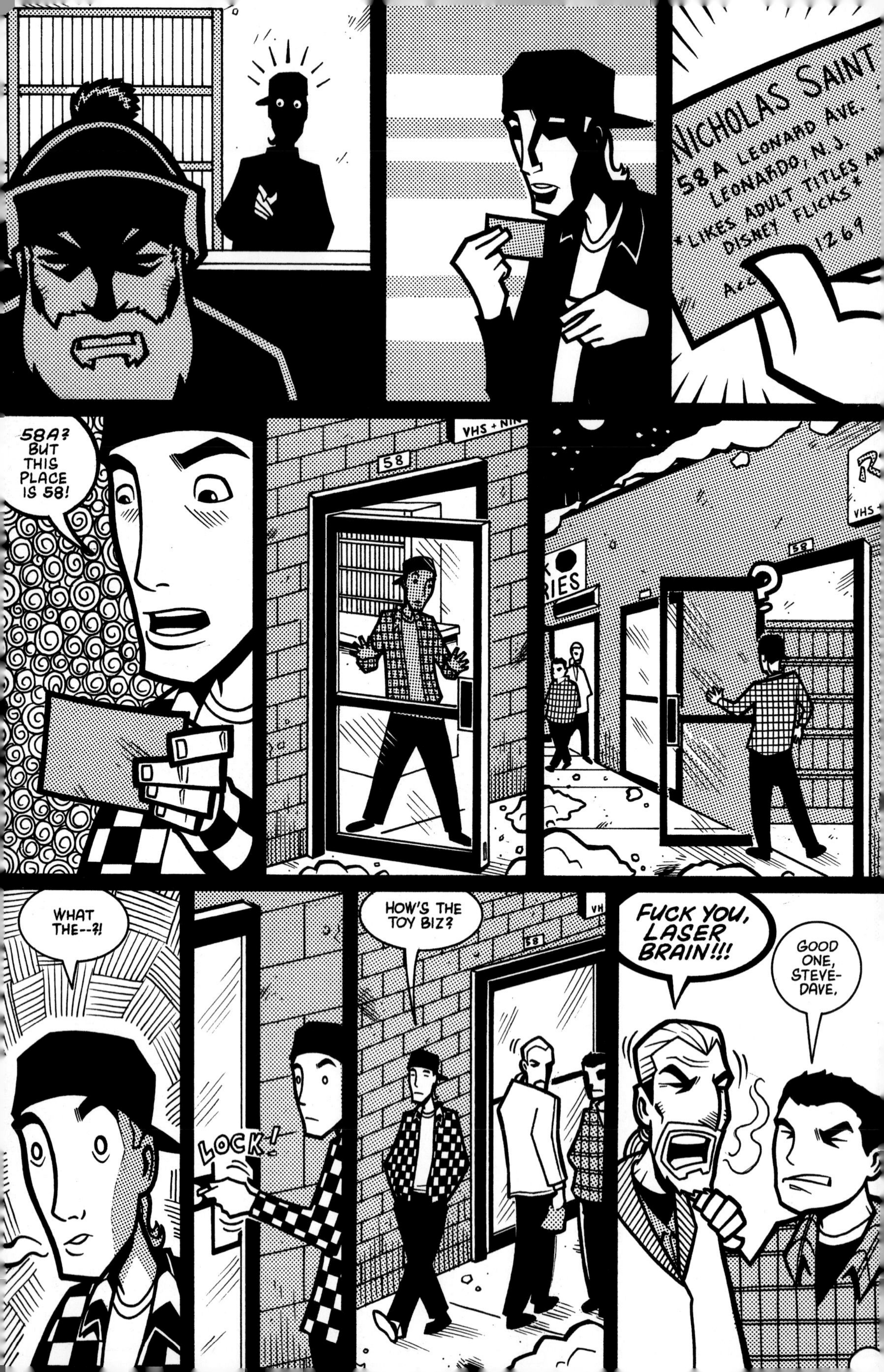

NICHOLAS SAINT
58A LEONARD AVE.
LEONARDO, N.J.
* LIKES ADULT TITLES AN
DISNEY FLICKS *
1269
58A? BUT THIS PLACE IS 58!
VHS + NIN
58
58
RIES
VHS
WHAT THE--?!
LOCK!
HOW'S THE TOY BIZ?
58
FUCK YOU, LASER BRAIN!!!
GOOD ONE, STEVE-DAVE.

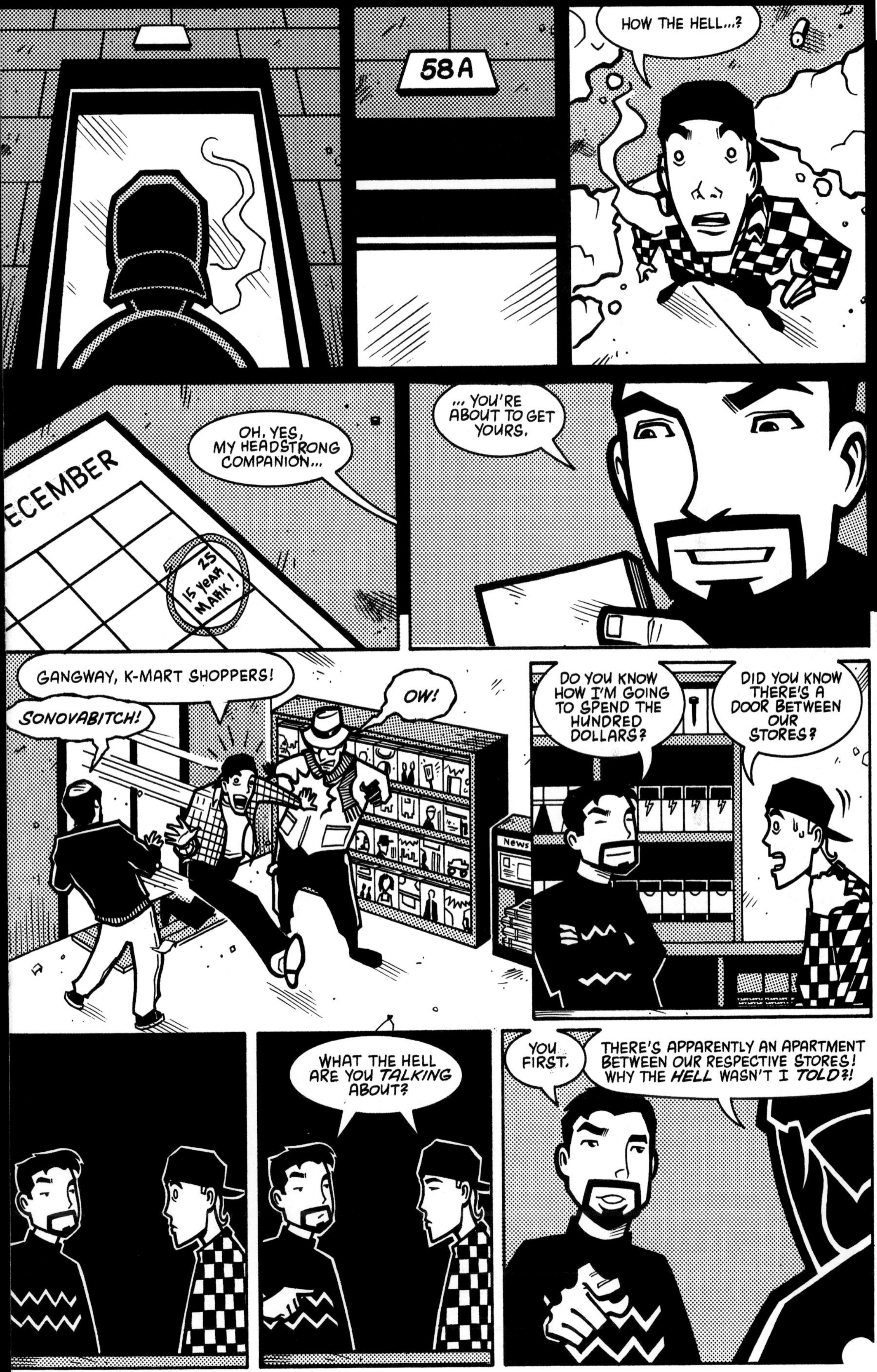
58A
HOW THE HELL...?
OH, YES, MY HEADSTRONG COMPANION...
DECEMBER
25
15 YEAR MARK!
...YOU'RE ABOUT TO GET YOURS.
GANGWAY, K-MART SHOPPERS!
SONOVABITCH!
OW!
News
DO YOU KNOW HOW I'M GOING TO SPEND THE HUNDRED DOLLARS?
DID YOU KNOW THERE'S A DOOR BETWEEN OUR STORES?
WHAT THE HELL ARE YOU TALKING ABOUT?
YOU FIRST.
THERE'S APPARENTLY AN APARTMENT BETWEEN OUR RESPECTIVE STORES! WHY THE HELL WASN'T I TOLD?!

YOU'RE JUST NOTICING THAT NOW?

YOU MEAN IT'S ALWAYS BEEN THERE?! HOW THE HELL DID THAT SLIP BY ME?

HISTORICALLY, YOU'VE ALWAYS BEEN UNABLE TO GRASP MOST OF LIFE'S SIMPLE CONCEPTS, RANDAL.

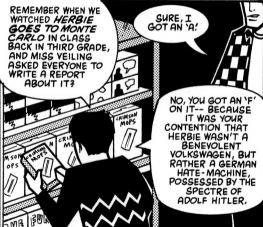

REMEMBER WHEN WE WATCHED *HERBIE GOES TO MONTE CARLO* IN CLASS BACK IN THIRD GRADE, AND MISS VEILING ASKED EVERYONE TO WRITE A REPORT ABOUT IT?

SURE, I GOT AN 'A!

NO, YOU GOT AN 'F' ON IT-- BECAUSE IT WAS YOUR CONTENTION THAT HERBIE WASN'T A BENEVOLENT VOLKSWAGEN, BUT RATHER A GERMAN HATE-MACHINE, POSSESSED BY THE SPECTRE OF ADOLF HITLER.

IT WAS A SENTIENT GERMAN CAR WHOSE CONTEMPT FOR JEWS WAS DISTURBINGLY APPARENT, FOR CHRISSAKES! HERBIE REPRESENTED THE REPACKAGING OF THIRD REICH IDEALS INTO SOMETHING AMERICANS WOULD SWALLOW EASIER: AN AFFORDABLE CAR.

IT WAS CALLED *THE LOVE BUG*, YOU IDIOT!

YES, BUT LOVE OF *WHAT?* READ BETWEEN THE LINES, MY FRIEND: IT WAS THE LOVE OF HATING JEWS!

THAT'S THE MOVIE *I* SAW, AND I'M STANDING BY MY ASSESSMENT, ALMOST TWENTY YEARS LATER.

THE YEARS HAVE NOT BEEN KIND TO YOU, MY MISGUIDED FRIEND. NOR HAVE THEY BEEN KIND TO YOUR MEMORY.

WHAT ARE YOU BABBLING ABOUT, NOW?

RECALL, IF YOU WILL, A COCKSURE PUBESCENT, WHO ONE CHRISTMAS RECEIVED WHAT HE CONSIDERED, AT THAT TIME IN HIS LIFE, TO BE THE ULTIMATE TREASURE-- A GIFT HE SWORE COULD NEVER BE TOPPED, AND WOULD NEVER BE FORGOTTEN.

SO CERTAIN OF HIS ALLEGIANCE TO SAID GIFT WAS HE, THAT A BOLD PROCLAMATION WAS MADE, WHICH HAD HIM SWEARING HE WOULD FOR- EVER BRANDISH THIS TOKEN PROUDLY, FOR YEARS TO COME, AND IN THE FACE OF HIS MUCH MORE REALISTIC FRIEND'S POSIT THAT THE GIFT WOULD, NO DOUBT, BE FORGOTTEN WITHIN TEN YEARS, SO SURE WAS THE CLUELESS YOUTH OF HIS CONVICTIONS THAT HE PROPOSED A FOOLHARDY WAGER.

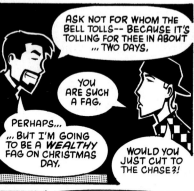

ASK NOT FOR WHOM THE BELL TOLLS-- BECAUSE IT'S TOLLING FOR THEE IN ABOUT ... TWO DAYS.

YOU ARE SUCH A FAG.

PERHAPS... ...BUT I'M GOING TO BE A *WEALTHY* FAG ON CHRISTMAS DAY.

WHAT DID YOU GET FOR CHRISTMAS FIFTEEN YEARS AGO?

WOULD YOU JUST CUT TO THE CHASE?!

ARE YOU STONED?! I DON'T REMEMBER WHAT I GOT FOR LUNCH YESTERDAY, LET ALONE WHAT I GOT FOR CHRISTMAS FIFTEEN YEARS AGO!

I'LL GIVE YOU A HINT...

BOOM-BOOM! SHOUT! BOOM-BOOM! SHOUT! BOOM-BOOM! SHOUT!

SHOUT AT THE DEVIL!

Oh, my God...

THAT'S RIGHT, MY FRIEND! FIFTEEN YEARS AGO THIS CHRISTMAS, YOU RECEIVED A DENIM JACKET WITH A MÖTLEY CRÜE ALBUM COVER PAINTED ON THE BACK!

Good God, I did...

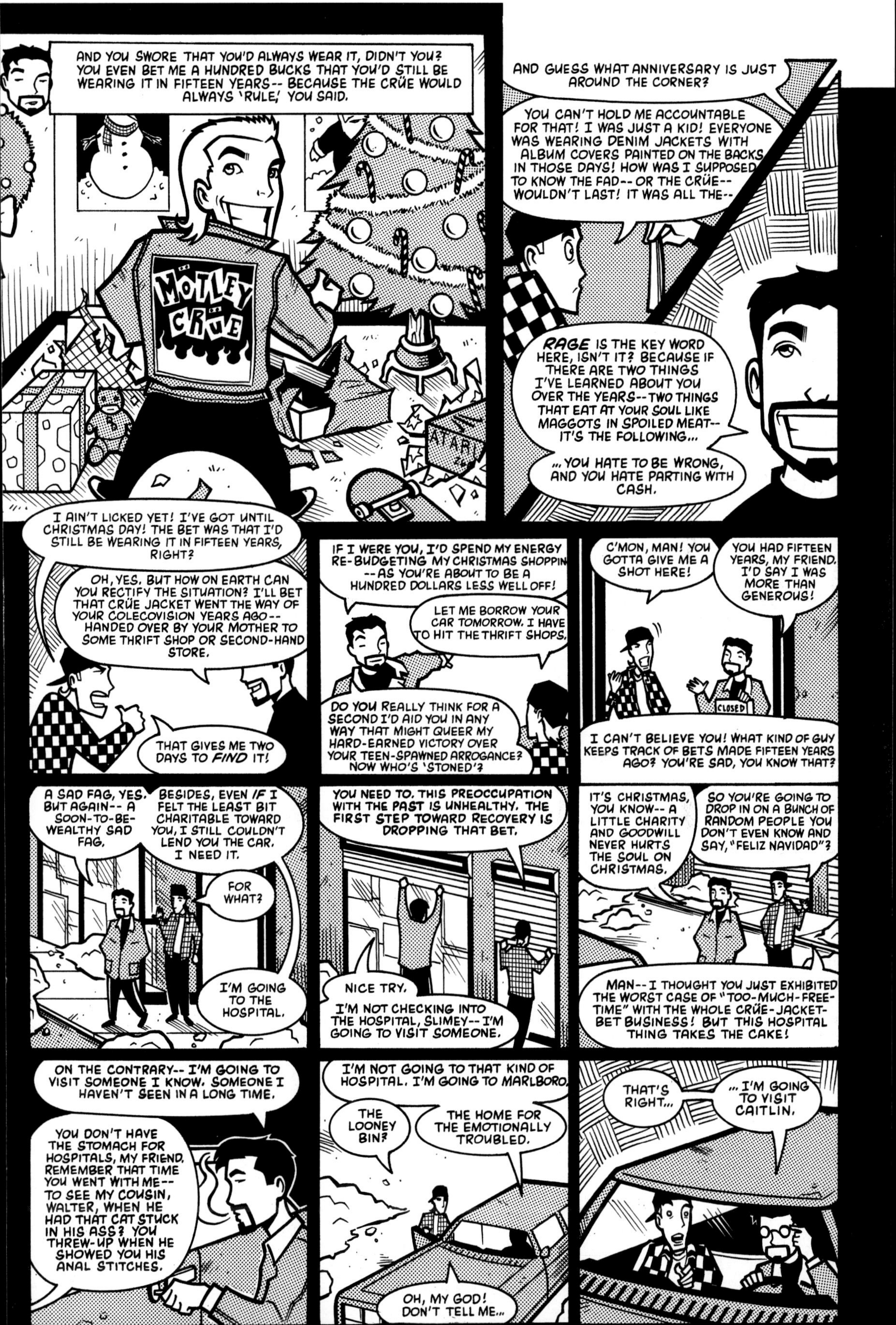
AND YOU SWORE THAT YOU'D ALWAYS WEAR IT, DIDN'T YOU? YOU EVEN BET ME A HUNDRED BUCKS THAT YOU'D STILL BE WEARING IT IN FIFTEEN YEARS-- BECAUSE THE CRÜE WOULD ALWAYS 'RULE,' YOU SAID.
MÖTLEY CRÜE
ATARI
AND GUESS WHAT ANNIVERSARY IS JUST AROUND THE CORNER?
YOU CAN'T HOLD ME ACCOUNTABLE FOR THAT! I WAS JUST A KID! EVERYONE WAS WEARING DENIM JACKETS WITH ALBUM COVERS PAINTED ON THE BACKS IN THOSE DAYS! HOW WAS I SUPPOSED TO KNOW THE FAD-- OR THE CRÜE-- WOULDN'T LAST! IT WAS ALL THE--
RAGE IS THE KEY WORD HERE, ISN'T IT? BECAUSE IF THERE ARE TWO THINGS I'VE LEARNED ABOUT YOU OVER THE YEARS-- TWO THINGS THAT EAT AT YOUR SOUL LIKE MAGGOTS IN SPOILED MEAT-- IT'S THE FOLLOWING...
...YOU HATE TO BE WRONG, AND YOU HATE PARTING WITH CASH.
I AIN'T LICKED YET! I'VE GOT UNTIL CHRISTMAS DAY! THE BET WAS THAT I'D STILL BE WEARING IT IN FIFTEEN YEARS, RIGHT?
OH, YES. BUT HOW ON EARTH CAN YOU RECTIFY THE SITUATION? I'LL BET THAT CRÜE JACKET WENT THE WAY OF YOUR COLECOVISION YEARS AGO-- HANDED OVER BY YOUR MOTHER TO SOME THRIFT SHOP OR SECOND-HAND STORE.
THAT GIVES ME TWO DAYS TO FIND IT!
IF I WERE YOU, I'D SPEND MY ENERGY RE-BUDGETING MY CHRISTMAS SHOPPIN --AS YOU'RE ABOUT TO BE A HUNDRED DOLLARS LESS WELL OFF!
LET ME BORROW YOUR CAR TOMORROW. I HAVE TO HIT THE THRIFT SHOPS.
DO YOU REALLY THINK FOR A SECOND I'D AID YOU IN ANY WAY THAT MIGHT QUEER MY HARD-EARNED VICTORY OVER YOUR TEEN-SPAWNED ARROGANCE? NOW WHO'S 'STONED'?
C'MON, MAN! YOU GOTTA GIVE ME A SHOT HERE!
YOU HAD FIFTEEN YEARS, MY FRIEND. I'D SAY I WAS MORE THAN GENEROUS!
CLOSED
I CAN'T BELIEVE YOU! WHAT KIND OF GUY KEEPS TRACK OF BETS MADE FIFTEEN YEARS AGO? YOU'RE SAD, YOU KNOW THAT?
A SAD FAG, YES. BUT AGAIN-- A SOON-TO-BE-WEALTHY SAD FAG.
BESIDES, EVEN IF I FELT THE LEAST BIT CHARITABLE TOWARD YOU, I STILL COULDN'T LEND YOU THE CAR. I NEED IT.
FOR WHAT?
I'M GOING TO THE HOSPITAL.
YOU NEED TO. THIS PREOCCUPATION WITH THE PAST IS UNHEALTHY. THE FIRST STEP TOWARD RECOVERY IS DROPPING THAT BET.
NICE TRY.
I'M NOT CHECKING INTO THE HOSPITAL, SLIMEY-- I'M GOING TO VISIT SOMEONE.
IT'S CHRISTMAS, YOU KNOW-- A LITTLE CHARITY AND GOODWILL NEVER HURTS THE SOUL ON CHRISTMAS.
SO YOU'RE GOING TO DROP IN ON A BUNCH OF RANDOM PEOPLE YOU DON'T EVEN KNOW AND SAY, "FELIZ NAVIDAD"?
MAN-- I THOUGHT YOU JUST EXHIBITED THE WORST CASE OF "TOO-MUCH-FREE-TIME" WITH THE WHOLE CRÜE-JACKET-BET BUSINESS! BUT THIS HOSPITAL THING TAKES THE CAKE!
ON THE CONTRARY-- I'M GOING TO VISIT SOMEONE I KNOW. SOMEONE I HAVEN'T SEEN IN A LONG TIME.
YOU DON'T HAVE THE STOMACH FOR HOSPITALS, MY FRIEND. REMEMBER THAT TIME YOU WENT WITH ME-- TO SEE MY COUSIN, WALTER, WHEN HE HAD THAT CAT STUCK IN HIS ASS? YOU THREW-UP WHEN HE SHOWED YOU HIS ANAL STITCHES.
I'M NOT GOING TO THAT KIND OF HOSPITAL. I'M GOING TO MARLBORO.
THE LOONEY BIN?
THE HOME FOR THE EMOTIONALLY TROUBLED.
OH, MY GOD! DON'T TELL ME...
THAT'S RIGHT...
...I'M GOING TO VISIT CAITLIN.

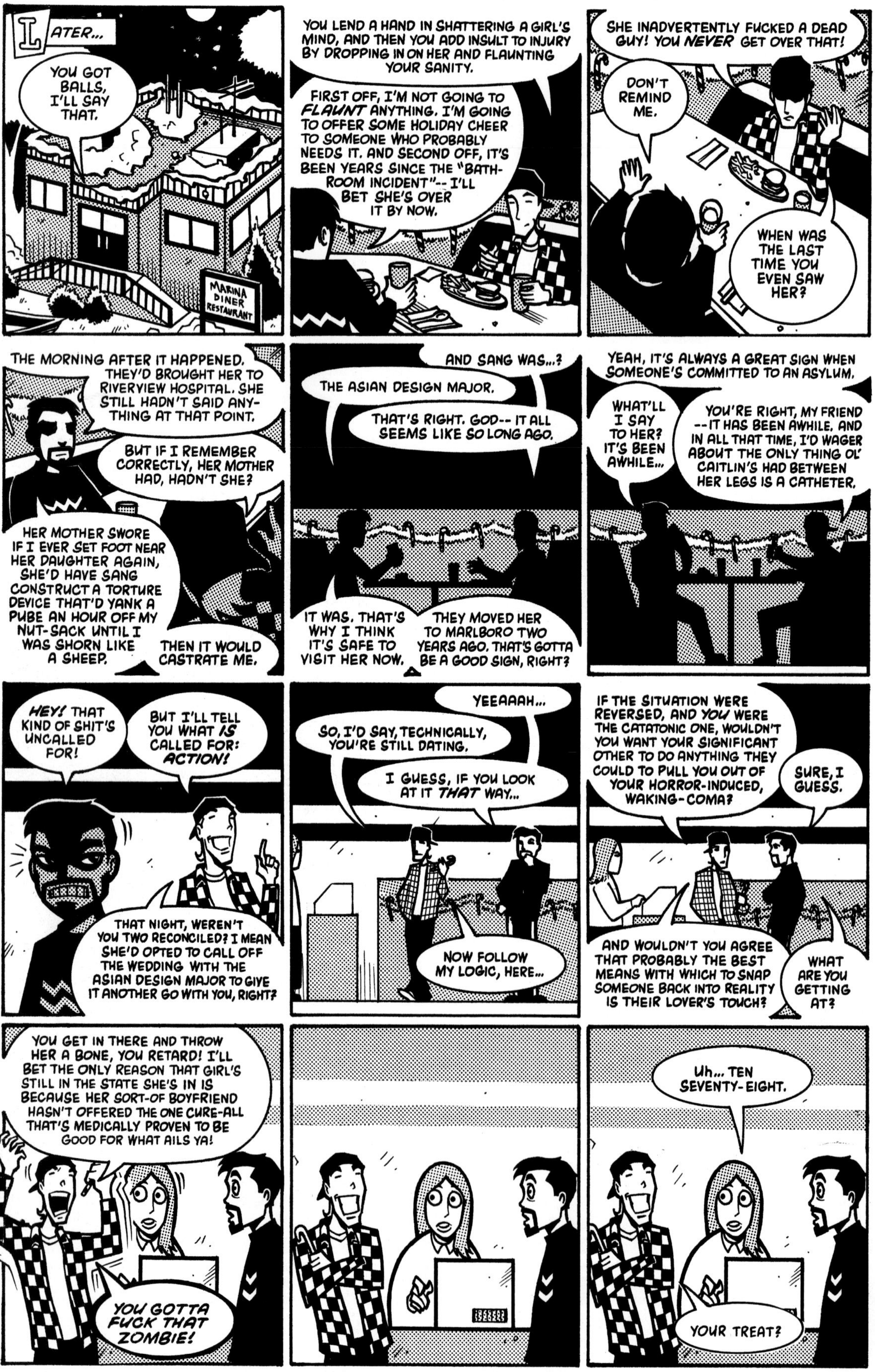
LATER...
YOU GOT BALLS, I'LL SAY THAT.
MARINA DINER RESTAURANT
YOU LEND A HAND IN SHATTERING A GIRL'S MIND, AND THEN YOU ADD INSULT TO INJURY BY DROPPING IN ON HER AND FLAUNTING YOUR SANITY.
FIRST OFF, I'M NOT GOING TO FLAUNT ANYTHING. I'M GOING TO OFFER SOME HOLIDAY CHEER TO SOMEONE WHO PROBABLY NEEDS IT. AND SECOND OFF, IT'S BEEN YEARS SINCE THE "BATH-ROOM INCIDENT"-- I'LL BET SHE'S OVER IT BY NOW.
SHE INADVERTENTLY FUCKED A DEAD GUY! YOU NEVER GET OVER THAT!
DON'T REMIND ME.
WHEN WAS THE LAST TIME YOU EVEN SAW HER?
THE MORNING AFTER IT HAPPENED. THEY'D BROUGHT HER TO RIVERVIEW HOSPITAL. SHE STILL HADN'T SAID ANY-THING AT THAT POINT.
BUT IF I REMEMBER CORRECTLY, HER MOTHER HAD, HADN'T SHE?
HER MOTHER SWORE IF I EVER SET FOOT NEAR HER DAUGHTER AGAIN, SHE'D HAVE SANG CONSTRUCT A TORTURE DEVICE THAT'D YANK A PUBE AN HOUR OFF MY NUT-SACK UNTIL I WAS SHORN LIKE A SHEEP.
THEN IT WOULD CASTRATE ME.
AND SANG WAS...?
THE ASIAN DESIGN MAJOR.
THAT'S RIGHT. GOD-- IT ALL SEEMS LIKE SO LONG AGO.
IT WAS. THAT'S WHY I THINK IT'S SAFE TO VISIT HER NOW.
THEY MOVED HER TO MARLBORO TWO YEARS AGO. THAT'S GOTTA BE A GOOD SIGN, RIGHT?
YEAH, IT'S ALWAYS A GREAT SIGN WHEN SOMEONE'S COMMITTED TO AN ASYLUM.
WHAT'LL I SAY TO HER? IT'S BEEN AWHILE...
YOU'RE RIGHT, MY FRIEND --IT HAS BEEN AWHILE. AND IN ALL THAT TIME, I'D WAGER ABOUT THE ONLY THING OL' CAITLIN'S HAD BETWEEN HER LEGS IS A CATHETER.
HEY! THAT KIND OF SHIT'S UNCALLED FOR!
BUT I'LL TELL YOU WHAT IS CALLED FOR: ACTION!
THAT NIGHT, WEREN'T YOU TWO RECONCILED? I MEAN SHE'D OPTED TO CALL OFF THE WEDDING WITH THE ASIAN DESIGN MAJOR TO GIVE IT ANOTHER GO WITH YOU, RIGHT?
YEEAAAH...
SO, I'D SAY, TECHNICALLY, YOU'RE STILL DATING.
I GUESS, IF YOU LOOK AT IT THAT WAY...
NOW FOLLOW MY LOGIC, HERE...
IF THE SITUATION WERE REVERSED, AND YOU WERE THE CATATONIC ONE, WOULDN'T YOU WANT YOUR SIGNIFICANT OTHER TO DO ANYTHING THEY COULD TO PULL YOU OUT OF YOUR HORROR-INDUCED, WAKING-COMA?
SURE, I GUESS.
AND WOULDN'T YOU AGREE THAT PROBABLY THE BEST MEANS WITH WHICH TO SNAP SOMEONE BACK INTO REALITY IS THEIR LOVER'S TOUCH?
WHAT ARE YOU GETTING AT?
YOU GET IN THERE AND THROW HER A BONE, YOU RETARD! I'LL BET THE ONLY REASON THAT GIRL'S STILL IN THE STATE SHE'S IN IS BECAUSE HER SORT-OF BOYFRIEND HASN'T OFFERED THE ONE CURE-ALL THAT'S MEDICALLY PROVEN TO BE GOOD FOR WHAT AILS YA!
YOU GOTTA FUCK THAT ZOMBIE!
Uh... TEN SEVENTY-EIGHT.
YOUR TREAT?

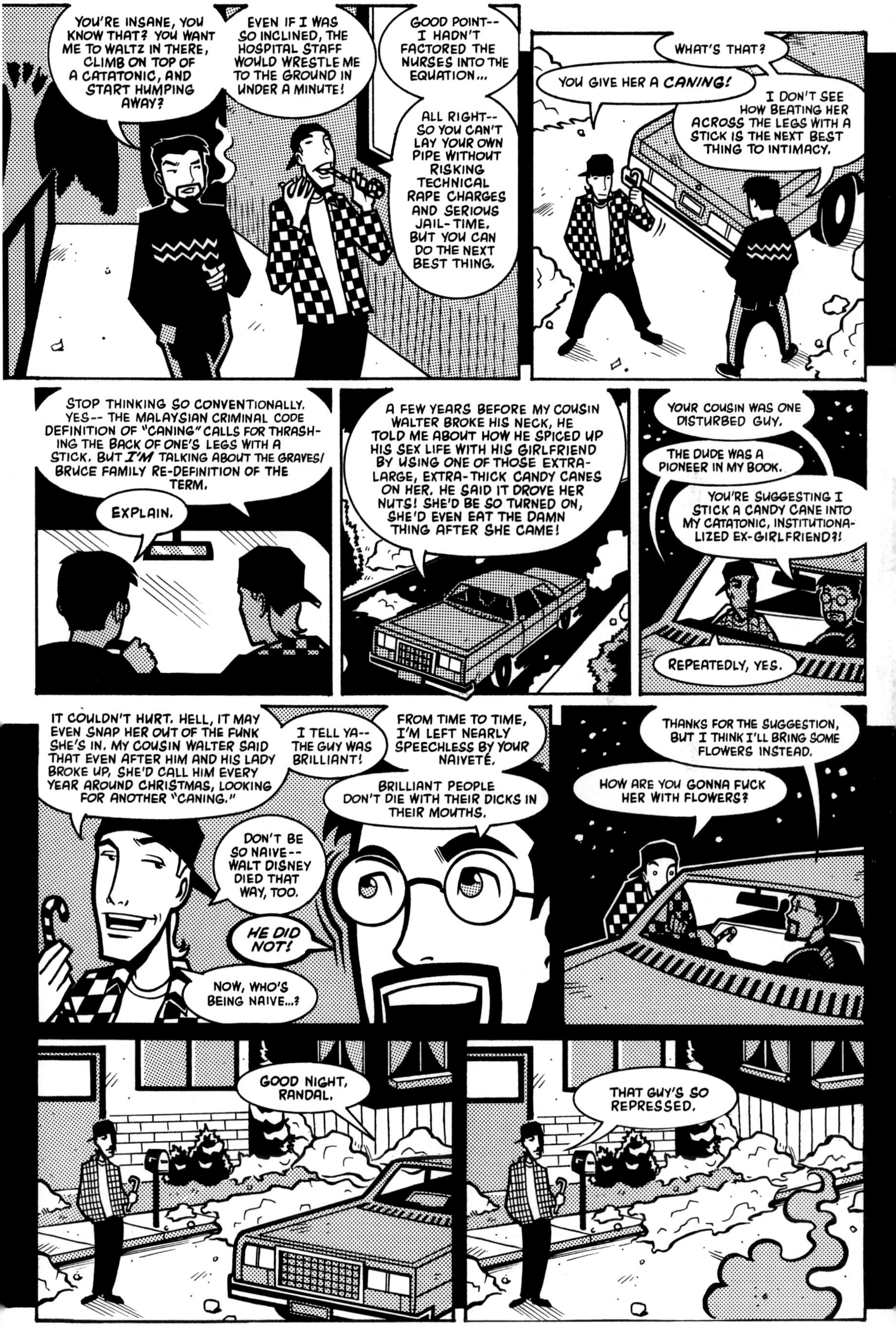
YOU'RE INSANE, YOU KNOW THAT? YOU WANT ME TO WALTZ IN THERE, CLIMB ON TOP OF A CATATONIC, AND START HUMPING AWAY?
EVEN IF I WAS SO INCLINED, THE HOSPITAL STAFF WOULD WRESTLE ME TO THE GROUND IN UNDER A MINUTE!
GOOD POINT-- I HADN'T FACTORED THE NURSES INTO THE EQUATION...
ALL RIGHT-- SO YOU CAN'T LAY YOUR OWN PIPE WITHOUT RISKING TECHNICAL RAPE CHARGES AND SERIOUS JAIL-TIME. BUT YOU CAN DO THE NEXT BEST THING.
YOU GIVE HER A CANING!
WHAT'S THAT?
I DON'T SEE HOW BEATING HER ACROSS THE LEGS WITH A STICK IS THE NEXT BEST THING TO INTIMACY.
STOP THINKING SO CONVENTIONALLY. YES-- THE MALAYSIAN CRIMINAL CODE DEFINITION OF "CANING" CALLS FOR THRASHING THE BACK OF ONE'S LEGS WITH A STICK. BUT I'M TALKING ABOUT THE GRAVES/BRUCE FAMILY RE-DEFINITION OF THE TERM.
EXPLAIN.
A FEW YEARS BEFORE MY COUSIN WALTER BROKE HIS NECK, HE TOLD ME ABOUT HOW HE SPICED UP HIS SEX LIFE WITH HIS GIRLFRIEND BY USING ONE OF THOSE EXTRA-LARGE, EXTRA-THICK CANDY CANES ON HER. HE SAID IT DROVE HER NUTS! SHE'D BE SO TURNED ON, SHE'D EVEN EAT THE DAMN THING AFTER SHE CAME!
YOUR COUSIN WAS ONE DISTURBED GUY.
THE DUDE WAS A PIONEER IN MY BOOK.
YOU'RE SUGGESTING I STICK A CANDY CANE INTO MY CATATONIC, INSTITUTIONALIZED EX-GIRLFRIEND?!
REPEATEDLY, YES.
IT COULDN'T HURT. HELL, IT MAY EVEN SNAP HER OUT OF THE FUNK SHE'S IN. MY COUSIN WALTER SAID THAT EVEN AFTER HIM AND HIS LADY BROKE UP, SHE'D CALL HIM EVERY YEAR AROUND CHRISTMAS, LOOKING FOR ANOTHER "CANING."
I TELL YA-- THE GUY WAS BRILLIANT!
FROM TIME TO TIME, I'M LEFT NEARLY SPEECHLESS BY YOUR NAIVETÉ.
BRILLIANT PEOPLE DON'T DIE WITH THEIR DICKS IN THEIR MOUTHS.
DON'T BE SO NAIVE-- WALT DISNEY DIED THAT WAY, TOO.
HE DID NOT!
NOW, WHO'S BEING NAIVE...?
THANKS FOR THE SUGGESTION, BUT I THINK I'LL BRING SOME FLOWERS INSTEAD.
HOW ARE YOU GONNA FUCK HER WITH FLOWERS?
GOOD NIGHT, RANDAL.
THAT GUY'S SO REPRESSED.

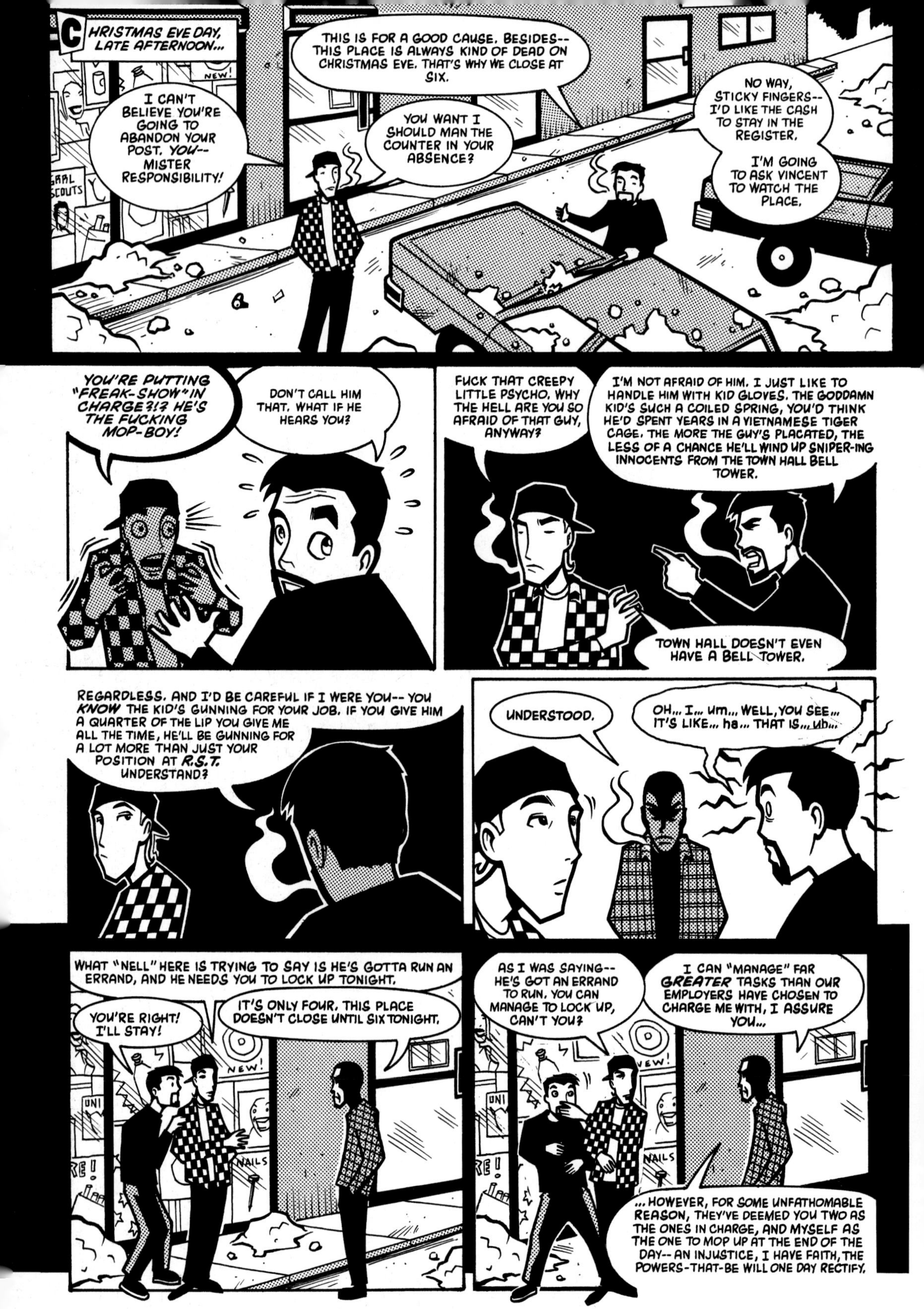
CHRISTMAS EVE DAY, LATE AFTERNOON...
I CAN'T BELIEVE YOU'RE GOING TO ABANDON YOUR POST. YOU-- MISTER RESPONSIBILITY!
THIS IS FOR A GOOD CAUSE. BESIDES-- THIS PLACE IS ALWAYS KIND OF DEAD ON CHRISTMAS EVE. THAT'S WHY WE CLOSE AT SIX.
YOU WANT I SHOULD MAN THE COUNTER IN YOUR ABSENCE?
NO WAY, STICKY FINGERS-- I'D LIKE THE CASH TO STAY IN THE REGISTER.
I'M GOING TO ASK VINCENT TO WATCH THE PLACE.
NEW!
YOU'RE PUTTING "FREAK-SHOW" IN CHARGE?!? HE'S THE FUCKING MOP-BOY!
DON'T CALL HIM THAT. WHAT IF HE HEARS YOU?
FUCK THAT CREEPY LITTLE PSYCHO. WHY THE HELL ARE YOU SO AFRAID OF THAT GUY, ANYWAY?
I'M NOT AFRAID OF HIM. I JUST LIKE TO HANDLE HIM WITH KID GLOVES. THE GODDAMN KID'S SUCH A COILED SPRING, YOU'D THINK HE'D SPENT YEARS IN A VIETNAMESE TIGER CAGE. THE MORE THE GUY'S PLACATED, THE LESS OF A CHANCE HE'LL WIND UP SNIPER-ING INNOCENTS FROM THE TOWN HALL BELL TOWER.
TOWN HALL DOESN'T EVEN HAVE A BELL TOWER.
REGARDLESS. AND I'D BE CAREFUL IF I WERE YOU-- YOU KNOW THE KID'S GUNNING FOR YOUR JOB. IF YOU GIVE HIM A QUARTER OF THE LIP YOU GIVE ME ALL THE TIME, HE'LL BE GUNNING FOR A LOT MORE THAN JUST YOUR POSITION AT R.S.T. UNDERSTAND?
UNDERSTOOD.
OH... I... um... WELL, YOU SEE... IT'S LIKE... ha... THAT IS... uh...
WHAT "NELL" HERE IS TRYING TO SAY IS HE'S GOTTA RUN AN ERRAND, AND HE NEEDS YOU TO LOCK UP TONIGHT.
YOU'RE RIGHT! I'LL STAY!
IT'S ONLY FOUR. THIS PLACE DOESN'T CLOSE UNTIL SIX TONIGHT.
NEW!
UNI
NAILS
AS I WAS SAYING-- HE'S GOT AN ERRAND TO RUN. YOU CAN MANAGE TO LOCK UP, CAN'T YOU?
I CAN "MANAGE" FAR GREATER TASKS THAN OUR EMPLOYERS HAVE CHOSEN TO CHARGE ME WITH, I ASSURE YOU...
...HOWEVER, FOR SOME UNFATHOMABLE REASON, THEY'VE DEEMED YOU TWO AS THE ONES IN CHARGE, AND MYSELF AS THE ONE TO MOP UP AT THE END OF THE DAY-- AN INJUSTICE, I HAVE FAITH, THE POWERS-THAT-BE WILL ONE DAY RECTIFY.

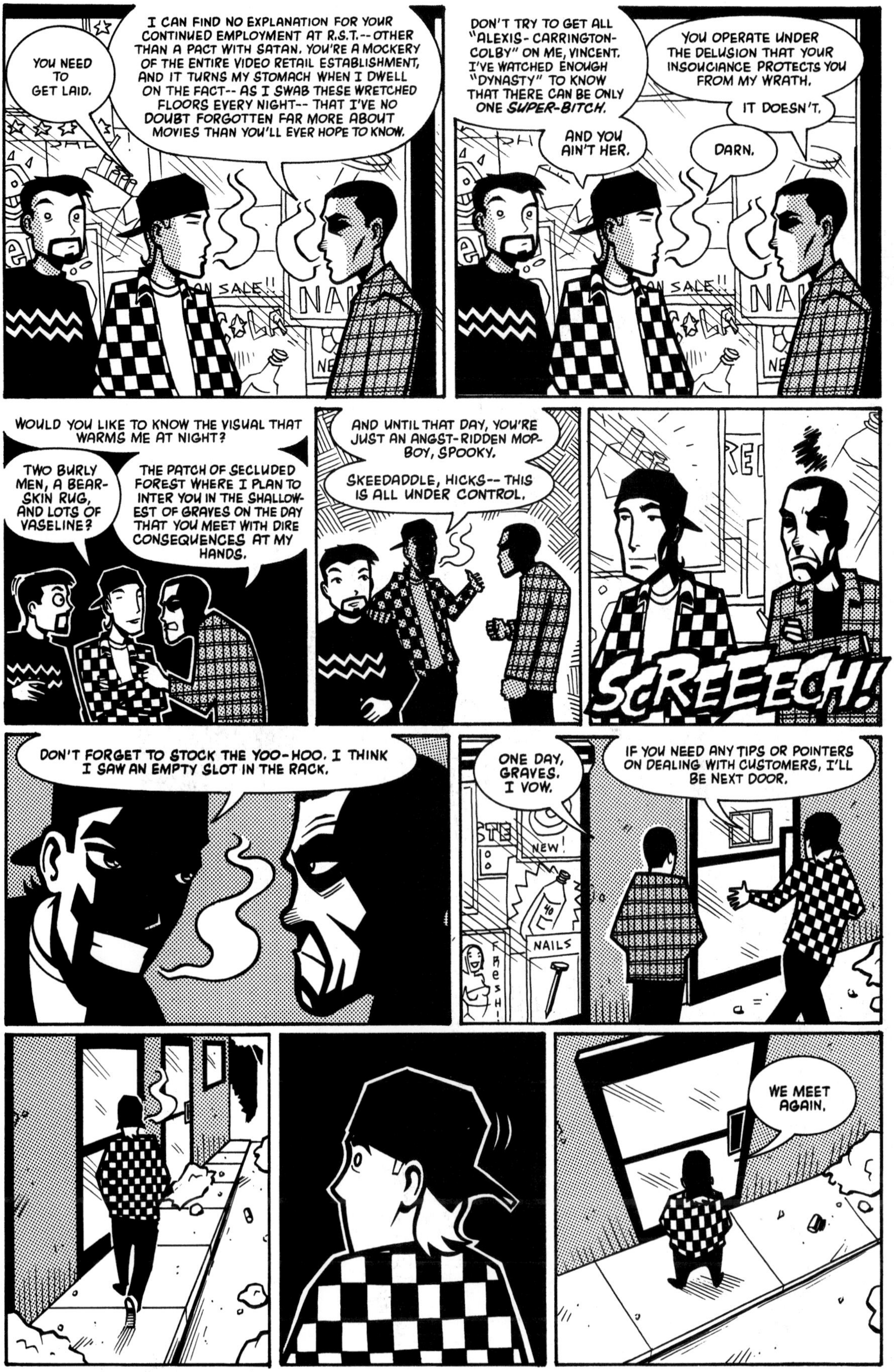
YOU NEED TO GET LAID.
I CAN FIND NO EXPLANATION FOR YOUR CONTINUED EMPLOYMENT AT R.S.T.-- OTHER THAN A PACT WITH SATAN. YOU'RE A MOCKERY OF THE ENTIRE VIDEO RETAIL ESTABLISHMENT, AND IT TURNS MY STOMACH WHEN I DWELL ON THE FACT-- AS I SWAB THESE WRETCHED FLOORS EVERY NIGHT-- THAT I'VE NO DOUBT FORGOTTEN FAR MORE ABOUT MOVIES THAN YOU'LL EVER HOPE TO KNOW.
DON'T TRY TO GET ALL "ALEXIS-CARRINGTON-COLBY" ON ME, VINCENT. I'VE WATCHED ENOUGH "DYNASTY" TO KNOW THAT THERE CAN BE ONLY ONE SUPER-BITCH.
AND YOU AIN'T HER.
YOU OPERATE UNDER THE DELUSION THAT YOUR INSOUCIANCE PROTECTS YOU FROM MY WRATH.
IT DOESN'T.
DARN.
WOULD YOU LIKE TO KNOW THE VISUAL THAT WARMS ME AT NIGHT?
TWO BURLY MEN, A BEAR-SKIN RUG, AND LOTS OF VASELINE?
THE PATCH OF SECLUDED FOREST WHERE I PLAN TO INTER YOU IN THE SHALLOW-EST OF GRAVES ON THE DAY THAT YOU MEET WITH DIRE CONSEQUENCES AT MY HANDS.
AND UNTIL THAT DAY, YOU'RE JUST AN ANGST-RIDDEN MOP-BOY, SPOOKY.
SKEEDADDLE, HICKS-- THIS IS ALL UNDER CONTROL.
SCREEECH!
DON'T FORGET TO STOCK THE YOO-HOO. I THINK I SAW AN EMPTY SLOT IN THE RACK.
ONE DAY, GRAVES. I VOW.
IF YOU NEED ANY TIPS OR POINTERS ON DEALING WITH CUSTOMERS, I'LL BE NEXT DOOR.
WE MEET AGAIN.

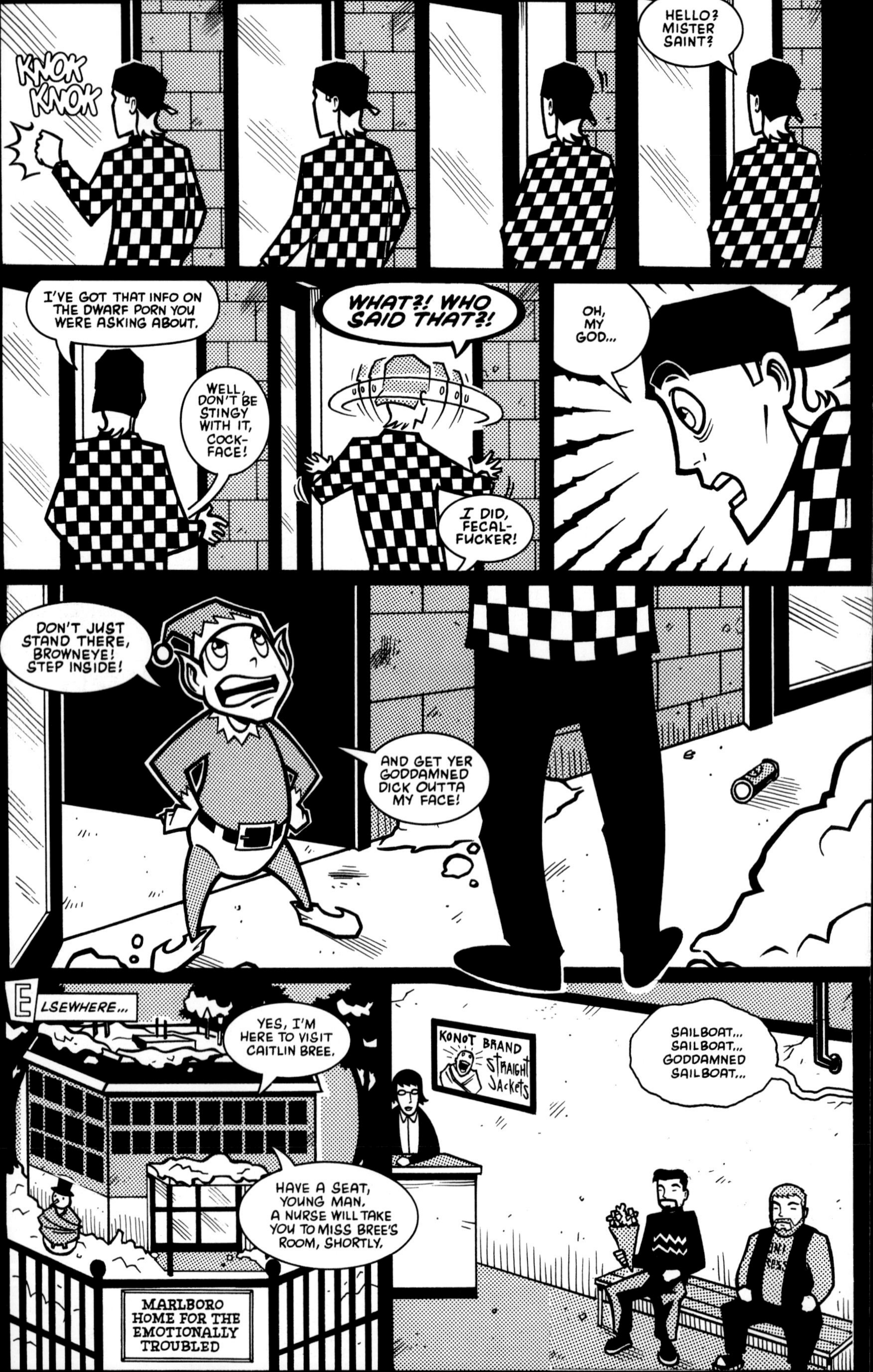
KNOK KNOK
HELLO? MISTER SAINT?
I'VE GOT THAT INFO ON THE DWARF PORN YOU WERE ASKING ABOUT.
WELL, DON'T BE STINGY WITH IT, COCK-FACE!
WHAT?! WHO SAID THAT?!
I DID, FECAL-FUCKER!
OH, MY GOD...
DON'T JUST STAND THERE, BROWNEYE! STEP INSIDE!
AND GET YER GODDAMNED DICK OUTTA MY FACE!
ELSEWHERE...
YES, I'M HERE TO VISIT CAITLIN BREE.
HAVE A SEAT, YOUNG MAN, A NURSE WILL TAKE YOU TO MISS BREE'S ROOM, SHORTLY.
MARLBORO HOME FOR THE EMOTIONALLY TROUBLED
KONOT BRAND STRAIGHT JACKETS
SAILBOAT... SAILBOAT... GODDAMNED SAILBOAT...

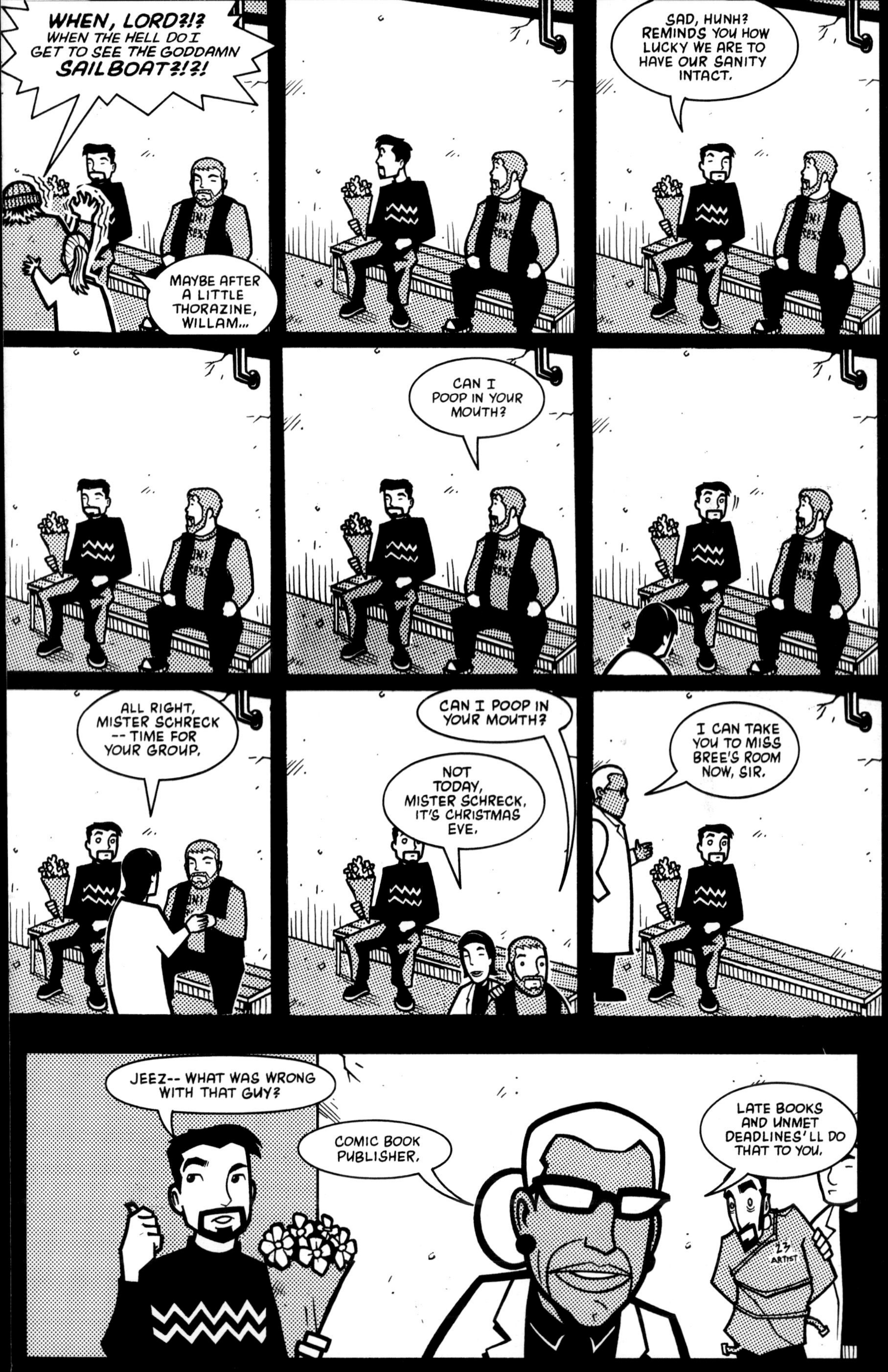
WHEN, LORD?!? WHEN THE HELL DO I GET TO SEE THE GODDAMN SAILBOAT?!?!
MAYBE AFTER A LITTLE THORAZINE, WILLAM...
SAD, HUNH? REMINDS YOU HOW LUCKY WE ARE TO HAVE OUR SANITY INTACT.
CAN I POOP IN YOUR MOUTH?
ALL RIGHT, MISTER SCHRECK -- TIME FOR YOUR GROUP.
CAN I POOP IN YOUR MOUTH?
NOT TODAY, MISTER SCHRECK, IT'S CHRISTMAS EVE.
I CAN TAKE YOU TO MISS BREE'S ROOM NOW, SIR.
JEEZ-- WHAT WAS WRONG WITH THAT GUY?
COMIC BOOK PUBLISHER.
LATE BOOKS AND UNMET DEADLINES'LL DO THAT TO YOU.
23 ARTIST

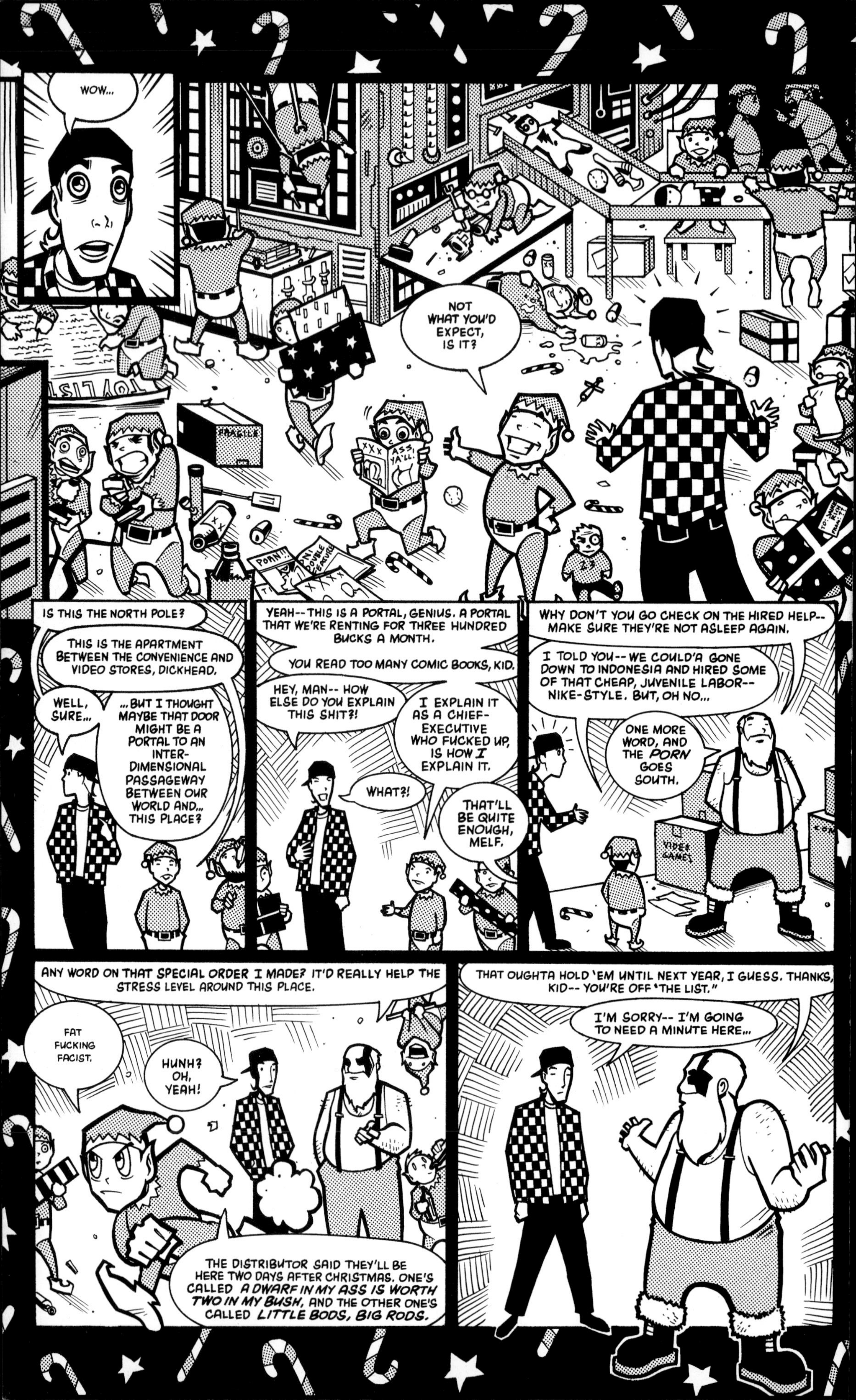
WOW...
NOT WHAT YOU'D EXPECT, IS IT?
IS THIS THE NORTH POLE?
THIS IS THE APARTMENT BETWEEN THE CONVENIENCE AND VIDEO STORES, DICKHEAD.
WELL, SURE...
...BUT I THOUGHT MAYBE THAT DOOR MIGHT BE A PORTAL TO AN INTER-DIMENSIONAL PASSAGEWAY BETWEEN OUR WORLD AND... THIS PLACE?
YEAH--THIS IS A PORTAL, GENIUS. A PORTAL THAT WE'RE RENTING FOR THREE HUNDRED BUCKS A MONTH.
YOU READ TOO MANY COMIC BOOKS, KID.
HEY, MAN-- HOW ELSE DO YOU EXPLAIN THIS SHIT?!
I EXPLAIN IT AS A CHIEF-EXECUTIVE WHO FUCKED UP, IS HOW *I* EXPLAIN IT.
WHAT?!
THAT'LL BE QUITE ENOUGH, MELF.
WHY DON'T YOU GO CHECK ON THE HIRED HELP-- MAKE SURE THEY'RE NOT ASLEEP AGAIN.
I TOLD YOU--WE COULD'A GONE DOWN TO INDONESIA AND HIRED SOME OF THAT CHEAP, JUVENILE LABOR-- NIKE-STYLE. BUT, OH NO...
ONE MORE WORD, AND THE *PORN* GOES SOUTH.
VIDEO GAMES
ANY WORD ON THAT *SPECIAL ORDER* I MADE? IT'D REALLY HELP THE STRESS LEVEL AROUND THIS PLACE.
FAT FUCKING FACIST.
HUNH? OH, YEAH!
THE DISTRIBUTOR SAID THEY'LL BE HERE TWO DAYS AFTER CHRISTMAS. ONE'S CALLED *A DWARF IN MY ASS IS WORTH TWO IN MY BUSH*, AND THE OTHER ONE'S CALLED *LITTLE BODS, BIG RODS.*
THAT OUGHTA HOLD 'EM UNTIL NEXT YEAR, I GUESS. THANKS, KID-- YOU'RE OFF "THE LIST."
I'M SORRY-- I'M GOING TO NEED A MINUTE HERE...

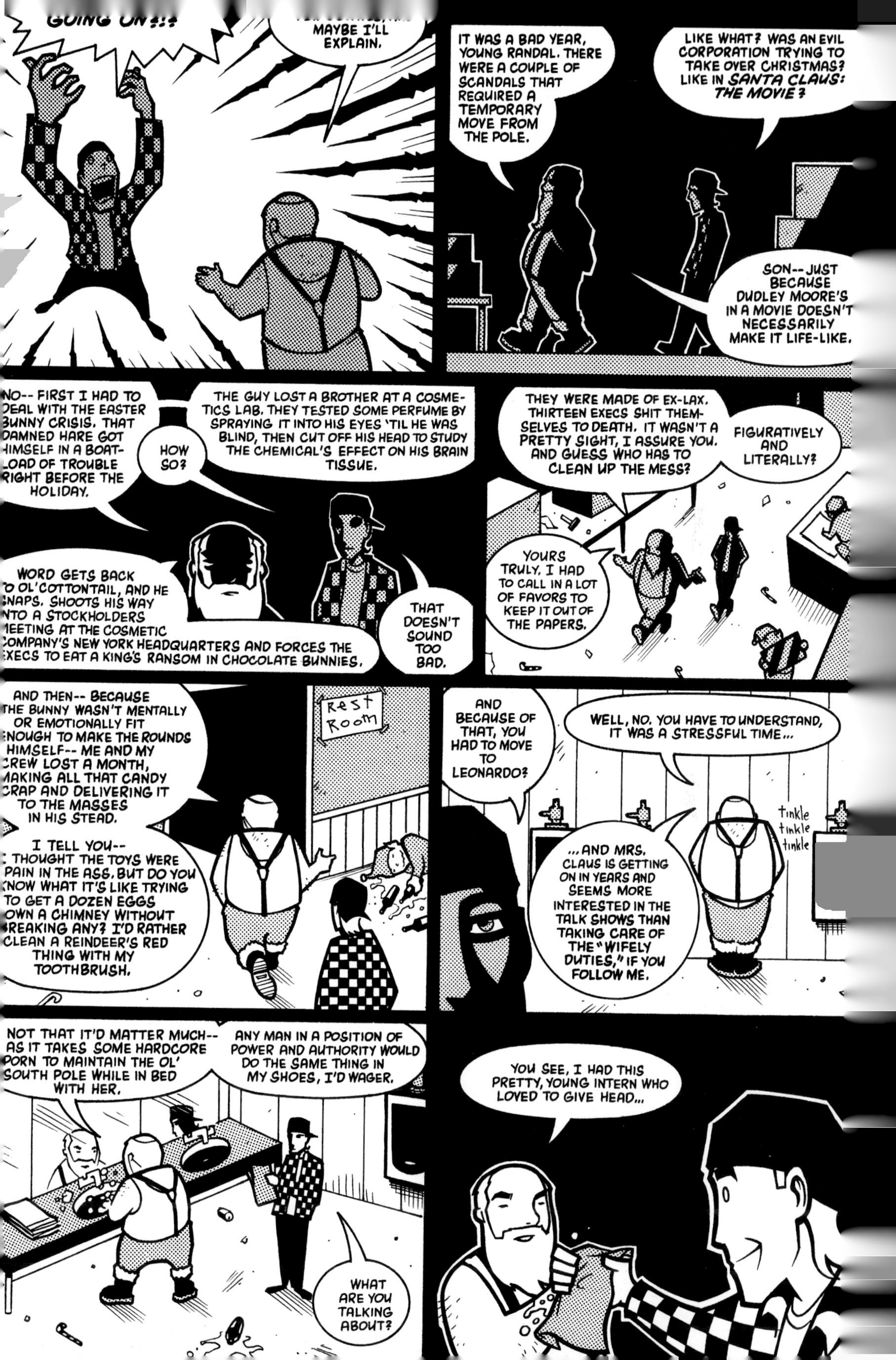
GOING ON!!!
MAYBE I'LL EXPLAIN.
IT WAS A BAD YEAR, YOUNG RANDAL. THERE WERE A COUPLE OF SCANDALS THAT REQUIRED A TEMPORARY MOVE FROM THE POLE.
LIKE WHAT? WAS AN EVIL CORPORATION TRYING TO TAKE OVER CHRISTMAS? LIKE IN SANTA CLAUS: THE MOVIE?
SON-- JUST BECAUSE DUDLEY MOORE'S IN A MOVIE DOESN'T NECESSARILY MAKE IT LIFE-LIKE.
NO-- FIRST I HAD TO DEAL WITH THE EASTER BUNNY CRISIS. THAT DAMNED HARE GOT HIMSELF IN A BOATLOAD OF TROUBLE RIGHT BEFORE THE HOLIDAY.
HOW SO?
THE GUY LOST A BROTHER AT A COSMETICS LAB. THEY TESTED SOME PERFUME BY SPRAYING IT INTO HIS EYES 'TIL HE WAS BLIND, THEN CUT OFF HIS HEAD TO STUDY THE CHEMICAL'S EFFECT ON HIS BRAIN TISSUE.
WORD GETS BACK TO OL' COTTONTAIL, AND HE SNAPS. SHOOTS HIS WAY INTO A STOCKHOLDERS MEETING AT THE COSMETIC COMPANY'S NEW YORK HEADQUARTERS AND FORCES THE EXECS TO EAT A KING'S RANSOM IN CHOCOLATE BUNNIES.
THAT DOESN'T SOUND TOO BAD.
THEY WERE MADE OF EX-LAX. THIRTEEN EXECS SHIT THEMSELVES TO DEATH. IT WASN'T A PRETTY SIGHT, I ASSURE YOU. AND GUESS WHO HAS TO CLEAN UP THE MESS?
FIGURATIVELY AND LITERALLY?
YOURS TRULY. I HAD TO CALL IN A LOT OF FAVORS TO KEEP IT OUT OF THE PAPERS.
AND THEN-- BECAUSE THE BUNNY WASN'T MENTALLY OR EMOTIONALLY FIT ENOUGH TO MAKE THE ROUNDS HIMSELF-- ME AND MY CREW LOST A MONTH, MAKING ALL THAT CANDY CRAP AND DELIVERING IT TO THE MASSES IN HIS STEAD.
I TELL YOU-- I THOUGHT THE TOYS WERE A PAIN IN THE ASS, BUT DO YOU KNOW WHAT IT'S LIKE TRYING TO GET A DOZEN EGGS DOWN A CHIMNEY WITHOUT BREAKING ANY? I'D RATHER CLEAN A REINDEER'S RED THING WITH MY TOOTHBRUSH.
Rest Room
AND BECAUSE OF THAT, YOU HAD TO MOVE TO LEONARDO?
WELL, NO. YOU HAVE TO UNDERSTAND, IT WAS A STRESSFUL TIME...
...AND MRS. CLAUS IS GETTING ON IN YEARS AND SEEMS MORE INTERESTED IN THE TALK SHOWS THAN TAKING CARE OF THE "WIFELY DUTIES," IF YOU FOLLOW ME.
tinkle tinkle tinkle
NOT THAT IT'D MATTER MUCH-- AS IT TAKES SOME HARDCORE PORN TO MAINTAIN THE OL' SOUTH POLE WHILE IN BED WITH HER.
ANY MAN IN A POSITION OF POWER AND AUTHORITY WOULD DO THE SAME THING IN MY SHOES, I'D WAGER.
WHAT ARE YOU TALKING ABOUT?
YOU SEE, I HAD THIS PRETTY, YOUNG INTERN WHO LOVED TO GIVE HEAD...

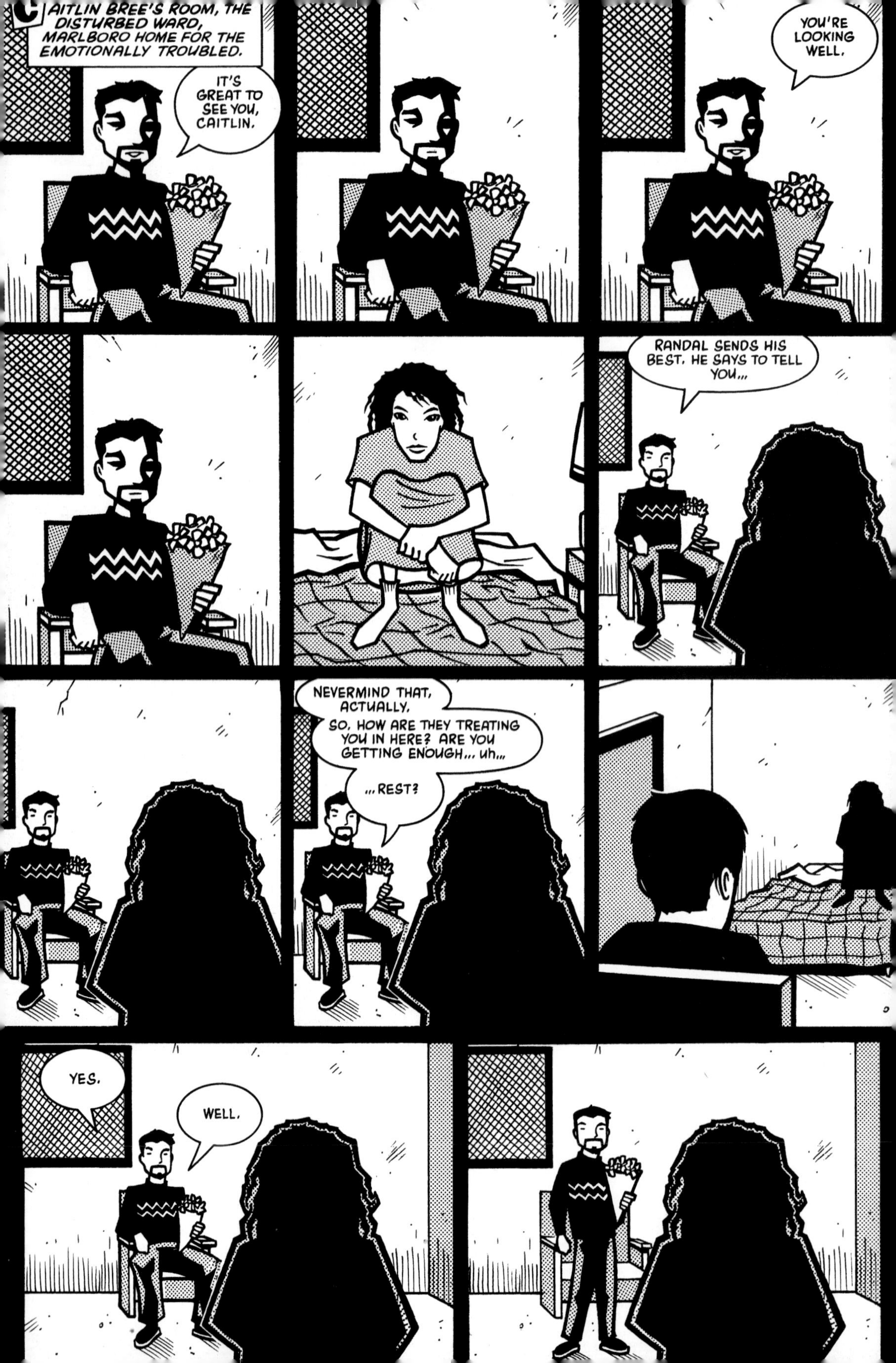
CAITLIN BREE'S ROOM, THE DISTURBED WARD, MARLBORO HOME FOR THE EMOTIONALLY TROUBLED.
IT'S GREAT TO SEE YOU, CAITLIN.
YOU'RE LOOKING WELL.
RANDAL SENDS HIS BEST. HE SAYS TO TELL YOU...
NEVERMIND THAT, ACTUALLY.
SO, HOW ARE THEY TREATING YOU IN HERE? ARE YOU GETTING ENOUGH... uh...
...REST?
YES.
WELL.

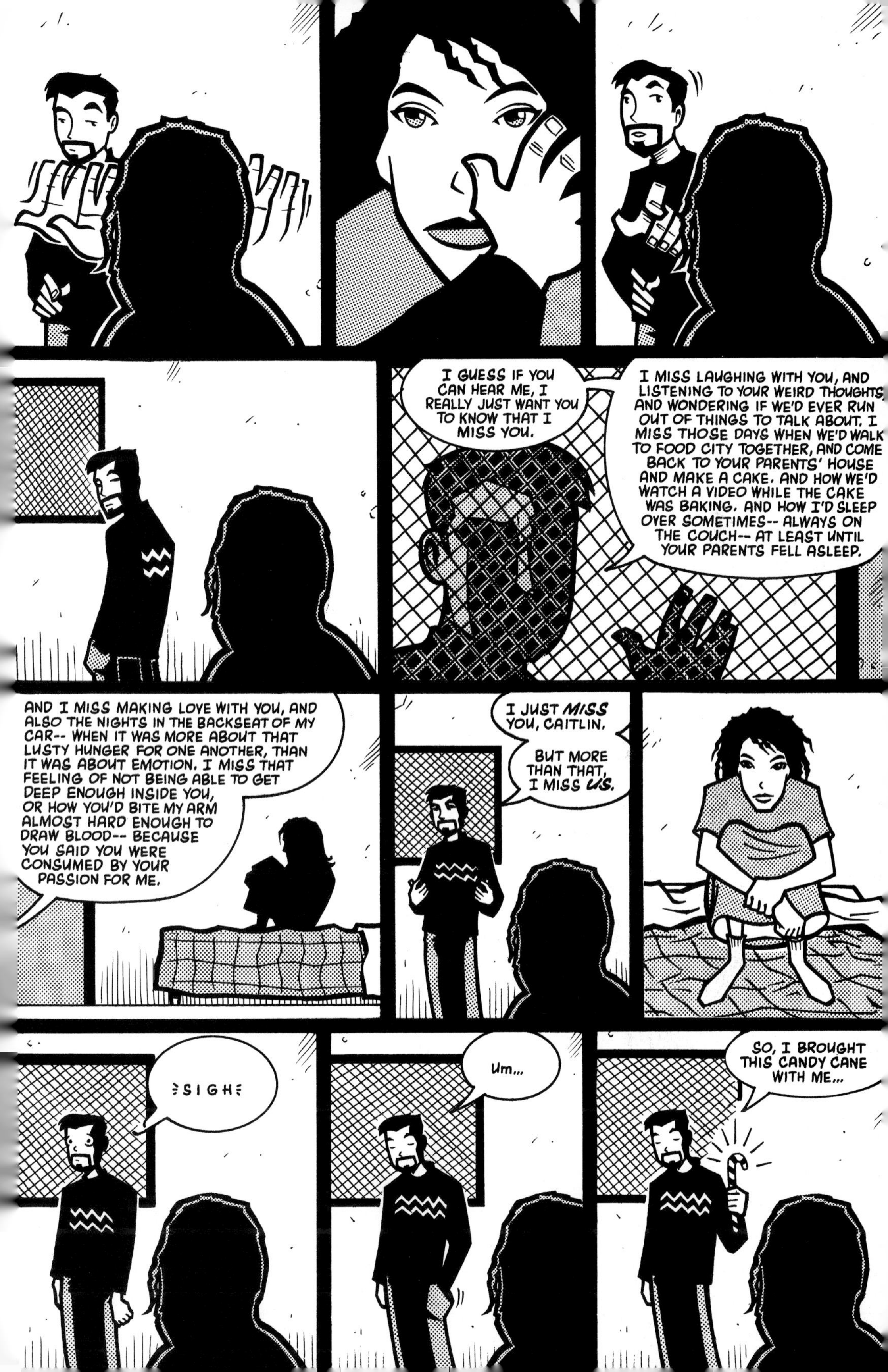
I GUESS IF YOU CAN HEAR ME, I REALLY JUST WANT YOU TO KNOW THAT I MISS YOU.
I MISS LAUGHING WITH YOU, AND LISTENING TO YOUR WEIRD THOUGHTS, AND WONDERING IF WE'D EVER RUN OUT OF THINGS TO TALK ABOUT. I MISS THOSE DAYS WHEN WE'D WALK TO FOOD CITY TOGETHER, AND COME BACK TO YOUR PARENTS' HOUSE AND MAKE A CAKE. AND HOW WE'D WATCH A VIDEO WHILE THE CAKE WAS BAKING. AND HOW I'D SLEEP OVER SOMETIMES-- ALWAYS ON THE COUCH-- AT LEAST UNTIL YOUR PARENTS FELL ASLEEP.
AND I MISS MAKING LOVE WITH YOU, AND ALSO THE NIGHTS IN THE BACKSEAT OF MY CAR-- WHEN IT WAS MORE ABOUT THAT LUSTY HUNGER FOR ONE ANOTHER, THAN IT WAS ABOUT EMOTION. I MISS THAT FEELING OF NOT BEING ABLE TO GET DEEP ENOUGH INSIDE YOU, OR HOW YOU'D BITE MY ARM ALMOST HARD ENOUGH TO DRAW BLOOD-- BECAUSE YOU SAID YOU WERE CONSUMED BY YOUR PASSION FOR ME.
I JUST *MISS* YOU, CAITLIN.
BUT MORE THAN THAT, I MISS *US*.
SIGH
Um...
SO, I BROUGHT THIS CANDY CANE WITH ME...

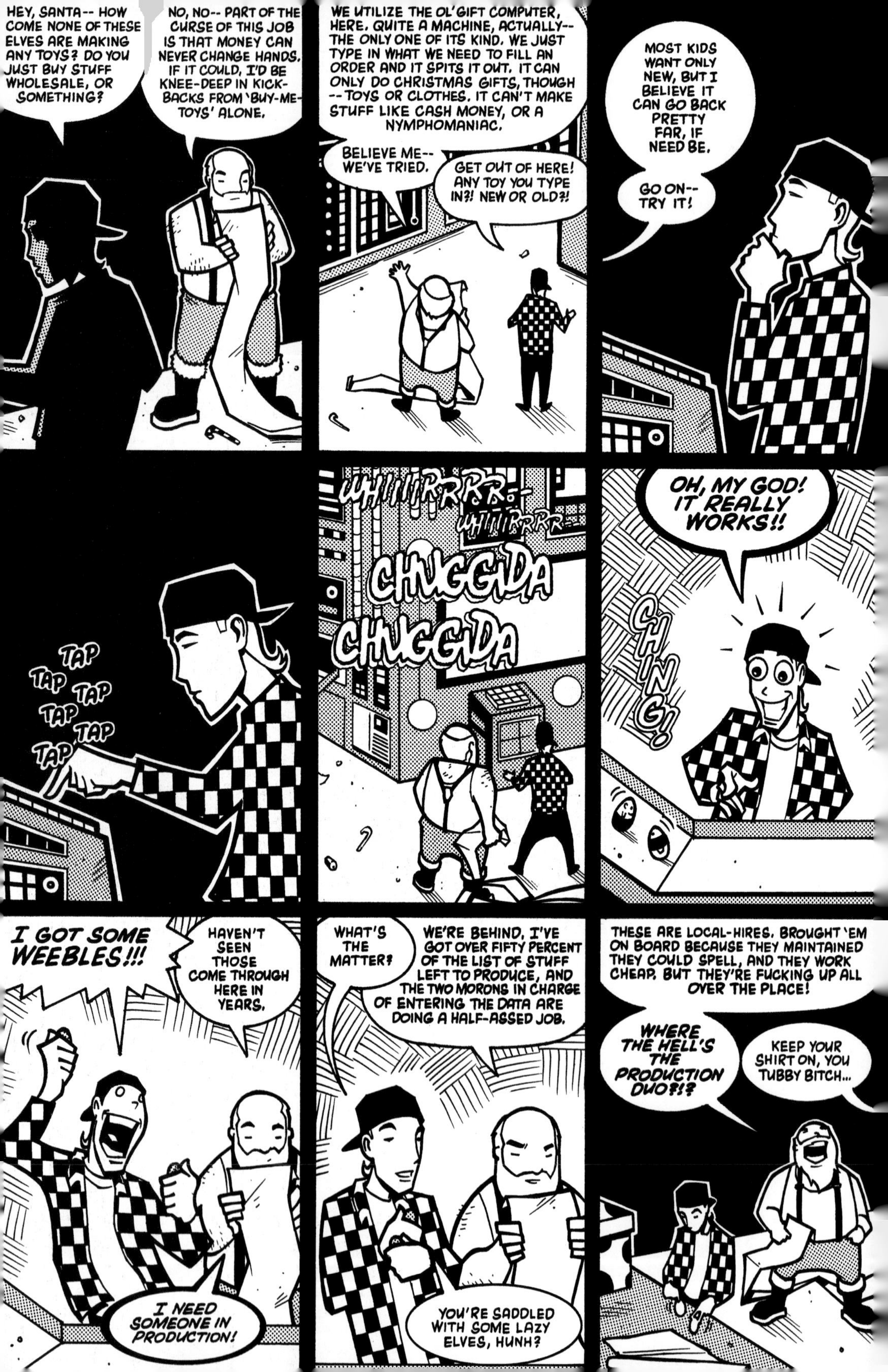
HEY, SANTA-- HOW COME NONE OF THESE ELVES ARE MAKING ANY TOYS? DO YOU JUST BUY STUFF WHOLESALE, OR SOMETHING?
NO, NO-- PART OF THE CURSE OF THIS JOB IS THAT MONEY CAN NEVER CHANGE HANDS. IF IT COULD, I'D BE KNEE-DEEP IN KICK-BACKS FROM 'BUY-ME-TOYS' ALONE.
WE UTILIZE THE OL' GIFT COMPUTER, HERE. QUITE A MACHINE, ACTUALLY-- THE ONLY ONE OF ITS KIND. WE JUST TYPE IN WHAT WE NEED TO FILL AN ORDER AND IT SPITS IT OUT. IT CAN ONLY DO CHRISTMAS GIFTS, THOUGH --TOYS OR CLOTHES. IT CAN'T MAKE STUFF LIKE CASH MONEY, OR A NYMPHOMANIAC.
BELIEVE ME-- WE'VE TRIED.
GET OUT OF HERE! ANY TOY YOU TYPE IN?! NEW OR OLD?!
MOST KIDS WANT ONLY NEW, BUT I BELIEVE IT CAN GO BACK PRETTY FAR, IF NEED BE.
GO ON-- TRY IT!
TAP TAP TAP TAP TAP TAP
WHIIIRRRR- WHIIIRRRR
CHUGGIDA CHUGGIDA
OH, MY GOD! IT REALLY WORKS!!
CHING!
I GOT SOME WEEBLES!!!
HAVEN'T SEEN THOSE COME THROUGH HERE IN YEARS.
I NEED SOMEONE IN PRODUCTION!
WHAT'S THE MATTER?
WE'RE BEHIND. I'VE GOT OVER FIFTY PERCENT OF THE LIST OF STUFF LEFT TO PRODUCE, AND THE TWO MORONS IN CHARGE OF ENTERING THE DATA ARE DOING A HALF-ASSED JOB.
YOU'RE SADDLED WITH SOME LAZY ELVES, HUNH?
THESE ARE LOCAL-HIRES. BROUGHT 'EM ON BOARD BECAUSE THEY MAINTAINED THEY COULD SPELL, AND THEY WORK CHEAP. BUT THEY'RE FUCKING UP ALL OVER THE PLACE!
WHERE THE HELL'S THE PRODUCTION DUO?!?
KEEP YOUR SHIRT ON, YOU TUBBY BITCH...

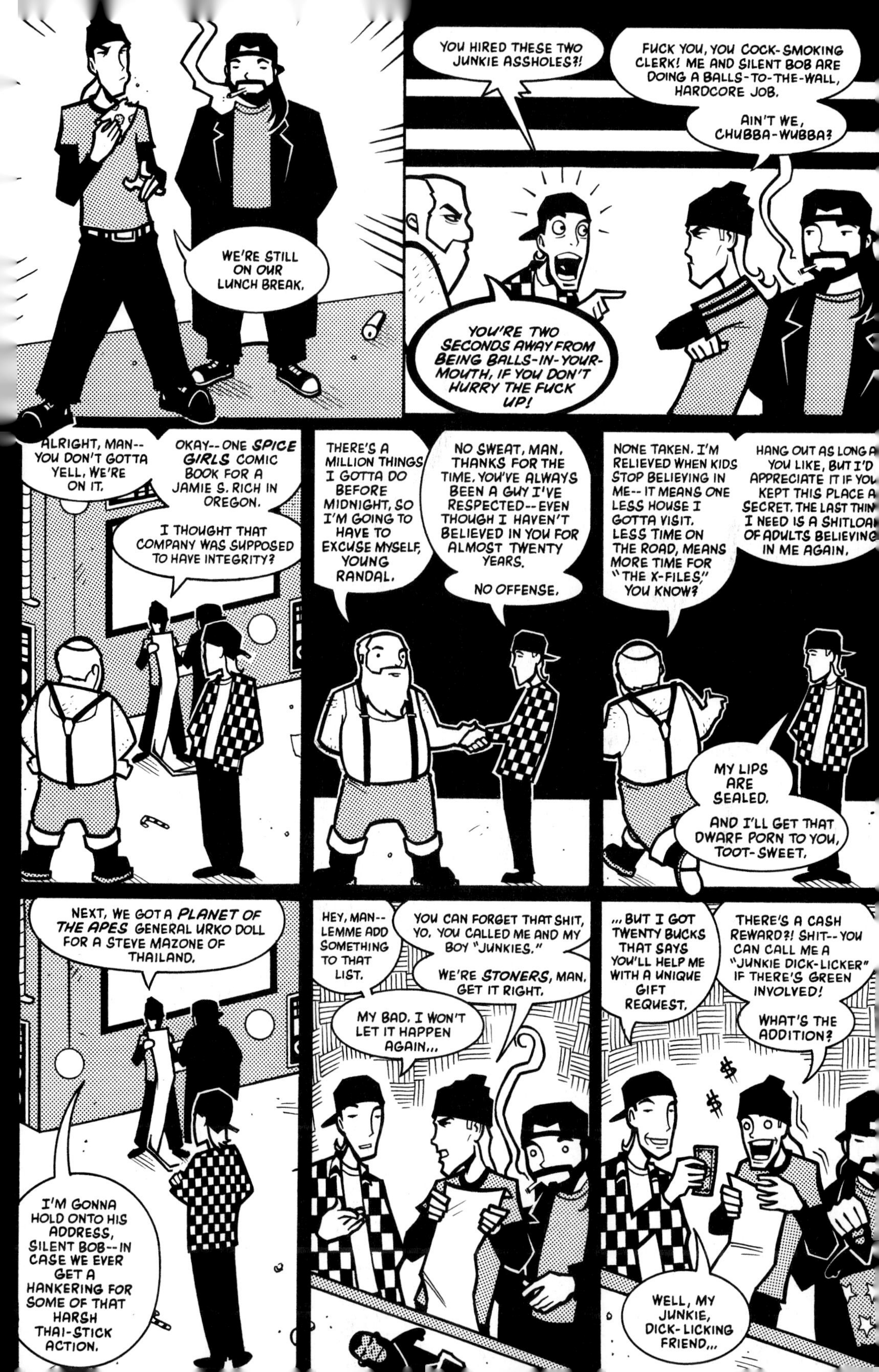
WE'RE STILL ON OUR LUNCH BREAK.
YOU HIRED THESE TWO JUNKIE ASSHOLES?!
FUCK YOU, YOU COCK-SMOKING CLERK! ME AND SILENT BOB ARE DOING A BALLS-TO-THE-WALL, HARDCORE JOB.
AIN'T WE, CHUBBA-WUBBA?
YOU'RE TWO SECONDS AWAY FROM BEING BALLS-IN-YOUR-MOUTH, IF YOU DON'T HURRY THE FUCK UP!
ALRIGHT, MAN-- YOU DON'T GOTTA YELL, WE'RE ON IT.
OKAY-- ONE SPICE GIRLS COMIC BOOK FOR A JAMIE S. RICH IN OREGON.
I THOUGHT THAT COMPANY WAS SUPPOSED TO HAVE INTEGRITY?
THERE'S A MILLION THINGS I GOTTA DO BEFORE MIDNIGHT, SO I'M GOING TO HAVE TO EXCUSE MYSELF, YOUNG RANDAL.
NO SWEAT, MAN. THANKS FOR THE TIME. YOU'VE ALWAYS BEEN A GUY I'VE RESPECTED-- EVEN THOUGH I HAVEN'T BELIEVED IN YOU FOR ALMOST TWENTY YEARS.
NO OFFENSE.
NONE TAKEN. I'M RELIEVED WHEN KIDS STOP BELIEVING IN ME-- IT MEANS ONE LESS HOUSE I GOTTA VISIT. LESS TIME ON THE ROAD, MEANS MORE TIME FOR "THE X-FILES," YOU KNOW?
HANG OUT AS LONG A YOU LIKE, BUT I'D APPRECIATE IT IF YOU KEPT THIS PLACE A SECRET. THE LAST THIN I NEED IS A SHITLOA OF ADULTS BELIEVING IN ME AGAIN.
MY LIPS ARE SEALED.
AND I'LL GET THAT DWARF PORN TO YOU, TOOT-SWEET.
NEXT, WE GOT A PLANET OF THE APES GENERAL URKO DOLL FOR A STEVE MAZONE OF THAILAND.
I'M GONNA HOLD ONTO HIS ADDRESS, SILENT BOB-- IN CASE WE EVER GET A HANKERING FOR SOME OF THAT HARSH THAI-STICK ACTION.
HEY, MAN-- LEMME ADD SOMETHING TO THAT LIST.
YOU CAN FORGET THAT SHIT, YO. YOU CALLED ME AND MY BOY "JUNKIES."
WE'RE STONERS, MAN. GET IT RIGHT.
MY BAD. I WON'T LET IT HAPPEN AGAIN...
...BUT I GOT TWENTY BUCKS THAT SAYS YOU'LL HELP ME WITH A UNIQUE GIFT REQUEST.
THERE'S A CASH REWARD?! SHIT-- YOU CAN CALL ME A "JUNKIE DICK-LICKER" IF THERE'S GREEN INVOLVED!
WHAT'S THE ADDITION?
WELL, MY JUNKIE, DICK-LICKING FRIEND...

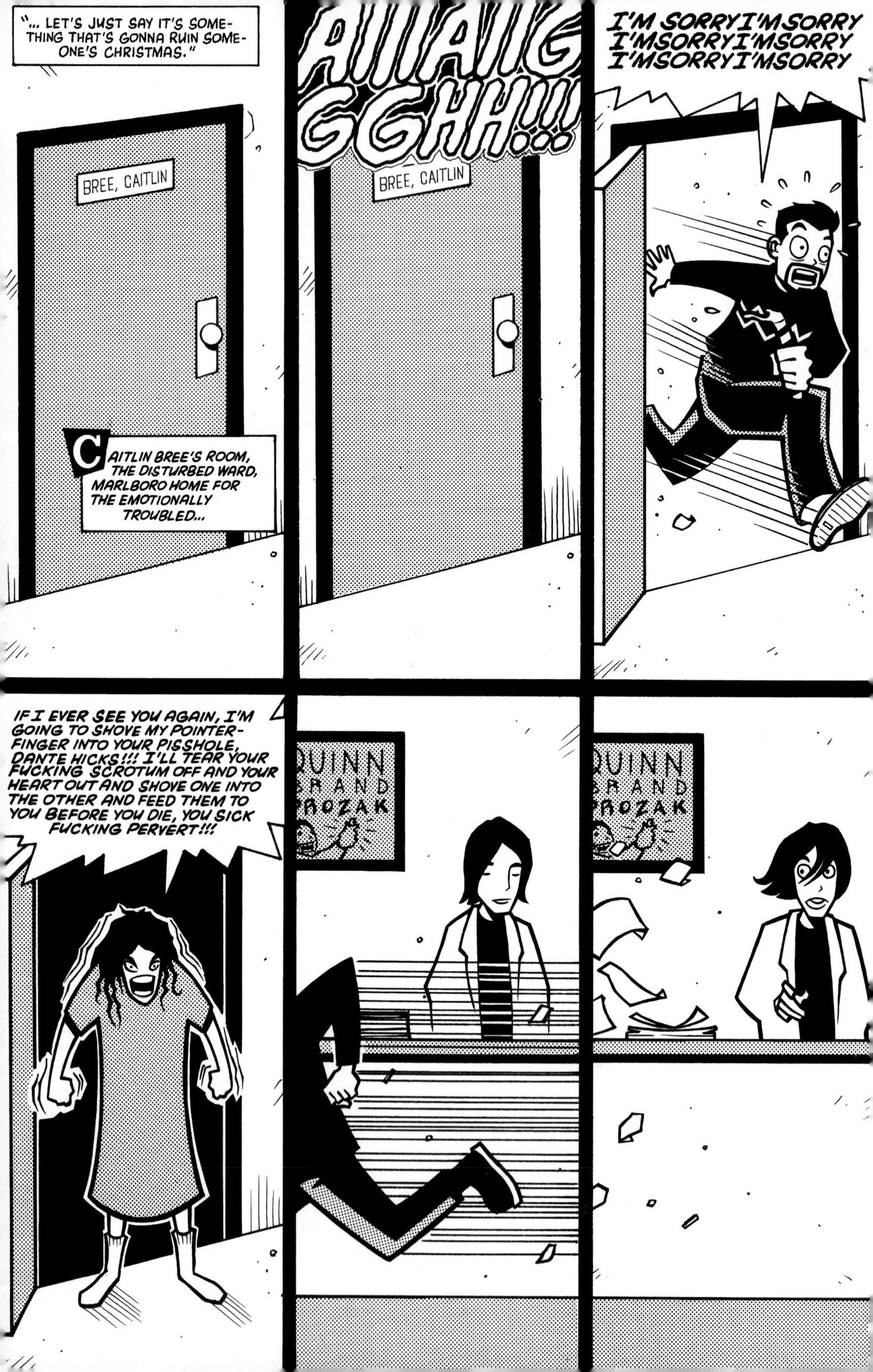
"... LET'S JUST SAY IT'S SOMETHING THAT'S GONNA RUIN SOMEONE'S CHRISTMAS."
BREE, CAITLIN
CAITLIN BREE'S ROOM, THE DISTURBED WARD, MARLBORO HOME FOR THE EMOTIONALLY TROUBLED...
AIIIAIIGGGHH!!!...
BREE, CAITLIN
I'M SORRY I'M SORRY I'M SORRY I'M SORRY I'M SORRY I'M SORRY
IF I EVER SEE YOU AGAIN, I'M GOING TO SHOVE MY POINTER-FINGER INTO YOUR PISSHOLE, DANTE HICKS!!! I'LL TEAR YOUR FUCKING SCROTUM OFF AND YOUR HEART OUT AND SHOVE ONE INTO THE OTHER AND FEED THEM TO YOU BEFORE YOU DIE, YOU SICK FUCKING PERVERT!!!
QUINN BRAND PROZAK
QUINN BRAND PROZAK

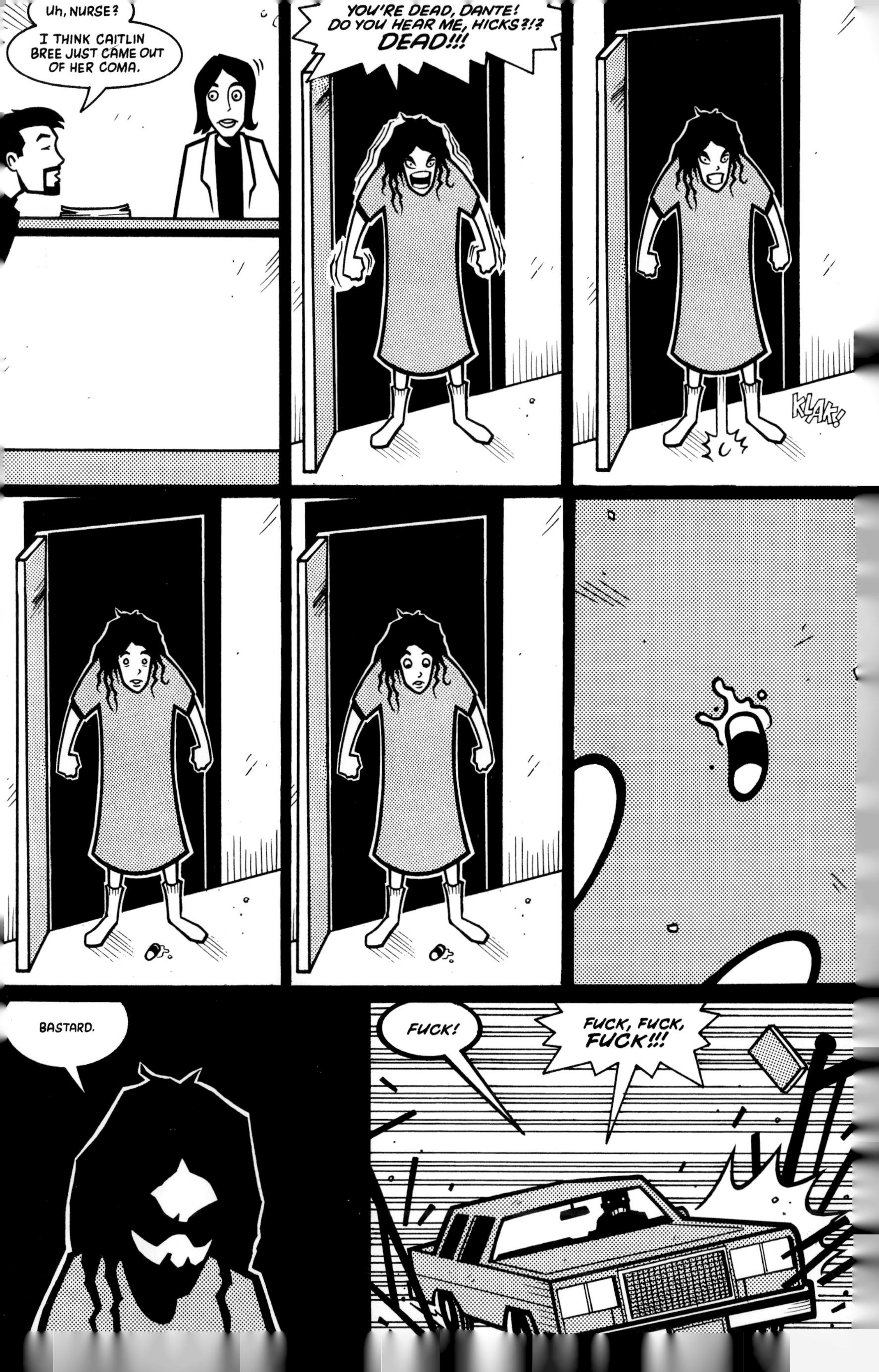
Uh, NURSE?
I THINK CAITLIN BREE JUST CAME OUT OF HER COMA.
YOU'RE DEAD, DANTE! DO YOU HEAR ME, HICKS?!? DEAD!!!
KLAK!
BASTARD.
FUCK!
FUCK, FUCK, FUCK!!!

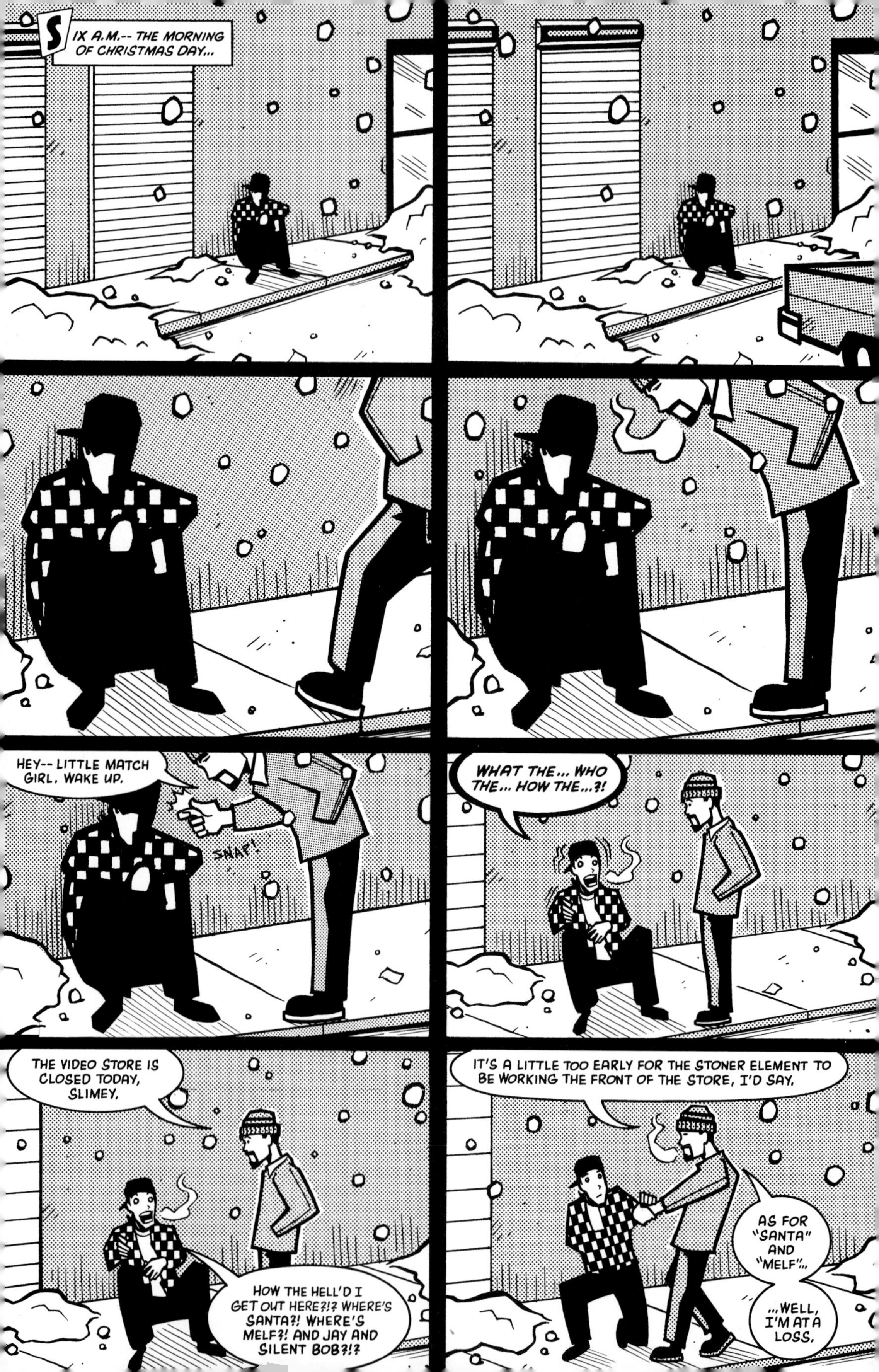
SIX A.M.-- THE MORNING OF CHRISTMAS DAY...
HEY-- LITTLE MATCH GIRL. WAKE UP.
SNAP!
WHAT THE... WHO THE... HOW THE...?!
THE VIDEO STORE IS CLOSED TODAY, SLIMEY.
HOW THE HELL'D I GET OUT HERE?!? WHERE'S SANTA?! WHERE'S MELF?! AND JAY AND SILENT BOB?!?
IT'S A LITTLE TOO EARLY FOR THE STONER ELEMENT TO BE WORKING THE FRONT OF THE STORE, I'D SAY.
AS FOR "SANTA" AND "MELF"...
...WELL, I'M AT A LOSS.

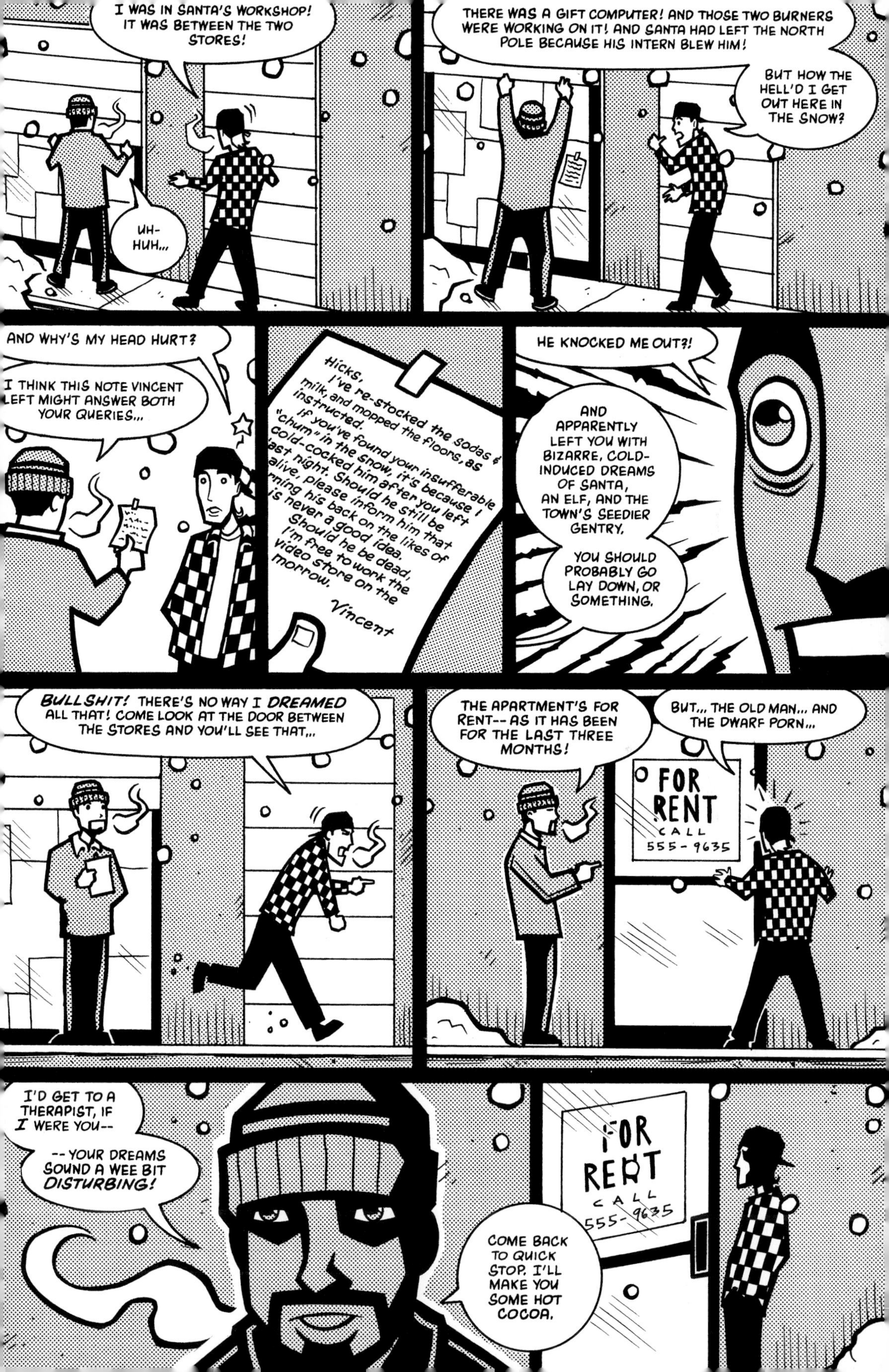
I WAS IN SANTA'S WORKSHOP! IT WAS BETWEEN THE TWO STORES!
UH-HUH...
THERE WAS A GIFT COMPUTER! AND THOSE TWO BURNERS WERE WORKING ON IT! AND SANTA HAD LEFT THE NORTH POLE BECAUSE HIS INTERN BLEW HIM!
BUT HOW THE HELL'D I GET OUT HERE IN THE SNOW?
AND WHY'S MY HEAD HURT?
I THINK THIS NOTE VINCENT LEFT MIGHT ANSWER BOTH YOUR QUERIES...
Hicks,
I've re-stocked the sodas & milk, and mopped the floors, as instructed.
If you've found your insufferable "chum" in the snow, it's because I cold-cocked him after you left last night. Should he still be alive, please inform him that turning his back on the likes of me is never a good idea.
Should he be dead, I'm free to work the video store on the morrow.
Vincent
HE KNOCKED ME OUT?!
AND APPARENTLY LEFT YOU WITH BIZARRE, COLD-INDUCED DREAMS OF SANTA, AN ELF, AND THE TOWN'S SEEDIER GENTRY.
YOU SHOULD PROBABLY GO LAY DOWN, OR SOMETHING.
BULLSHIT! THERE'S NO WAY I DREAMED ALL THAT! COME LOOK AT THE DOOR BETWEEN THE STORES AND YOU'LL SEE THAT...
THE APARTMENT'S FOR RENT-- AS IT HAS BEEN FOR THE LAST THREE MONTHS!
BUT... THE OLD MAN... AND THE DWARF PORN...
FOR RENT CALL 555-9635
I'D GET TO A THERAPIST, IF I WERE YOU--
-- YOUR DREAMS SOUND A WEE BIT DISTURBING!
FOR RENT CALL 555-9635
COME BACK TO QUICK STOP. I'LL MAKE YOU SOME HOT COCOA.

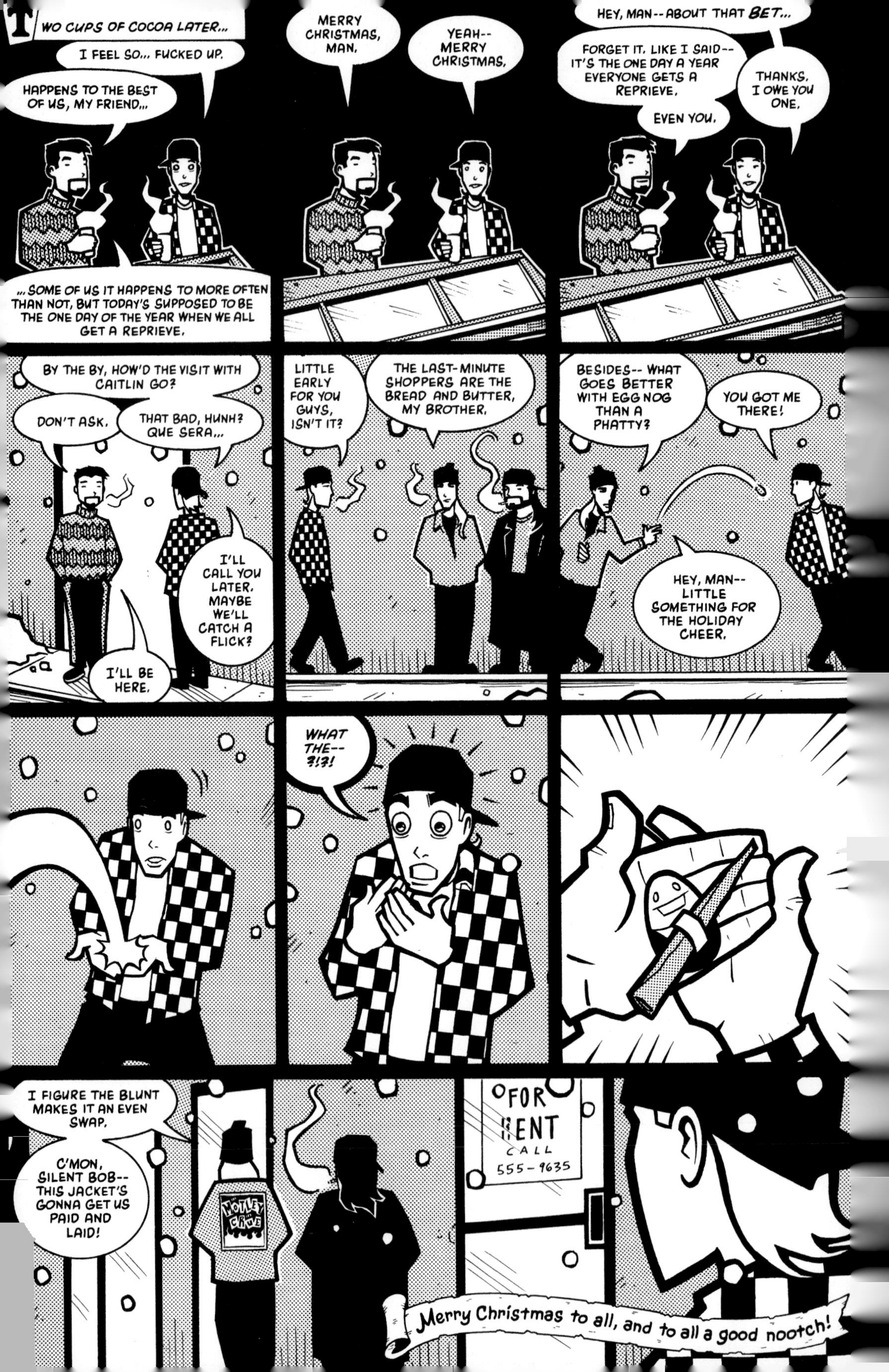
TWO CUPS OF COCOA LATER...
I FEEL SO... FUCKED UP.
HAPPENS TO THE BEST OF US, MY FRIEND...
...SOME OF US IT HAPPENS TO MORE OFTEN THAN NOT, BUT TODAY'S SUPPOSED TO BE THE ONE DAY OF THE YEAR WHEN WE ALL GET A REPRIEVE.
MERRY CHRISTMAS, MAN.
YEAH-- MERRY CHRISTMAS.
HEY, MAN-- ABOUT THAT BET...
FORGET IT. LIKE I SAID-- IT'S THE ONE DAY A YEAR EVERYONE GETS A REPRIEVE.
EVEN YOU.
THANKS, I OWE YOU ONE.
BY THE BY, HOW'D THE VISIT WITH CAITLIN GO?
DON'T ASK.
THAT BAD, HUNH? QUE SERA...
I'LL CALL YOU LATER. MAYBE WE'LL CATCH A FLICK?
I'LL BE HERE.
LITTLE EARLY FOR YOU GUYS, ISN'T IT?
THE LAST-MINUTE SHOPPERS ARE THE BREAD AND BUTTER, MY BROTHER.
BESIDES-- WHAT GOES BETTER WITH EGG NOG THAN A PHATTY?
YOU GOT ME THERE!
HEY, MAN-- LITTLE SOMETHING FOR THE HOLIDAY CHEER.
WHAT THE-- ?!?!
I FIGURE THE BLUNT MAKES IT AN EVEN SWAP.
C'MON, SILENT BOB-- THIS JACKET'S GONNA GET US PAID AND LAID!
MOTLEY CRUE
FOR RENT CALL 555-9635
Merry Christmas to all, and to all a good nootch!

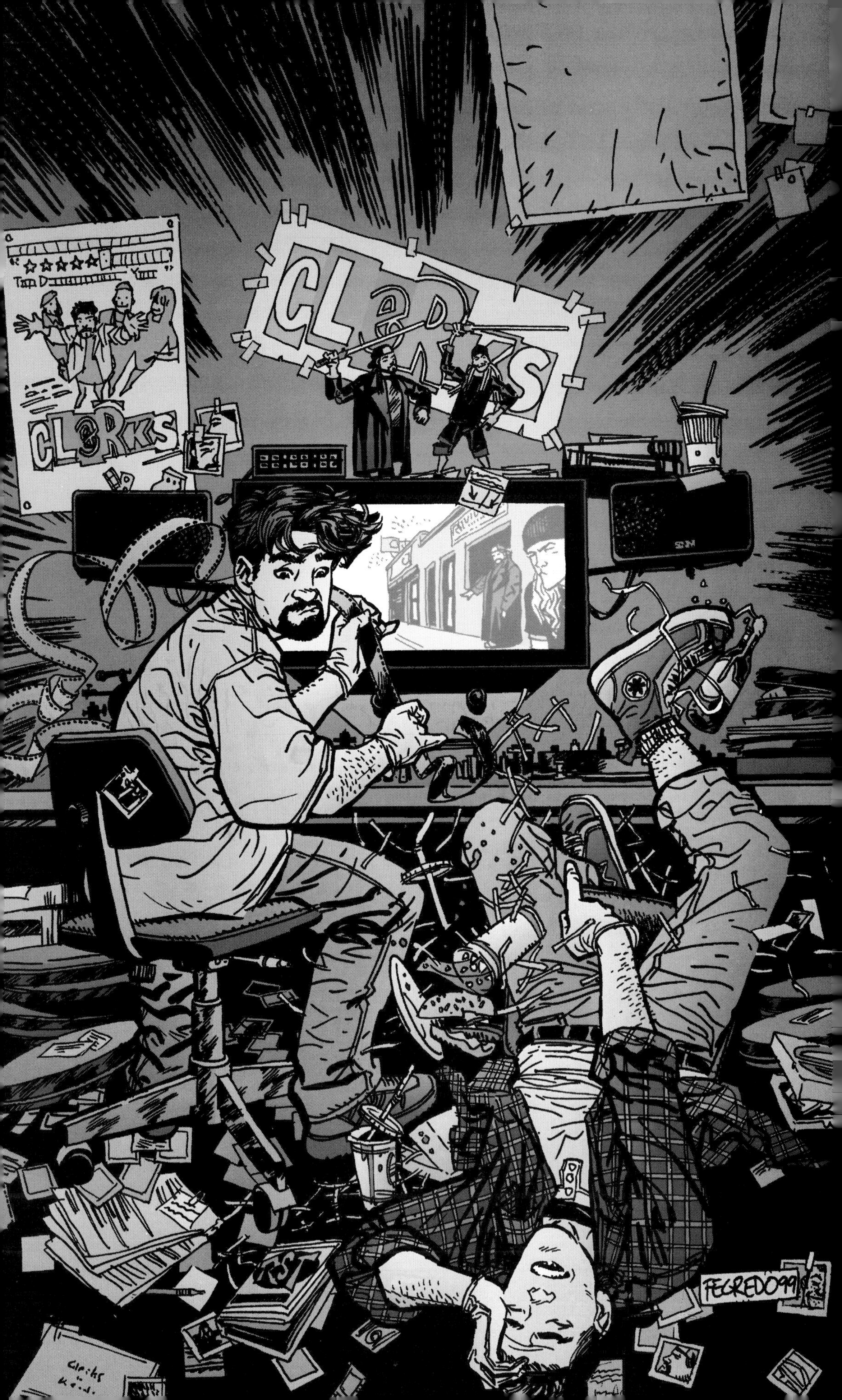
FEGREDO99

(The Lost Scene)

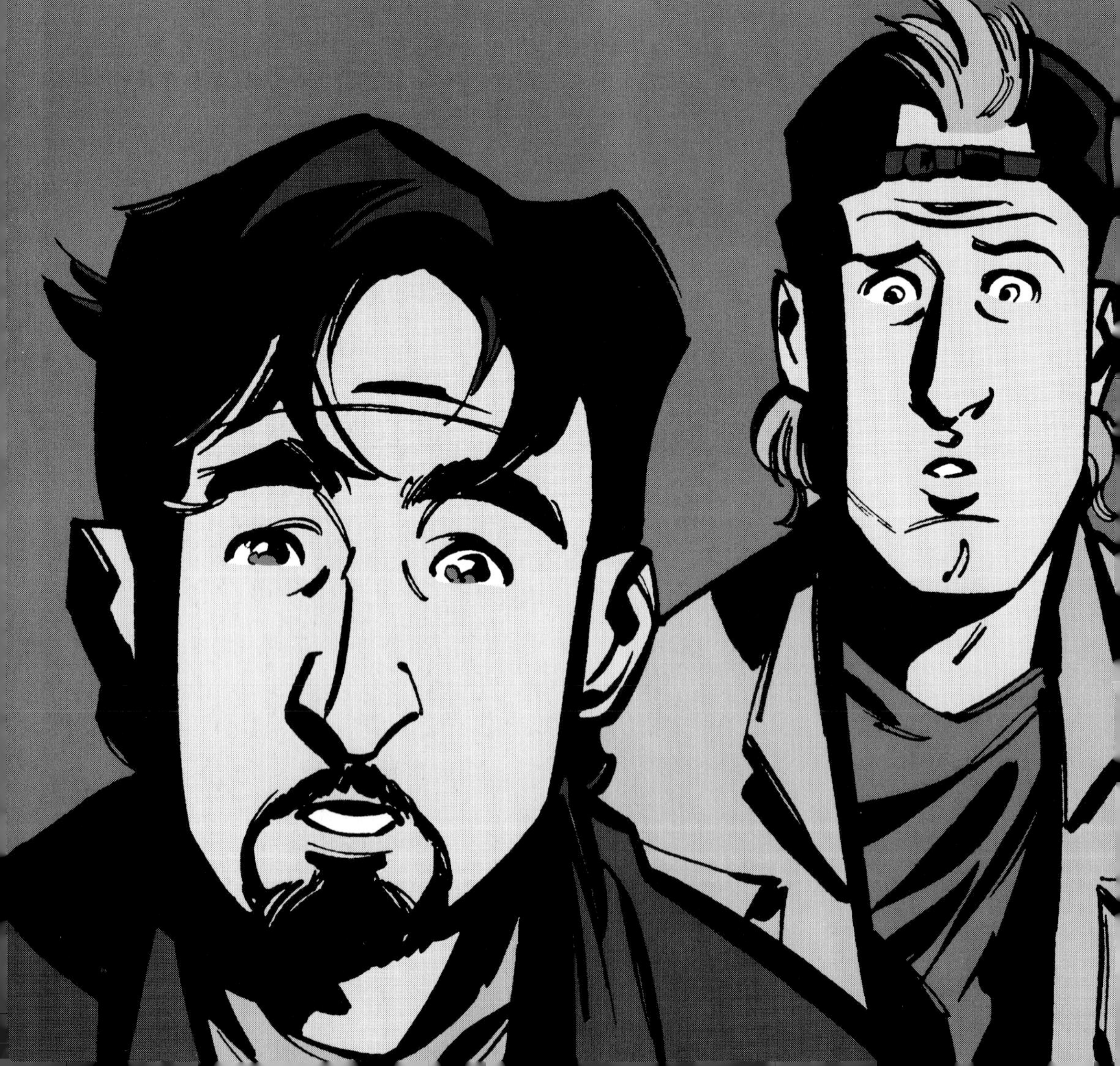

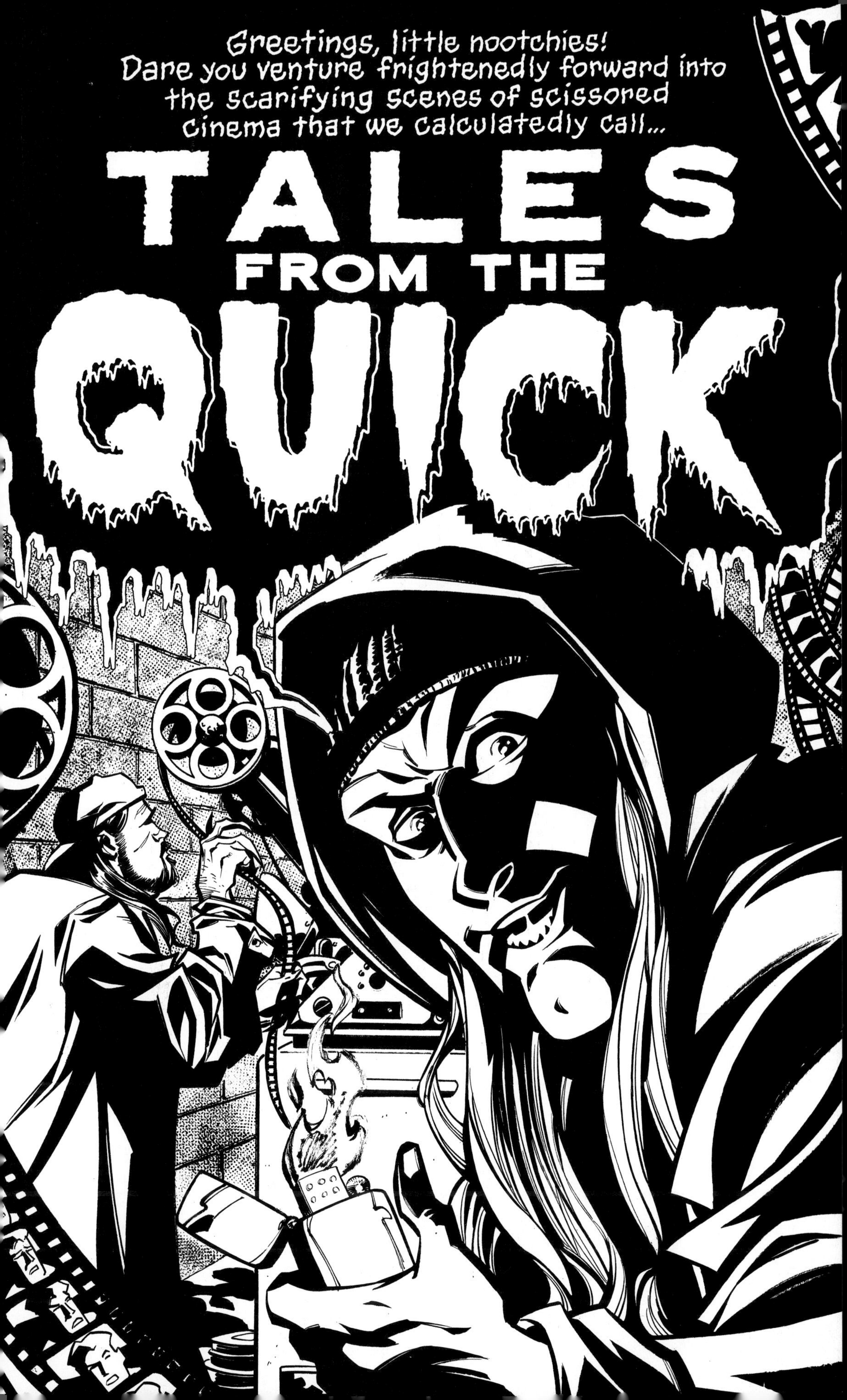
Greetings, little nootchies!
Dare you venture frighteningly forward into the scarifying scenes of scissored cinema that we calculatedly call...
TALES FROM THE QUICK

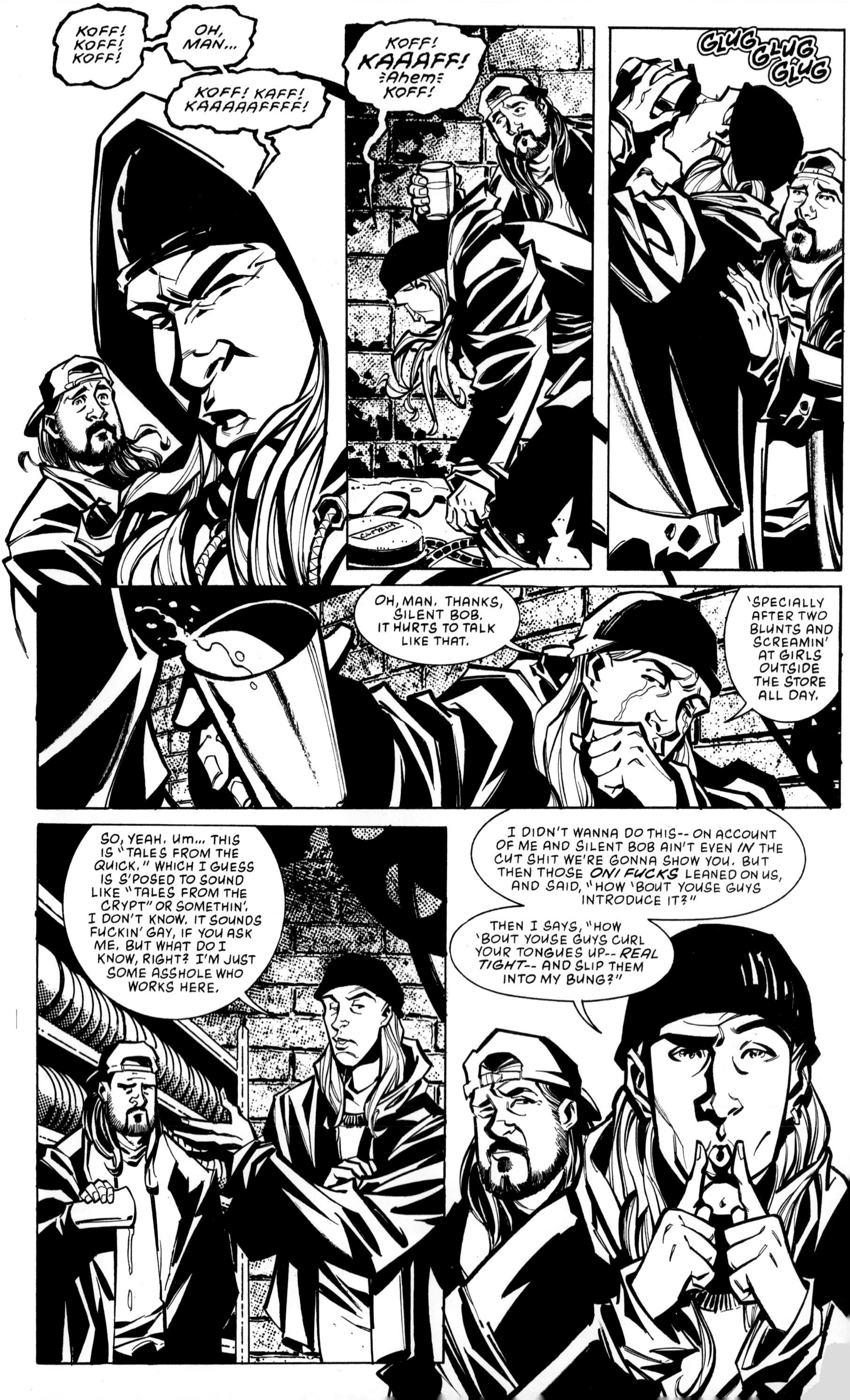
KOFF! KOFF! KOFF!
OH, MAN...
KOFF! KAFF! KAAAAAAFFFF!
KOFF! KAAAFF! Ahem KOFF!
GLUG GLUG GLUG
OH, MAN. THANKS, SILENT BOB. IT HURTS TO TALK LIKE THAT.
'SPECIALLY AFTER TWO BLUNTS AND SCREAMIN' AT GIRLS OUTSIDE THE STORE ALL DAY.
SO, YEAH. Um... THIS IS "TALES FROM THE QUICK," WHICH I GUESS IS S'POSED TO SOUND LIKE "TALES FROM THE CRYPT" OR SOMETHIN'. I DON'T KNOW. IT SOUNDS FUCKIN' GAY, IF YOU ASK ME. BUT WHAT DO I KNOW, RIGHT? I'M JUST SOME ASSHOLE WHO WORKS HERE.
I DIDN'T WANNA DO THIS-- ON ACCOUNT OF ME AND SILENT BOB AIN'T EVEN IN THE CUT SHIT WE'RE GONNA SHOW YOU. BUT THEN THOSE ONI FUCKS LEANED ON US, AND SAID, "HOW 'BOUT YOUSE GUYS INTRODUCE IT?"
THEN I SAYS, "HOW 'BOUT YOUSE GUYS CURL YOUR TONGUES UP-- REAL TIGHT-- AND SLIP THEM INTO MY BUNG?"

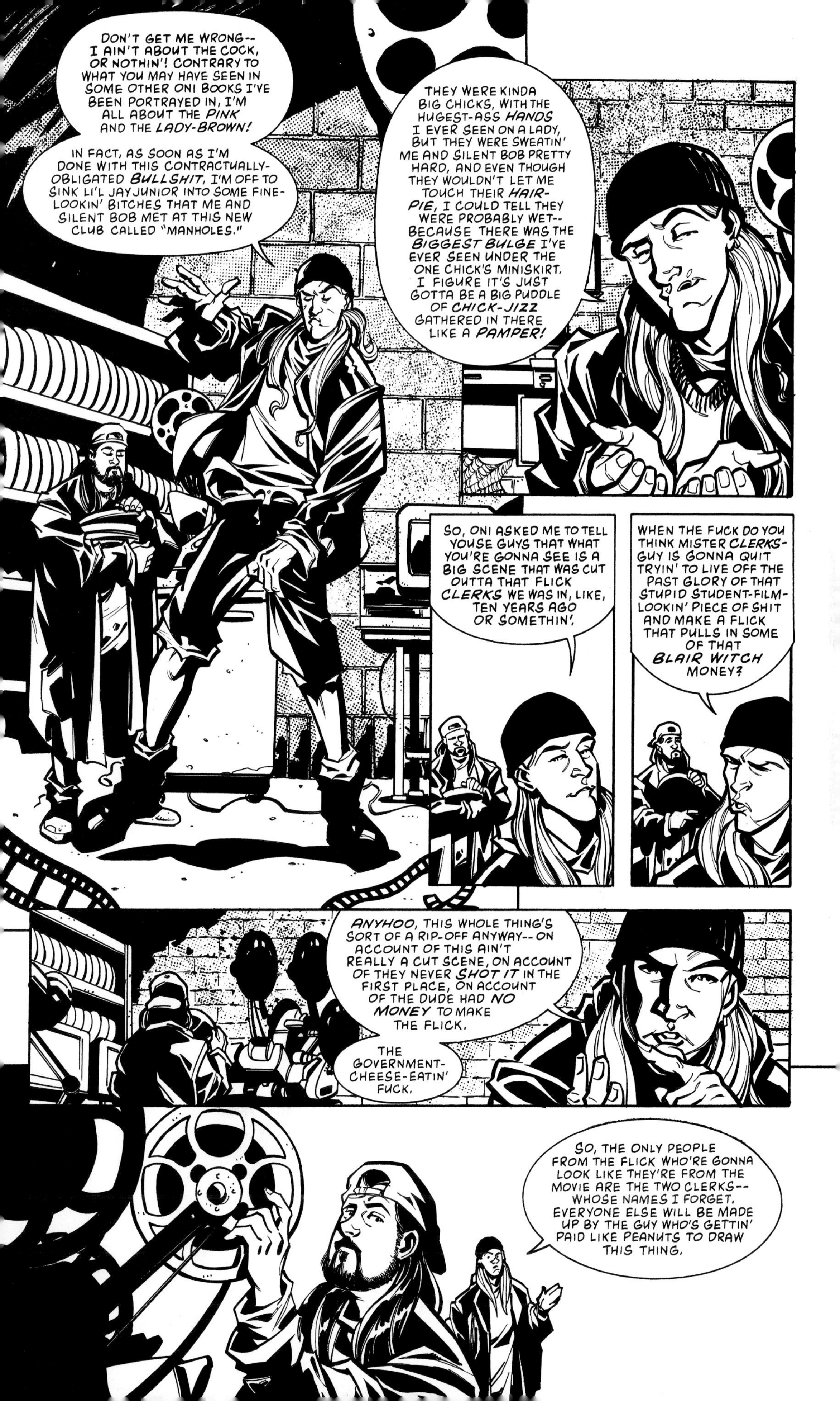
DON'T GET ME WRONG-- I AIN'T ABOUT THE COCK, OR NOTHIN'! CONTRARY TO WHAT YOU MAY HAVE SEEN IN SOME OTHER ONI BOOKS I'VE BEEN PORTRAYED IN, I'M ALL ABOUT THE PINK AND THE LADY-BROWN!
IN FACT, AS SOON AS I'M DONE WITH THIS CONTRACTUALLY-OBLIGATED BULLSHIT, I'M OFF TO SINK LI'L JAY JUNIOR INTO SOME FINE-LOOKIN' BITCHES THAT ME AND SILENT BOB MET AT THIS NEW CLUB CALLED "MANHOLES."
THEY WERE KINDA BIG CHICKS, WITH THE HUGEST-ASS HANDS I EVER SEEN ON A LADY, BUT THEY WERE SWEATIN' ME AND SILENT BOB PRETTY HARD, AND EVEN THOUGH THEY WOULDN'T LET ME TOUCH THEIR HAIR-PIE, I COULD TELL THEY WERE PROBABLY WET-- BECAUSE THERE WAS THE BIGGEST BULGE I'VE EVER SEEN UNDER THE ONE CHICK'S MINISKIRT. I FIGURE IT'S JUST GOTTA BE A BIG PUDDLE OF CHICK-JIZZ GATHERED IN THERE LIKE A PAMPER!
SO, ONI ASKED ME TO TELL YOUSE GUYS THAT WHAT YOU'RE GONNA SEE IS A BIG SCENE THAT WAS CUT OUTTA THAT FLICK CLERKS WE WAS IN, LIKE, TEN YEARS AGO OR SOMETHIN'.
WHEN THE FUCK DO YOU THINK MISTER CLERKS-GUY IS GONNA QUIT TRYIN' TO LIVE OFF THE PAST GLORY OF THAT STUPID STUDENT-FILM-LOOKIN' PIECE OF SHIT AND MAKE A FLICK THAT PULLS IN SOME OF THAT BLAIR WITCH MONEY?
ANYHOO, THIS WHOLE THING'S SORT OF A RIP-OFF ANYWAY-- ON ACCOUNT OF THIS AIN'T REALLY A CUT SCENE, ON ACCOUNT OF THEY NEVER SHOT IT IN THE FIRST PLACE, ON ACCOUNT OF THE DUDE HAD NO MONEY TO MAKE THE FLICK.
THE GOVERNMENT-CHEESE-EATIN' FUCK.
SO, THE ONLY PEOPLE FROM THE FLICK WHO'RE GONNA LOOK LIKE THEY'RE FROM THE MOVIE ARE THE TWO CLERKS-- WHOSE NAMES I FORGET. EVERYONE ELSE WILL BE MADE UP BY THE GUY WHO'S GETTIN' PAID LIKE PEANUTS TO DRAW THIS THING.

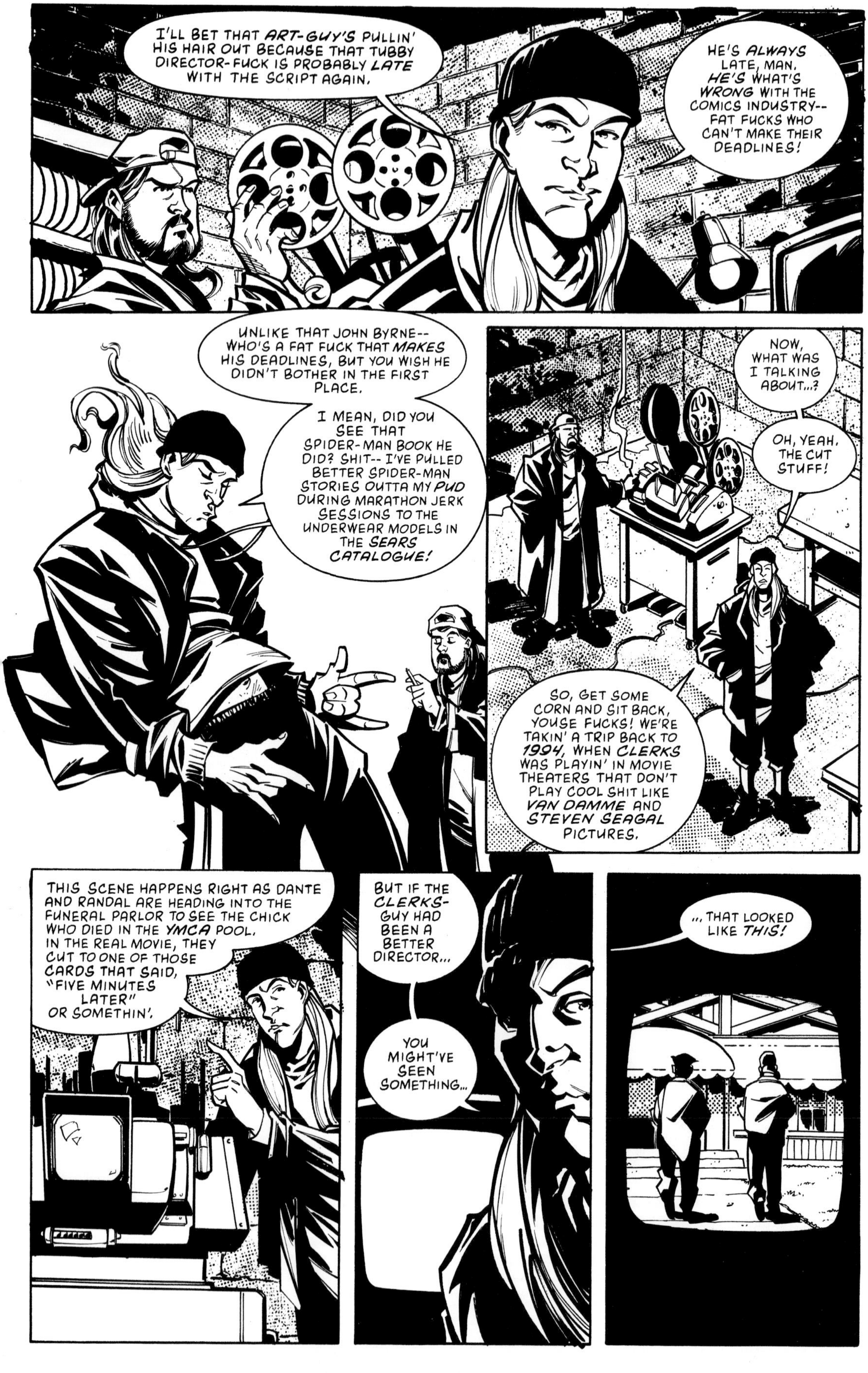
I'LL BET THAT ART-GUY'S PULLIN' HIS HAIR OUT BECAUSE THAT TUBBY DIRECTOR-FUCK IS PROBABLY LATE WITH THE SCRIPT AGAIN.
HE'S ALWAYS LATE, MAN. HE'S WHAT'S WRONG WITH THE COMICS INDUSTRY-- FAT FUCKS WHO CAN'T MAKE THEIR DEADLINES!
UNLIKE THAT JOHN BYRNE-- WHO'S A FAT FUCK THAT MAKES HIS DEADLINES, BUT YOU WISH HE DIDN'T BOTHER IN THE FIRST PLACE.
I MEAN, DID YOU SEE THAT SPIDER-MAN BOOK HE DID? SHIT-- I'VE PULLED BETTER SPIDER-MAN STORIES OUTTA MY PUD DURING MARATHON JERK SESSIONS TO THE UNDERWEAR MODELS IN THE SEARS CATALOGUE!
NOW, WHAT WAS I TALKING ABOUT...?
OH, YEAH, THE CUT STUFF!
SO, GET SOME CORN AND SIT BACK, YOUSE FUCKS! WE'RE TAKIN' A TRIP BACK TO 1994, WHEN CLERKS WAS PLAYIN' IN MOVIE THEATERS THAT DON'T PLAY COOL SHIT LIKE VAN DAMME AND STEVEN SEAGAL PICTURES.
THIS SCENE HAPPENS RIGHT AS DANTE AND RANDAL ARE HEADING INTO THE FUNERAL PARLOR TO SEE THE CHICK WHO DIED IN THE YMCA POOL. IN THE REAL MOVIE, THEY CUT TO ONE OF THOSE CARDS THAT SAID, "FIVE MINUTES LATER" OR SOMETHIN'.
BUT IF THE CLERKS-GUY HAD BEEN A BETTER DIRECTOR...
YOU MIGHT'VE SEEN SOMETHING...
...THAT LOOKED LIKE THIS!

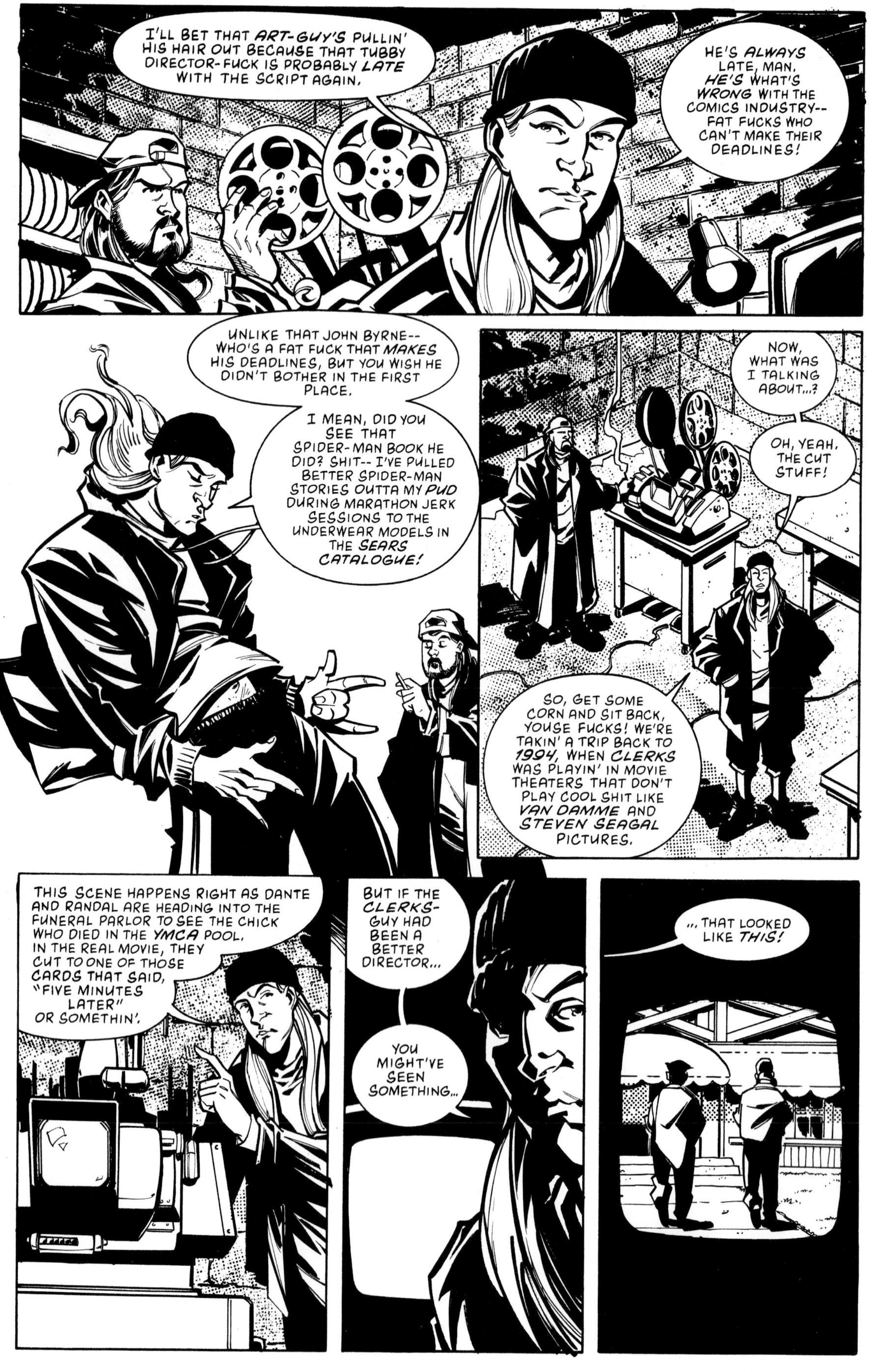
I'LL BET THAT ART-GUY'S PULLIN' HIS HAIR OUT BECAUSE THAT TUBBY DIRECTOR-FUCK IS PROBABLY LATE WITH THE SCRIPT AGAIN.
HE'S ALWAYS LATE, MAN. HE'S WHAT'S WRONG WITH THE COMICS INDUSTRY-- FAT FUCKS WHO CAN'T MAKE THEIR DEADLINES!
UNLIKE THAT JOHN BYRNE-- WHO'S A FAT FUCK THAT MAKES HIS DEADLINES, BUT YOU WISH HE DIDN'T BOTHER IN THE FIRST PLACE.
I MEAN, DID YOU SEE THAT SPIDER-MAN BOOK HE DID? SHIT-- I'VE PULLED BETTER SPIDER-MAN STORIES OUTTA MY PUD DURING MARATHON JERK SESSIONS TO THE UNDERWEAR MODELS IN THE SEARS CATALOGUE!
NOW, WHAT WAS I TALKING ABOUT...?
OH, YEAH, THE CUT STUFF!
SO, GET SOME CORN AND SIT BACK, YOUSE FUCKS! WE'RE TAKIN' A TRIP BACK TO 1994, WHEN CLERKS WAS PLAYIN' IN MOVIE THEATERS THAT DON'T PLAY COOL SHIT LIKE VAN DAMME AND STEVEN SEAGAL PICTURES.
THIS SCENE HAPPENS RIGHT AS DANTE AND RANDAL ARE HEADING INTO THE FUNERAL PARLOR TO SEE THE CHICK WHO DIED IN THE YMCA POOL. IN THE REAL MOVIE, THEY CUT TO ONE OF THOSE CARDS THAT SAID, "FIVE MINUTES LATER" OR SOMETHIN'.
BUT IF THE CLERKS-GUY HAD BEEN A BETTER DIRECTOR...
YOU MIGHT'VE SEEN SOMETHING...
...THAT LOOKED LIKE THIS!

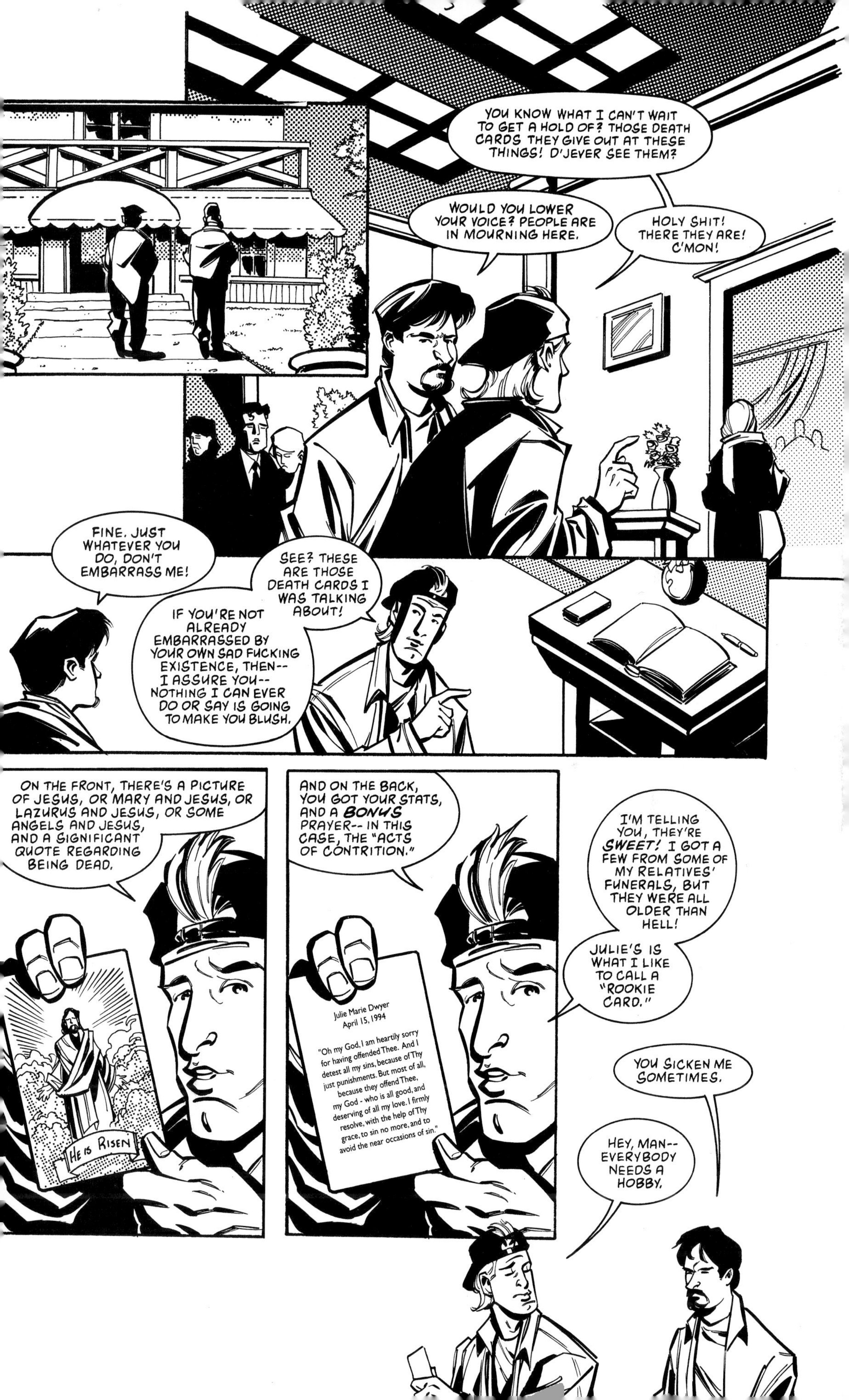
YOU KNOW WHAT I CAN'T WAIT TO GET A HOLD OF? THOSE DEATH CARDS THEY GIVE OUT AT THESE THINGS! D'JEVER SEE THEM?
WOULD YOU LOWER YOUR VOICE? PEOPLE ARE IN MOURNING HERE.
HOLY SHIT! THERE THEY ARE! C'MON!
FINE. JUST WHATEVER YOU DO, DON'T EMBARRASS ME!
SEE? THESE ARE THOSE DEATH CARDS I WAS TALKING ABOUT!
IF YOU'RE NOT ALREADY EMBARRASSED BY YOUR OWN SAD FUCKING EXISTENCE, THEN-- I ASSURE YOU-- NOTHING I CAN EVER DO OR SAY IS GOING TO MAKE YOU BLUSH.
ON THE FRONT, THERE'S A PICTURE OF JESUS, OR MARY AND JESUS, OR LAZURUS AND JESUS, OR SOME ANGELS AND JESUS, AND A SIGNIFICANT QUOTE REGARDING BEING DEAD.
HE IS RISEN
AND ON THE BACK, YOU GOT YOUR STATS, AND A BONUS PRAYER-- IN THIS CASE, THE "ACTS OF CONTRITION."
Julie Marie Dwyer
April 15, 1994
"Oh my God, I am heartily sorry for having offended Thee. And I detest all my sins, because of Thy just punishments. But most of all, because they offend Thee, my God - who is all good, and deserving of all my love. I firmly resolve, with the help of Thy grace, to sin no more, and to avoid the near occasions of sin."
I'M TELLING YOU, THEY'RE SWEET! I GOT A FEW FROM SOME OF MY RELATIVES' FUNERALS, BUT THEY WERE ALL OLDER THAN HELL!
JULIE'S IS WHAT I LIKE TO CALL A "ROOKIE CARD."
YOU SICKEN ME SOMETIMES.
HEY, MAN-- EVERYBODY NEEDS A HOBBY.

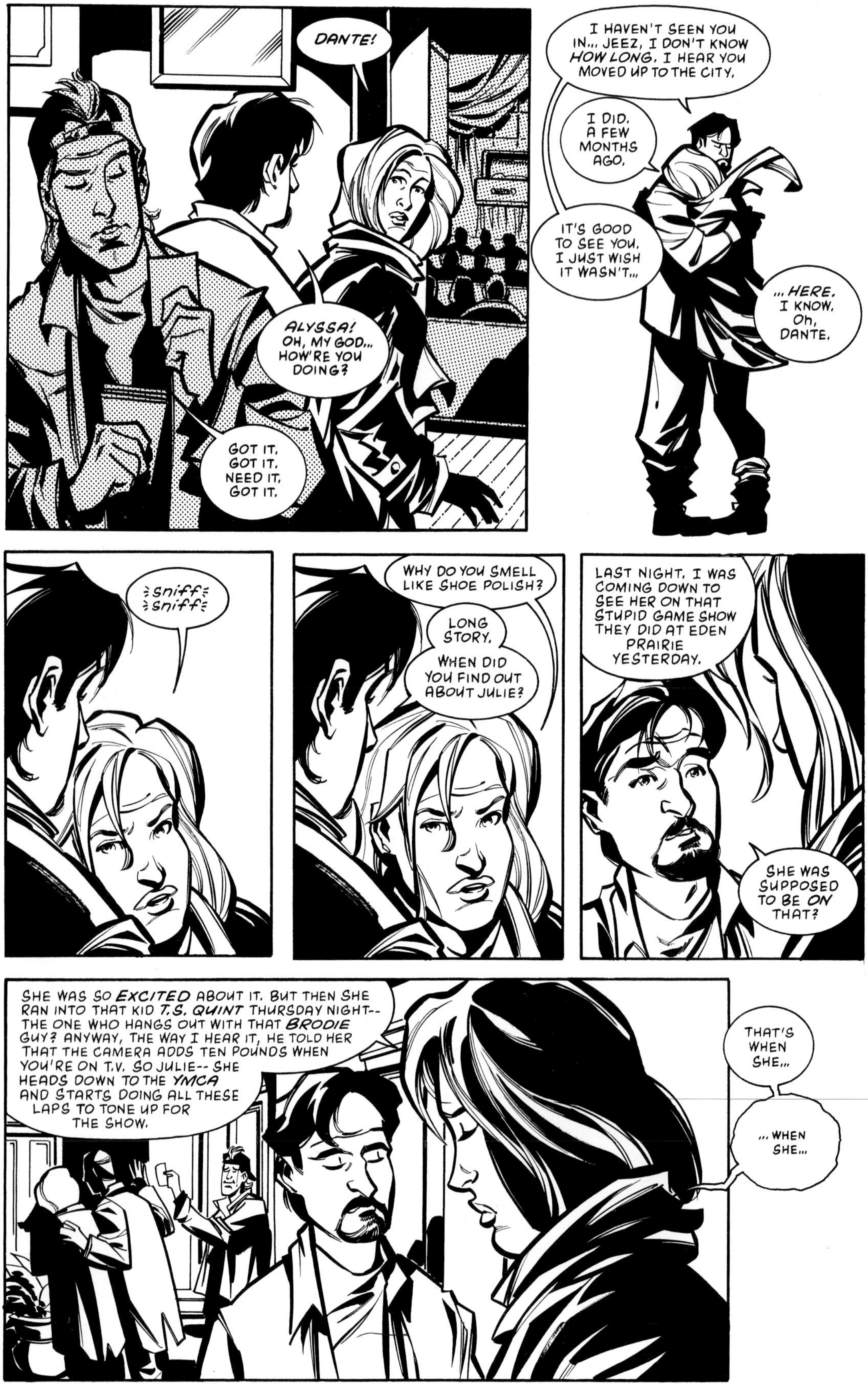
DANTE!
ALYSSA! OH, MY GOD... HOW'RE YOU DOING?
GOT IT. GOT IT. NEED IT. GOT IT.
I HAVEN'T SEEN YOU IN... JEEZ, I DON'T KNOW *HOW LONG*. I HEAR YOU MOVED UP TO THE CITY.
I DID. A FEW MONTHS AGO.
IT'S GOOD TO SEE YOU. I JUST WISH IT WASN'T...
...*HERE*. I KNOW. Oh, DANTE.
sniff sniff
WHY DO YOU SMELL LIKE SHOE POLISH?
LONG STORY.
WHEN DID YOU FIND OUT ABOUT JULIE?
LAST NIGHT. I WAS COMING DOWN TO SEE HER ON THAT STUPID GAME SHOW THEY DID AT EDEN PRAIRIE YESTERDAY.
SHE WAS SUPPOSED TO BE *ON* THAT?
SHE WAS SO *EXCITED* ABOUT IT. BUT THEN SHE RAN INTO THAT KID *T.S. QUINT* THURSDAY NIGHT-- THE ONE WHO HANGS OUT WITH THAT *BRODIE* GUY? ANYWAY, THE WAY I HEAR IT, HE TOLD HER THAT THE CAMERA ADDS TEN POUNDS WHEN YOU'RE ON T.V. SO JULIE-- SHE HEADS DOWN TO THE *YMCA* AND STARTS DOING ALL THESE LAPS TO TONE UP FOR THE SHOW.
THAT'S WHEN SHE...
...WHEN SHE...

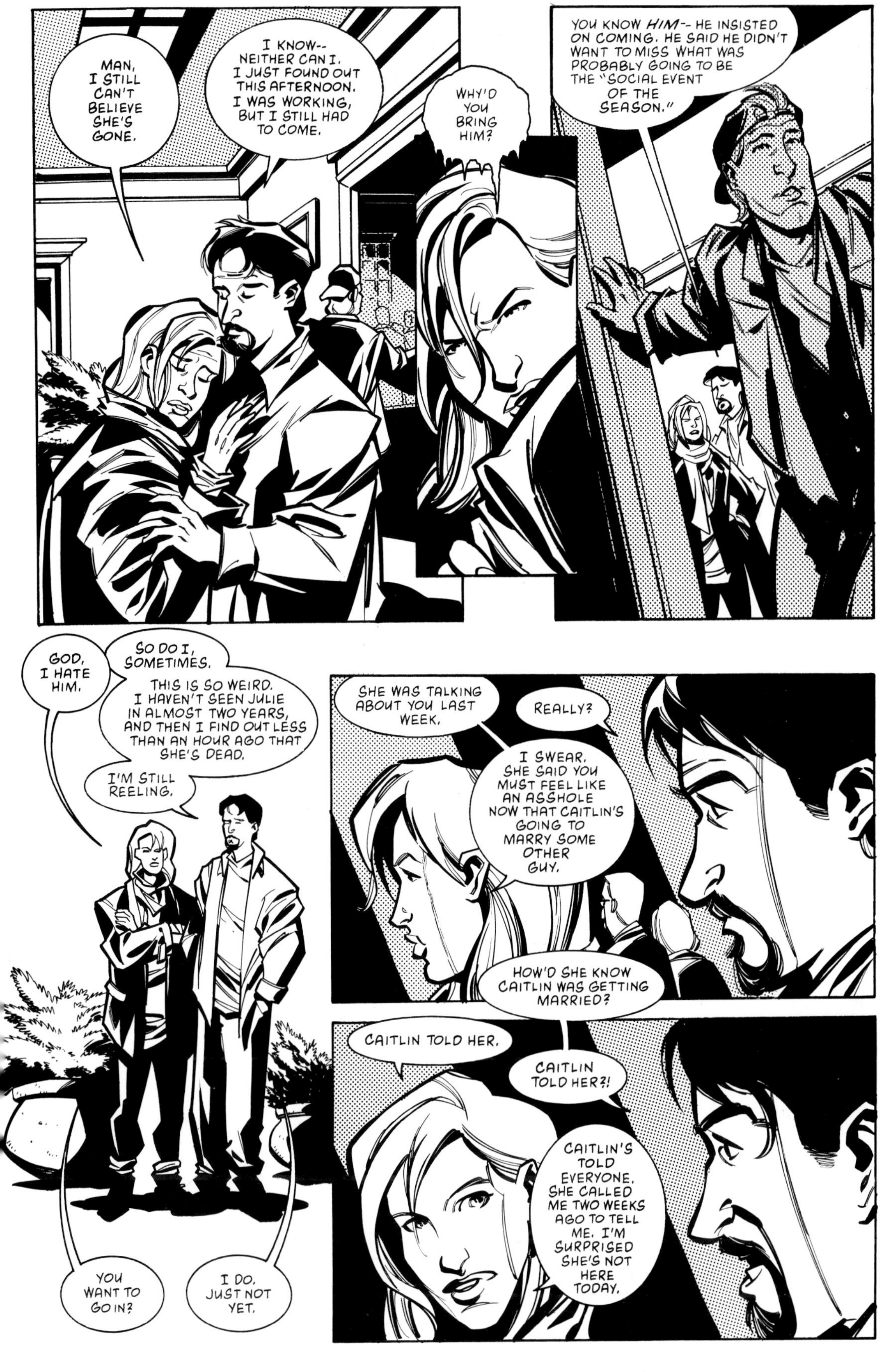
MAN, I STILL CAN'T BELIEVE SHE'S GONE.
I KNOW-- NEITHER CAN I. I JUST FOUND OUT THIS AFTERNOON. I WAS WORKING, BUT I STILL HAD TO COME.
WHY'D YOU BRING HIM?
YOU KNOW HIM-- HE INSISTED ON COMING. HE SAID HE DIDN'T WANT TO MISS WHAT WAS PROBABLY GOING TO BE THE "SOCIAL EVENT OF THE SEASON."
GOD, I HATE HIM.
SO DO I, SOMETIMES.
THIS IS SO WEIRD. I HAVEN'T SEEN JULIE IN ALMOST TWO YEARS, AND THEN I FIND OUT LESS THAN AN HOUR AGO THAT SHE'S DEAD.
I'M STILL REELING.
YOU WANT TO GO IN?
I DO, JUST NOT YET.
SHE WAS TALKING ABOUT YOU LAST WEEK.
REALLY?
I SWEAR. SHE SAID YOU MUST FEEL LIKE AN ASSHOLE NOW THAT CAITLIN'S GOING TO MARRY SOME OTHER GUY.
HOW'D SHE KNOW CAITLIN WAS GETTING MARRIED?
CAITLIN TOLD HER.
CAITLIN TOLD HER?!
CAITLIN'S TOLD EVERYONE. SHE CALLED ME TWO WEEKS AGO TO TELL ME. I'M SURPRISED SHE'S NOT HERE TODAY.

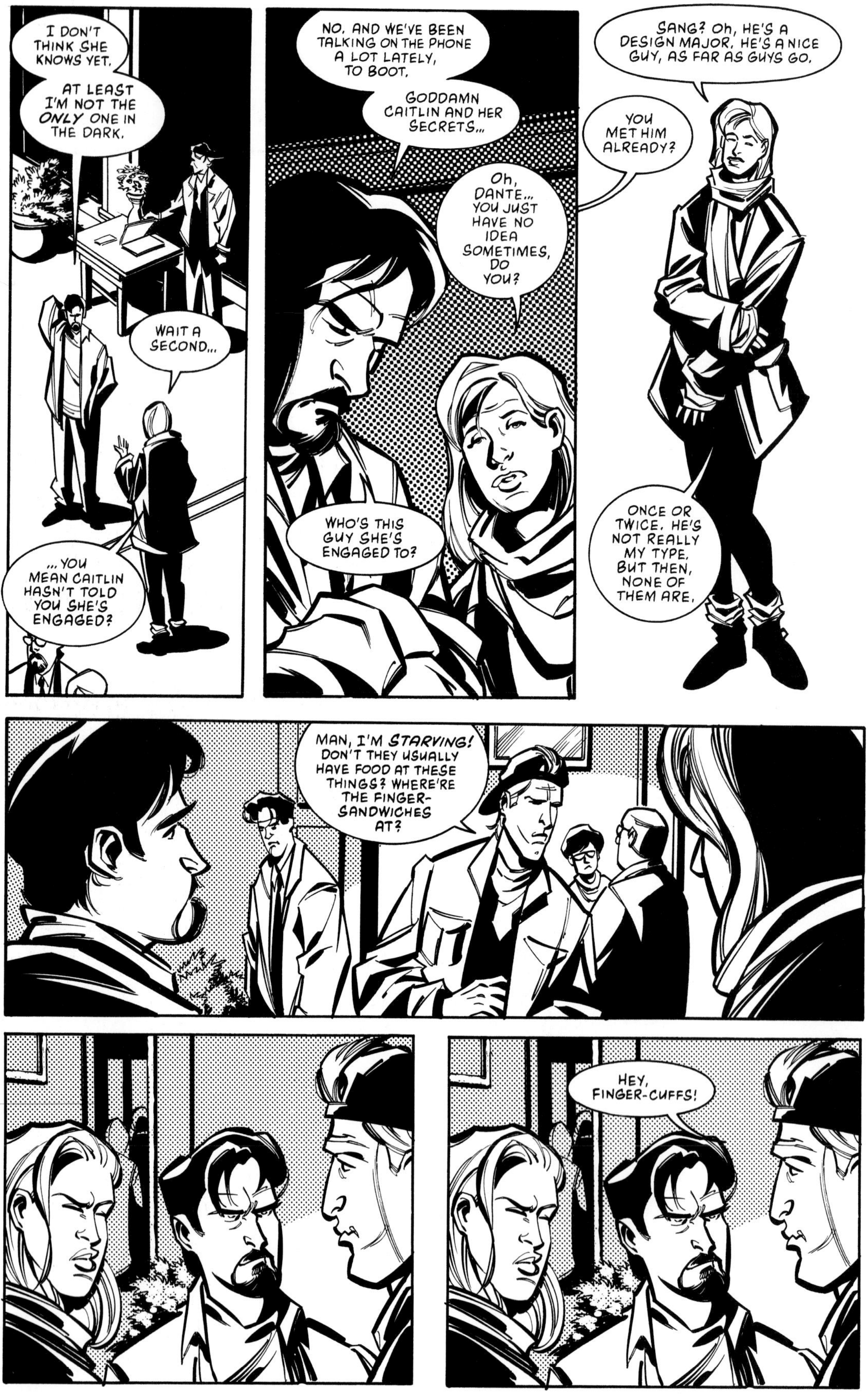
I DON'T THINK SHE KNOWS YET.
AT LEAST I'M NOT THE *ONLY* ONE IN THE DARK.
WAIT A SECOND...
...YOU MEAN CAITLIN HASN'T TOLD YOU SHE'S ENGAGED?
NO, AND WE'VE BEEN TALKING ON THE PHONE A LOT LATELY, TO BOOT.
GODDAMN CAITLIN AND HER SECRETS...
Oh, DANTE... YOU JUST HAVE NO IDEA SOMETIMES, DO YOU?
WHO'S THIS GUY SHE'S ENGAGED TO?
SANG? Oh, HE'S A DESIGN MAJOR, HE'S A NICE GUY, AS FAR AS GUYS GO.
YOU MET HIM ALREADY?
ONCE OR TWICE. HE'S NOT REALLY MY TYPE, BUT THEN, NONE OF THEM ARE.
MAN, I'M *STARVING!* DON'T THEY USUALLY HAVE FOOD AT THESE THINGS? WHERE'RE THE FINGER-SANDWICHES AT?
HEY, FINGER-CUFFS!

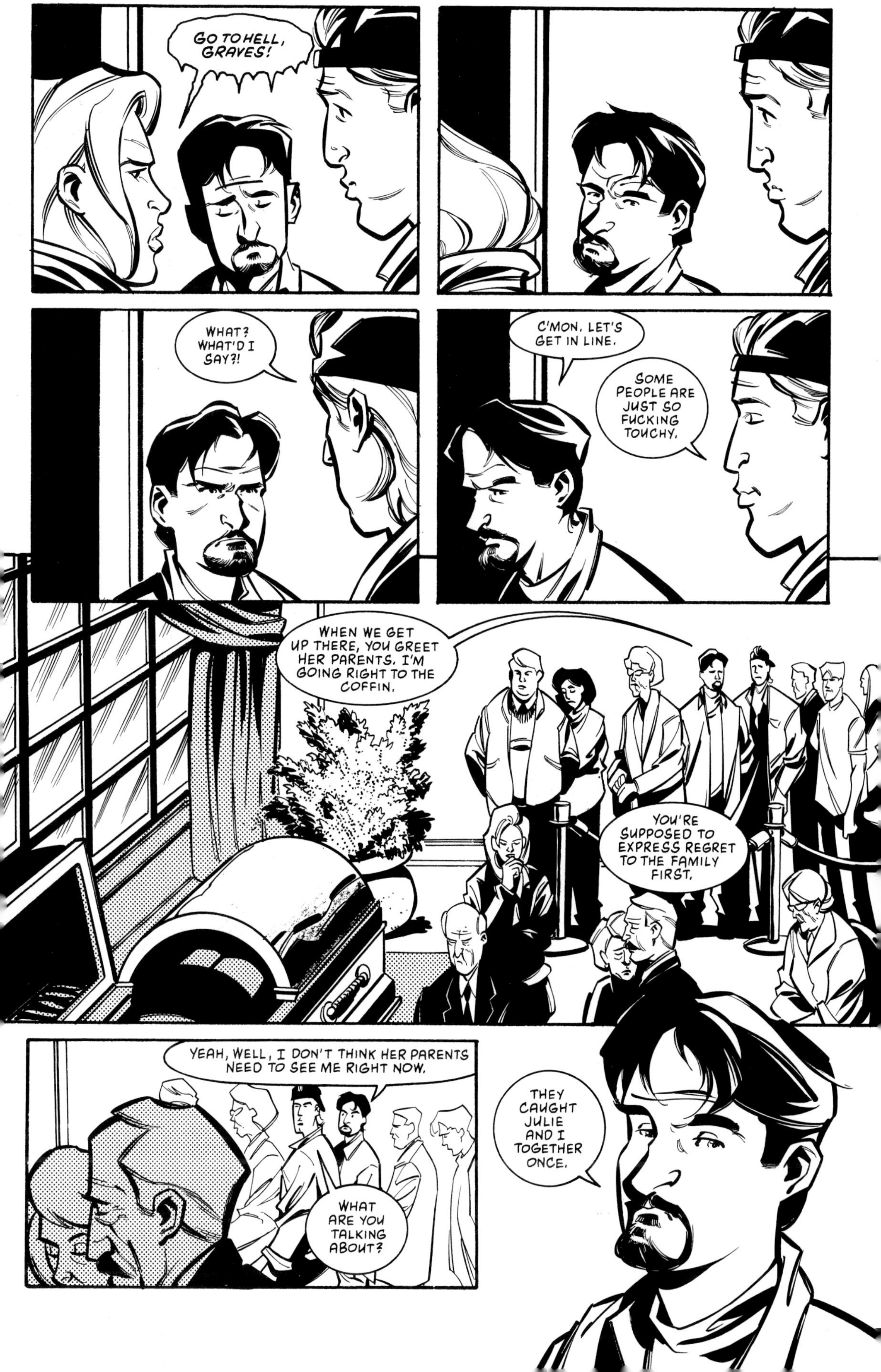
GO TO HELL, GRAVES!
WHAT? WHAT'D I SAY?!
C'MON. LET'S GET IN LINE.
SOME PEOPLE ARE JUST SO FUCKING TOUCHY.
WHEN WE GET UP THERE, YOU GREET HER PARENTS. I'M GOING RIGHT TO THE COFFIN.
YOU'RE SUPPOSED TO EXPRESS REGRET TO THE FAMILY FIRST.
YEAH, WELL, I DON'T THINK HER PARENTS NEED TO SEE ME RIGHT NOW.
WHAT ARE YOU TALKING ABOUT?
THEY CAUGHT JULIE AND I TOGETHER ONCE.

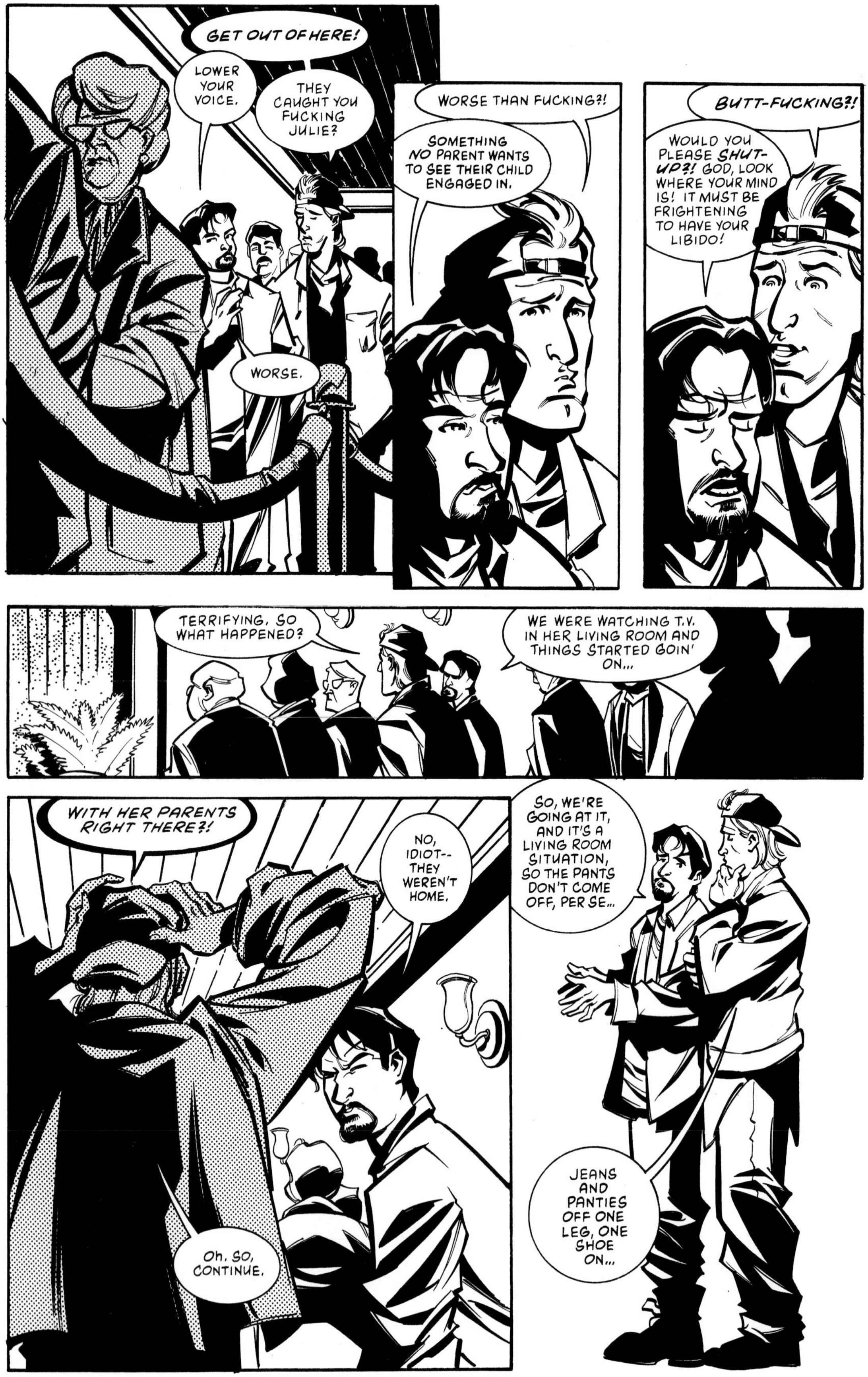
GET OUT OF HERE!
LOWER YOUR VOICE.
THEY CAUGHT YOU FUCKING JULIE?
WORSE.
WORSE THAN FUCKING?!
SOMETHING NO PARENT WANTS TO SEE THEIR CHILD ENGAGED IN.
BUTT-FUCKING?!
WOULD YOU PLEASE SHUT-UP?! GOD, LOOK WHERE YOUR MIND IS! IT MUST BE FRIGHTENING TO HAVE YOUR LIBIDO!
TERRIFYING. SO WHAT HAPPENED?
WE WERE WATCHING T.V. IN HER LIVING ROOM AND THINGS STARTED GOIN' ON...
WITH HER PARENTS RIGHT THERE?!
NO, IDIOT-- THEY WEREN'T HOME.
Oh. SO, CONTINUE.
SO, WE'RE GOING AT IT, AND IT'S A LIVING ROOM SITUATION, SO THE PANTS DON'T COME OFF, PER SE...
JEANS AND PANTIES OFF ONE LEG, ONE SHOE ON...

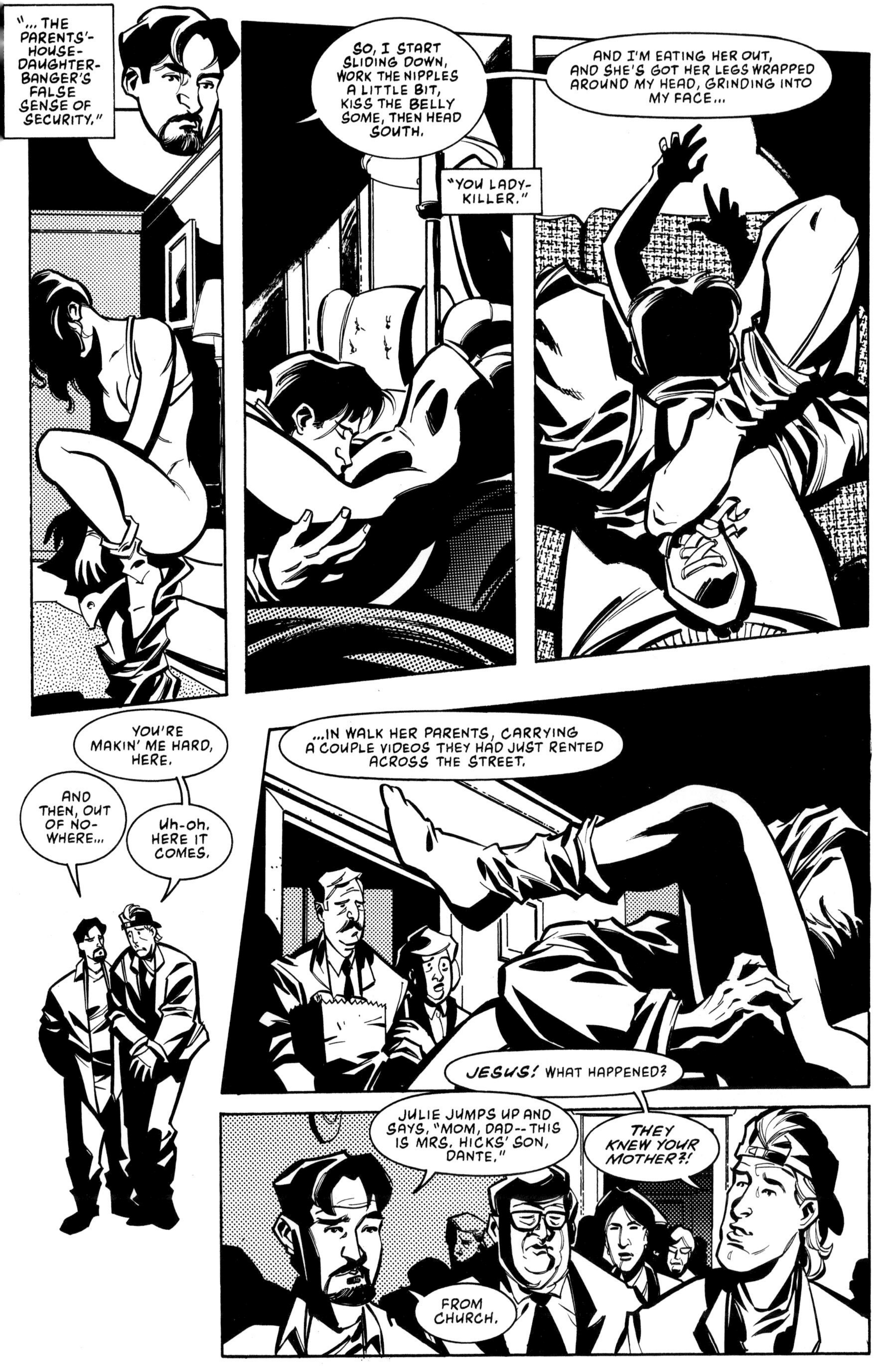
"... THE PARENTS'-HOUSE-DAUGHTER-BANGER'S FALSE SENSE OF SECURITY."
SO, I START SLIDING DOWN, WORK THE NIPPLES A LITTLE BIT, KISS THE BELLY SOME, THEN HEAD SOUTH.
"YOU LADY-KILLER."
AND I'M EATING HER OUT, AND SHE'S GOT HER LEGS WRAPPED AROUND MY HEAD, GRINDING INTO MY FACE...
YOU'RE MAKIN' ME HARD, HERE.
AND THEN, OUT OF NO-WHERE...
UH-OH. HERE IT COMES.
...IN WALK HER PARENTS, CARRYING A COUPLE VIDEOS THEY HAD JUST RENTED ACROSS THE STREET.
JESUS! WHAT HAPPENED?
JULIE JUMPS UP AND SAYS, "MOM, DAD-- THIS IS MRS. HICKS' SON, DANTE."
THEY KNEW YOUR MOTHER?!
FROM CHURCH.

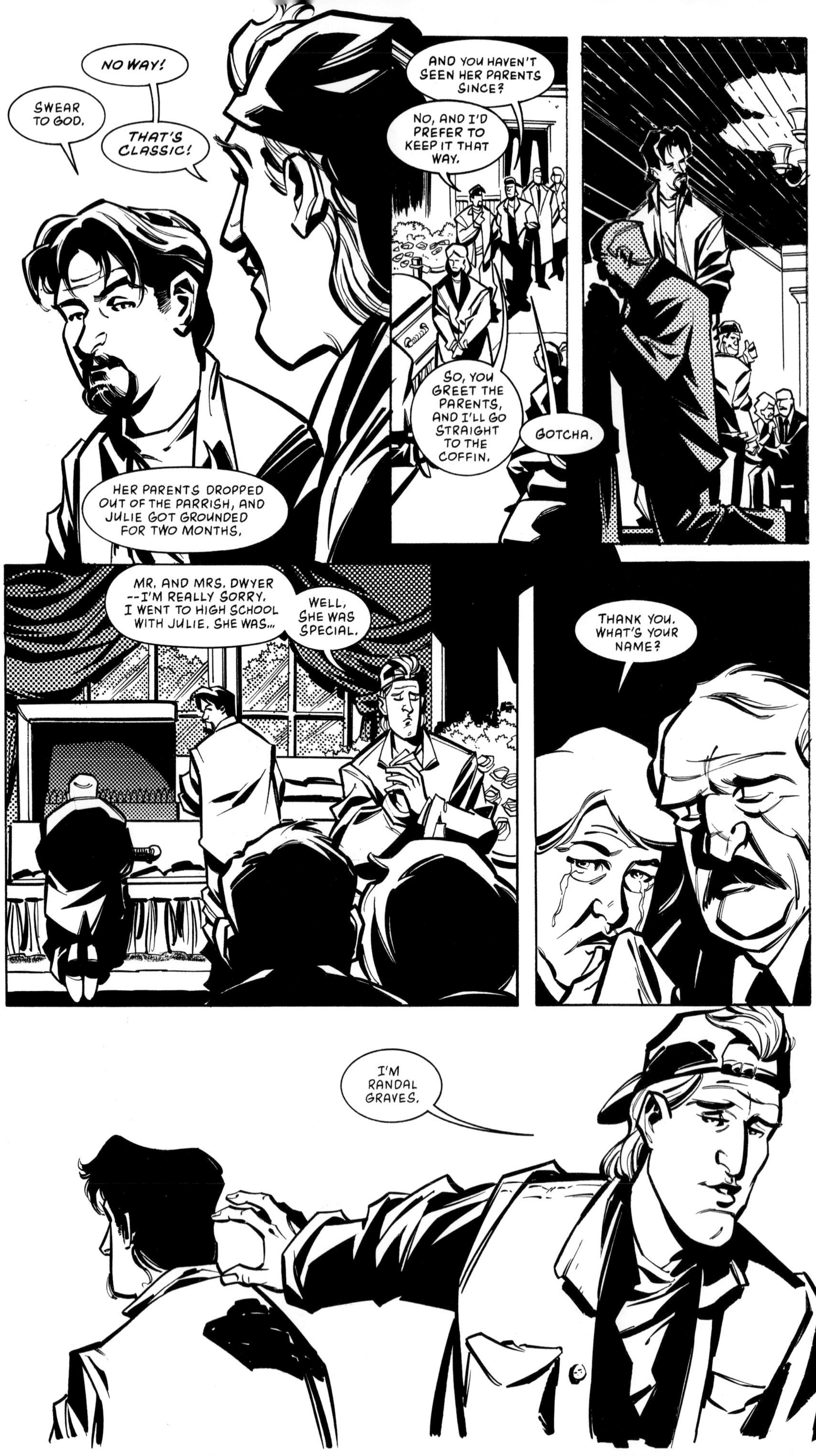
SWEAR TO GOD.
NO WAY!
THAT'S CLASSIC!
HER PARENTS DROPPED OUT OF THE PARRISH, AND JULIE GOT GROUNDED FOR TWO MONTHS.
AND YOU HAVEN'T SEEN HER PARENTS SINCE?
NO, AND I'D PREFER TO KEEP IT THAT WAY.
SO, YOU GREET THE PARENTS, AND I'LL GO STRAIGHT TO THE COFFIN.
GOTCHA.
MR. AND MRS. DWYER --I'M REALLY SORRY. I WENT TO HIGH SCHOOL WITH JULIE. SHE WAS...
WELL, SHE WAS SPECIAL.
THANK YOU. WHAT'S YOUR NAME?
I'M RANDAL GRAVES.

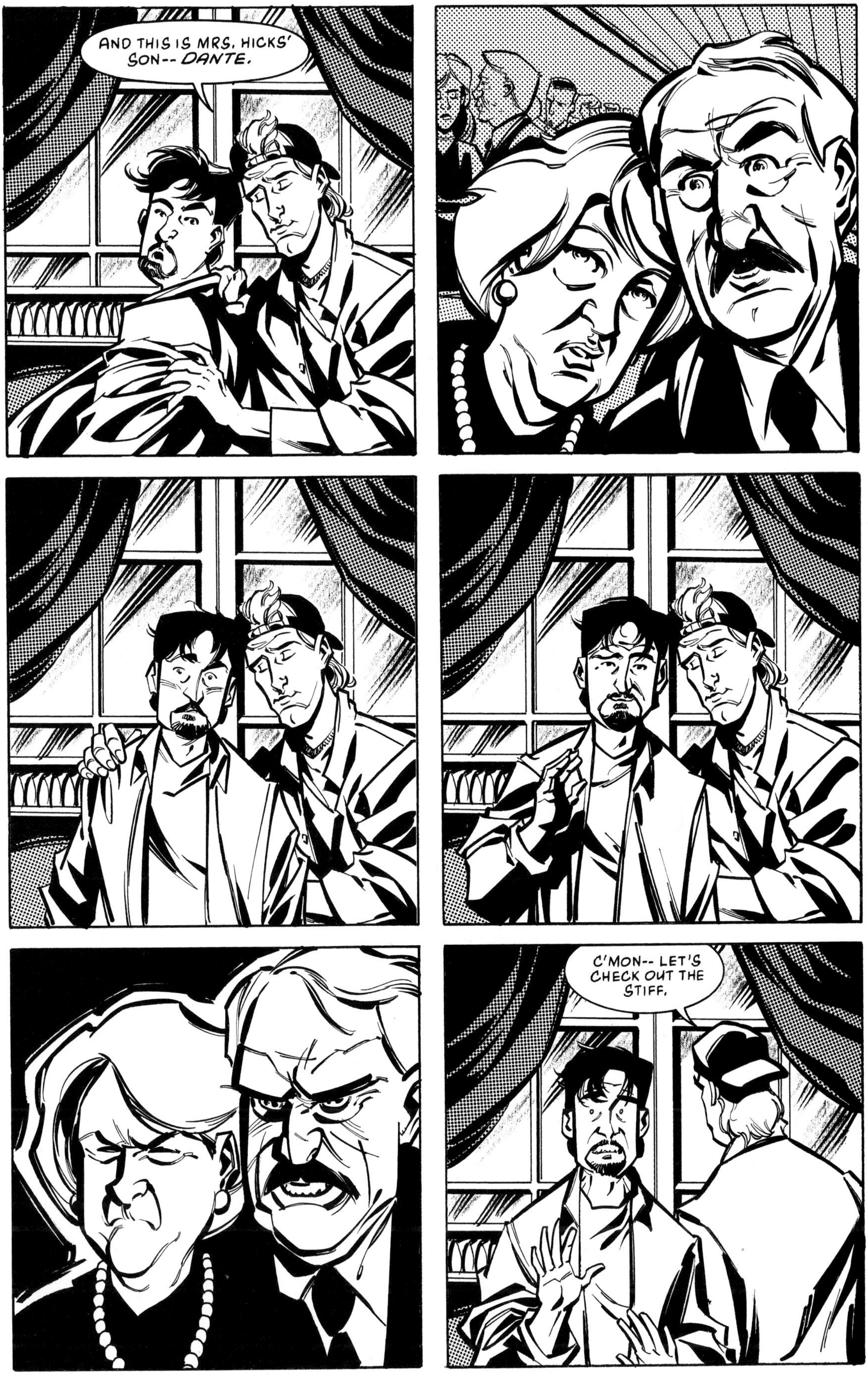
AND THIS IS MRS. HICKS' SON-- DANTE.
C'MON-- LET'S CHECK OUT THE STIFF.

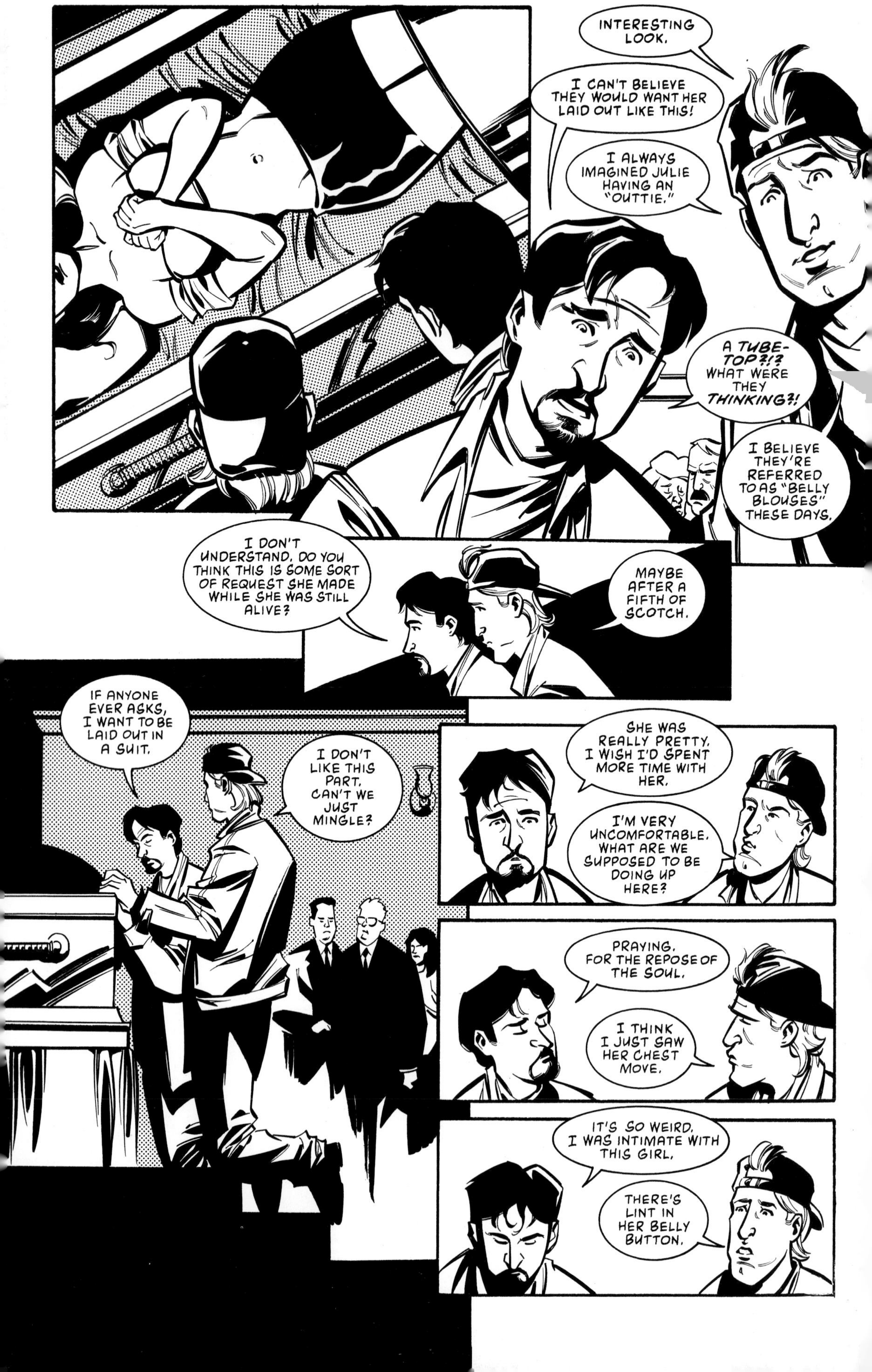
INTERESTING LOOK.
I CAN'T BELIEVE THEY WOULD WANT HER LAID OUT LIKE THIS!
I ALWAYS IMAGINED JULIE HAVING AN "OUTTIE."
A TUBE-TOP?!? WHAT WERE THEY THINKING?!
I BELIEVE THEY'RE REFERRED TO AS "BELLY BLOUSES" THESE DAYS.
I DON'T UNDERSTAND. DO YOU THINK THIS IS SOME SORT OF REQUEST SHE MADE WHILE SHE WAS STILL ALIVE?
MAYBE AFTER A FIFTH OF SCOTCH.
IF ANYONE EVER ASKS, I WANT TO BE LAID OUT IN A SUIT.
I DON'T LIKE THIS PART. CAN'T WE JUST MINGLE?
SHE WAS REALLY PRETTY. I WISH I'D SPENT MORE TIME WITH HER.
I'M VERY UNCOMFORTABLE. WHAT ARE WE SUPPOSED TO BE DOING UP HERE?
PRAYING. FOR THE REPOSE OF THE SOUL.
I THINK I JUST SAW HER CHEST MOVE.
IT'S SO WEIRD. I WAS INTIMATE WITH THIS GIRL.
THERE'S LINT IN HER BELLY BUTTON.

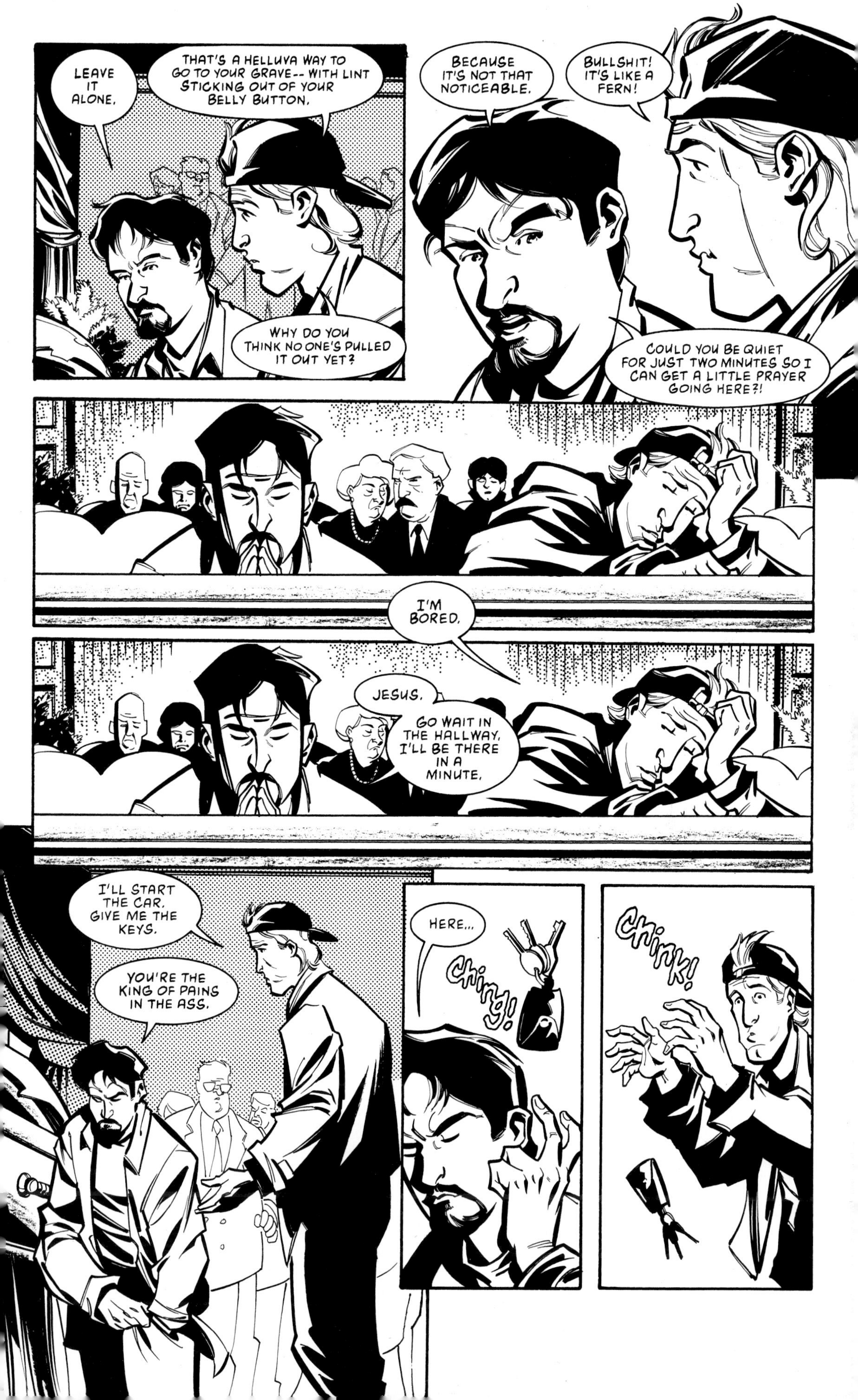
LEAVE IT ALONE.
THAT'S A HELLUVA WAY TO GO TO YOUR GRAVE-- WITH LINT STICKING OUT OF YOUR BELLY BUTTON.
WHY DO YOU THINK NO ONE'S PULLED IT OUT YET?
BECAUSE IT'S NOT THAT NOTICEABLE.
BULLSHIT! IT'S LIKE A FERN!
COULD YOU BE QUIET FOR JUST TWO MINUTES SO I CAN GET A LITTLE PRAYER GOING HERE?!
I'M BORED.
JESUS.
GO WAIT IN THE HALLWAY. I'LL BE THERE IN A MINUTE.
I'LL START THE CAR. GIVE ME THE KEYS.
YOU'RE THE KING OF PAINS IN THE ASS.
HERE...
Ching!
Chink!

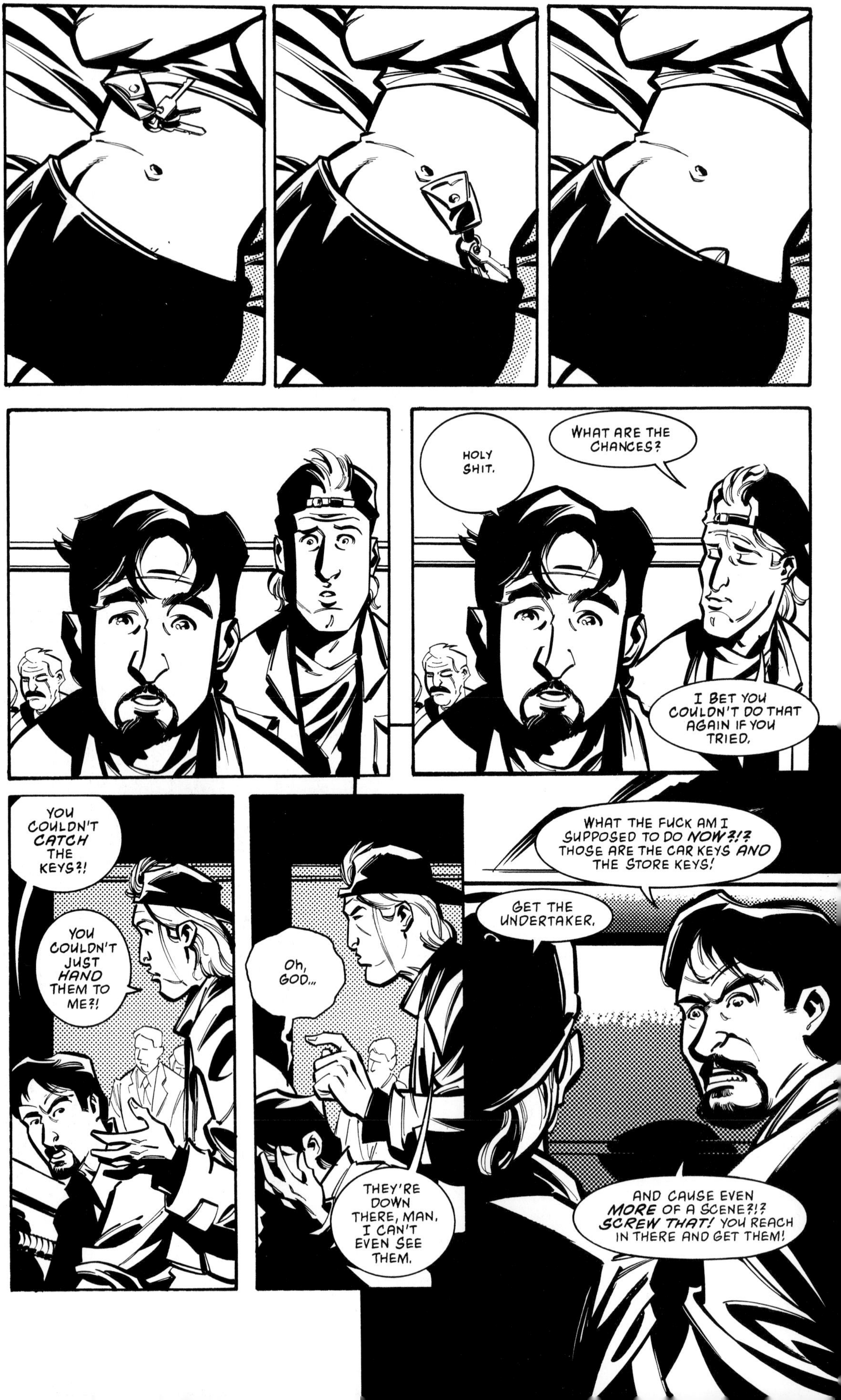

HOLY SHIT.
WHAT ARE THE CHANCES?
I BET YOU COULDN'T DO THAT AGAIN IF YOU TRIED.
YOU COULDN'T CATCH THE KEYS?!
YOU COULDN'T JUST HAND THEM TO ME?!
Oh, GOD...
THEY'RE DOWN THERE, MAN. I CAN'T EVEN SEE THEM.
WHAT THE FUCK AM I SUPPOSED TO DO NOW?!? THOSE ARE THE CAR KEYS AND THE STORE KEYS!
GET THE UNDERTAKER.
AND CAUSE EVEN MORE OF A SCENE?!? SCREW THAT! YOU REACH IN THERE AND GET THEM!

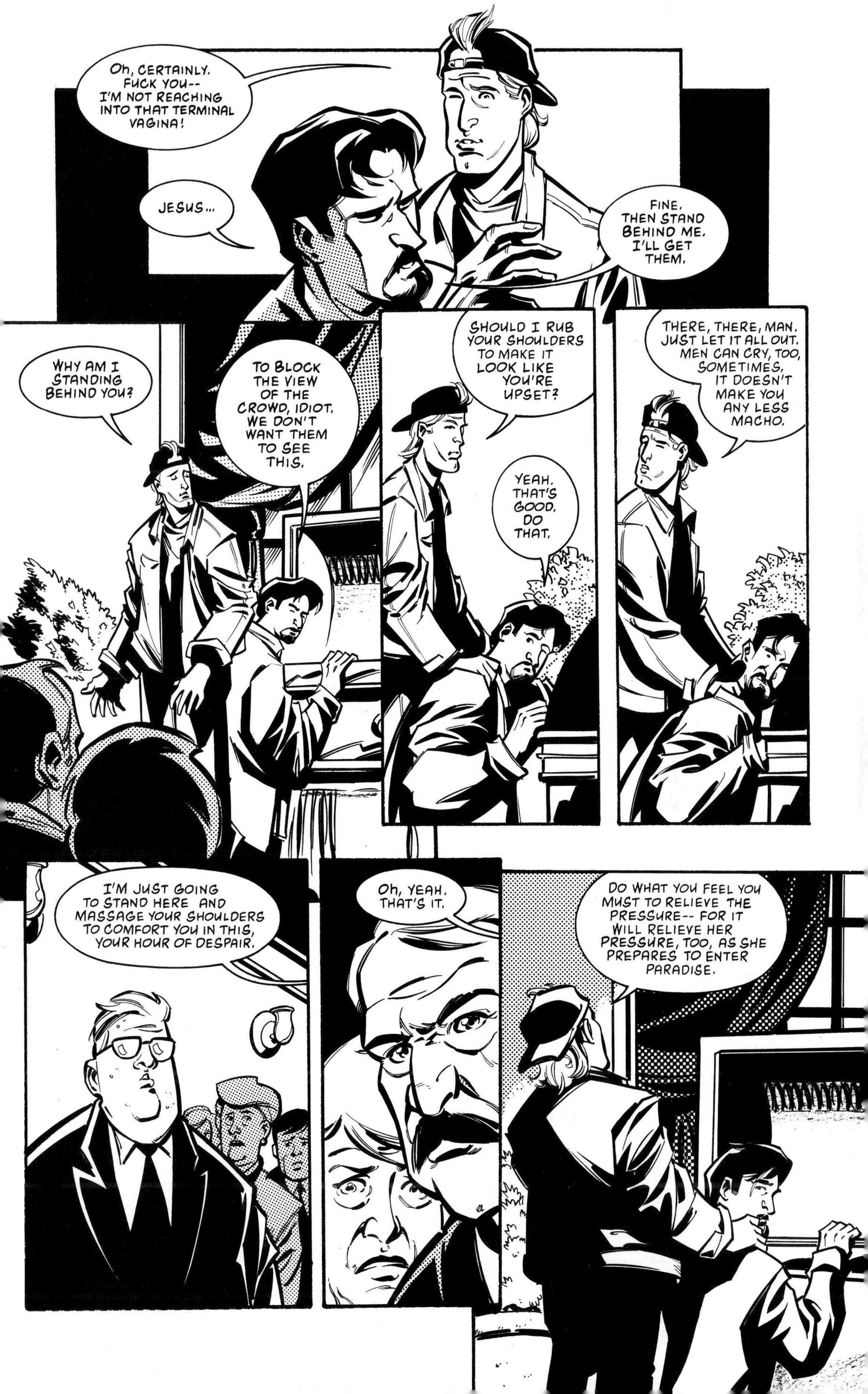
Oh, CERTAINLY. FUCK YOU-- I'M NOT REACHING INTO THAT TERMINAL VAGINA!
JESUS...
FINE. THEN STAND BEHIND ME. I'LL GET THEM.
WHY AM I STANDING BEHIND YOU?
TO BLOCK THE VIEW OF THE CROWD, IDIOT. WE DON'T WANT THEM TO SEE THIS.
SHOULD I RUB YOUR SHOULDERS TO MAKE IT LOOK LIKE YOU'RE UPSET?
YEAH. THAT'S GOOD. DO THAT.
THERE, THERE, MAN. JUST LET IT ALL OUT. MEN CAN CRY, TOO, SOMETIMES. IT DOESN'T MAKE YOU ANY LESS MACHO.
I'M JUST GOING TO STAND HERE AND MASSAGE YOUR SHOULDERS TO COMFORT YOU IN THIS, YOUR HOUR OF DESPAIR.
Oh, YEAH. THAT'S IT.
DO WHAT YOU FEEL YOU MUST TO RELIEVE THE PRESSURE-- FOR IT WILL RELIEVE HER PRESSURE, TOO, AS SHE PREPARES TO ENTER PARADISE.

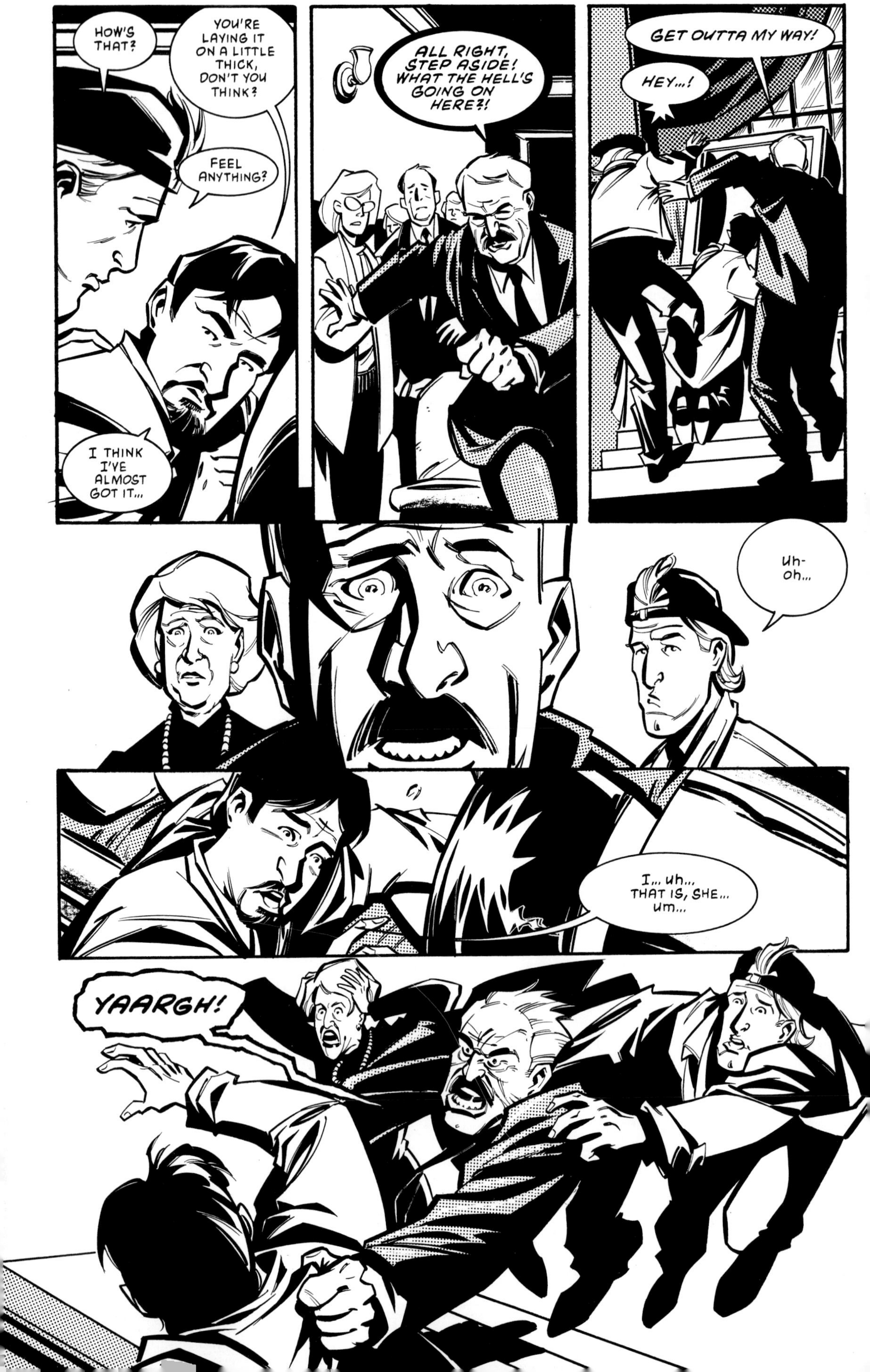
HOW'S THAT?
YOU'RE LAYING IT ON A LITTLE THICK, DON'T YOU THINK?
FEEL ANYTHING?
I THINK I'VE ALMOST GOT IT...
ALL RIGHT, STEP ASIDE! WHAT THE HELL'S GOING ON HERE?!
GET OUTTA MY WAY!
HEY...!
Uh-oh...
I... uh... THAT IS, SHE... um...
YAARGH!

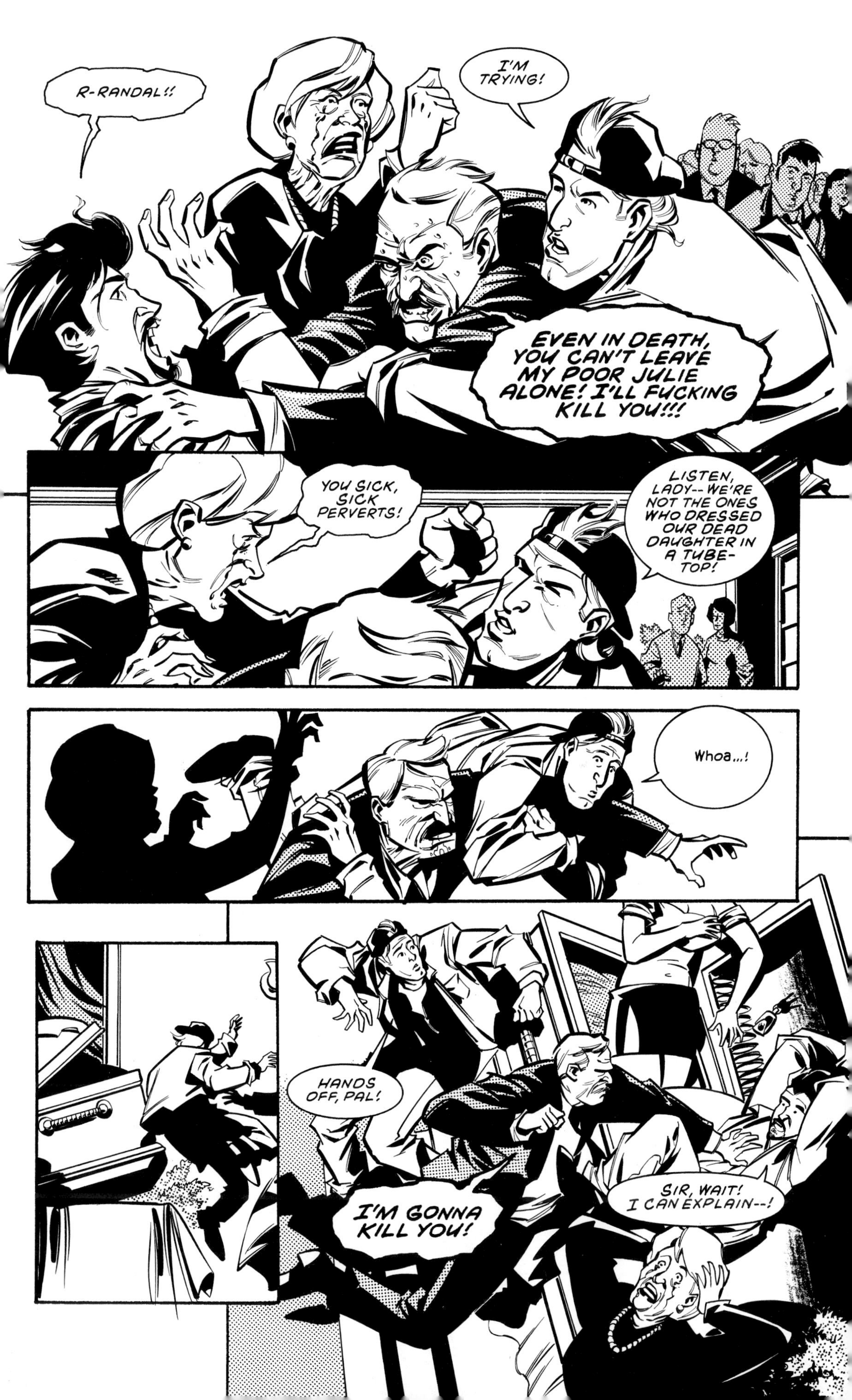
R-RANDAL!!
I'M TRYING!
EVEN IN DEATH, YOU CAN'T LEAVE MY POOR JULIE ALONE! I'LL FUCKING KILL YOU!!!
YOU SICK, SICK PERVERTS!
LISTEN, LADY-- WE'RE NOT THE ONES WHO DRESSED OUR DEAD DAUGHTER IN A TUBE-TOP!
Whoa...!
HANDS OFF, PAL!
I'M GONNA KILL YOU!
SIR, WAIT! I CAN EXPLAIN--!

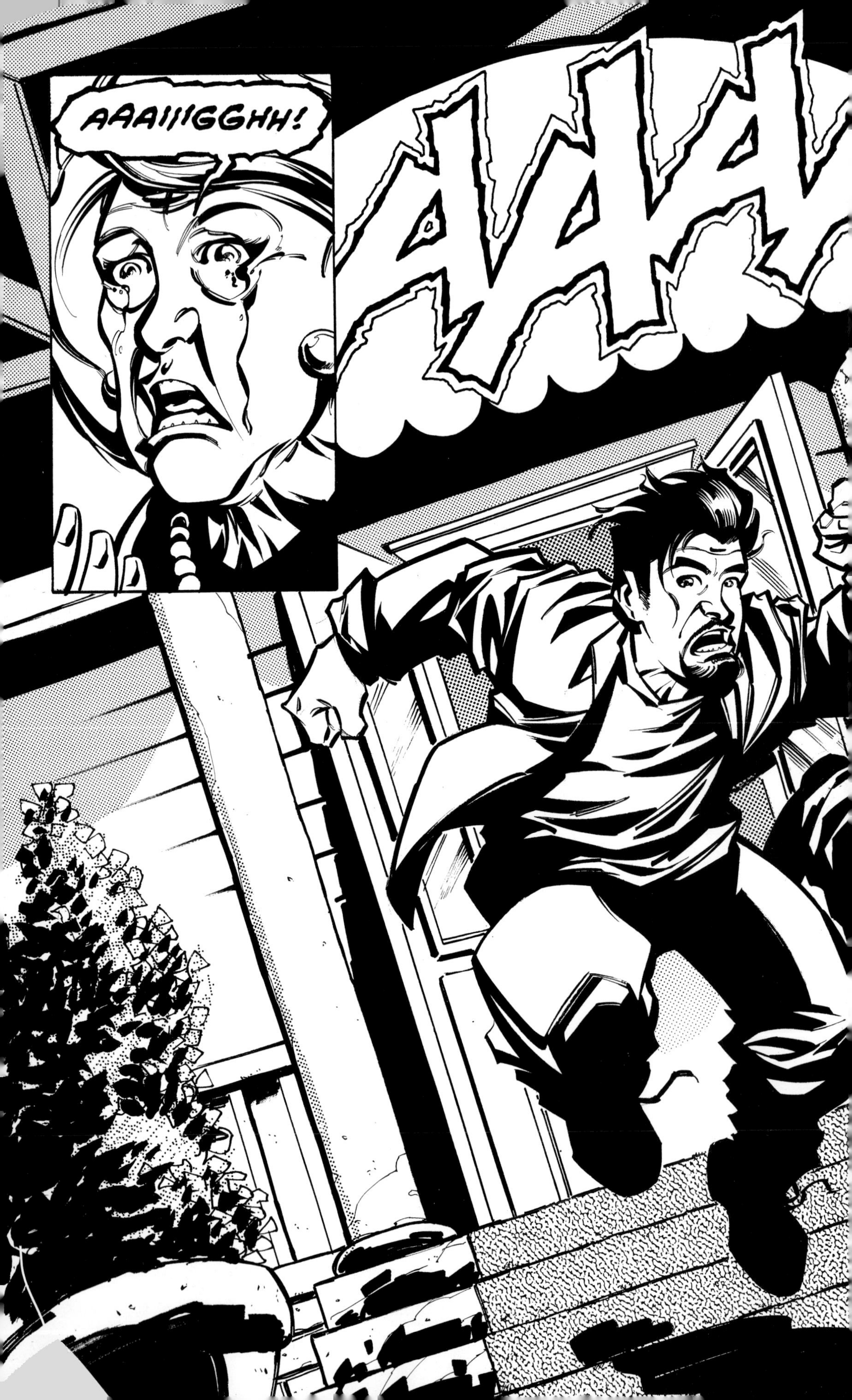
AAAIIIGGHH!

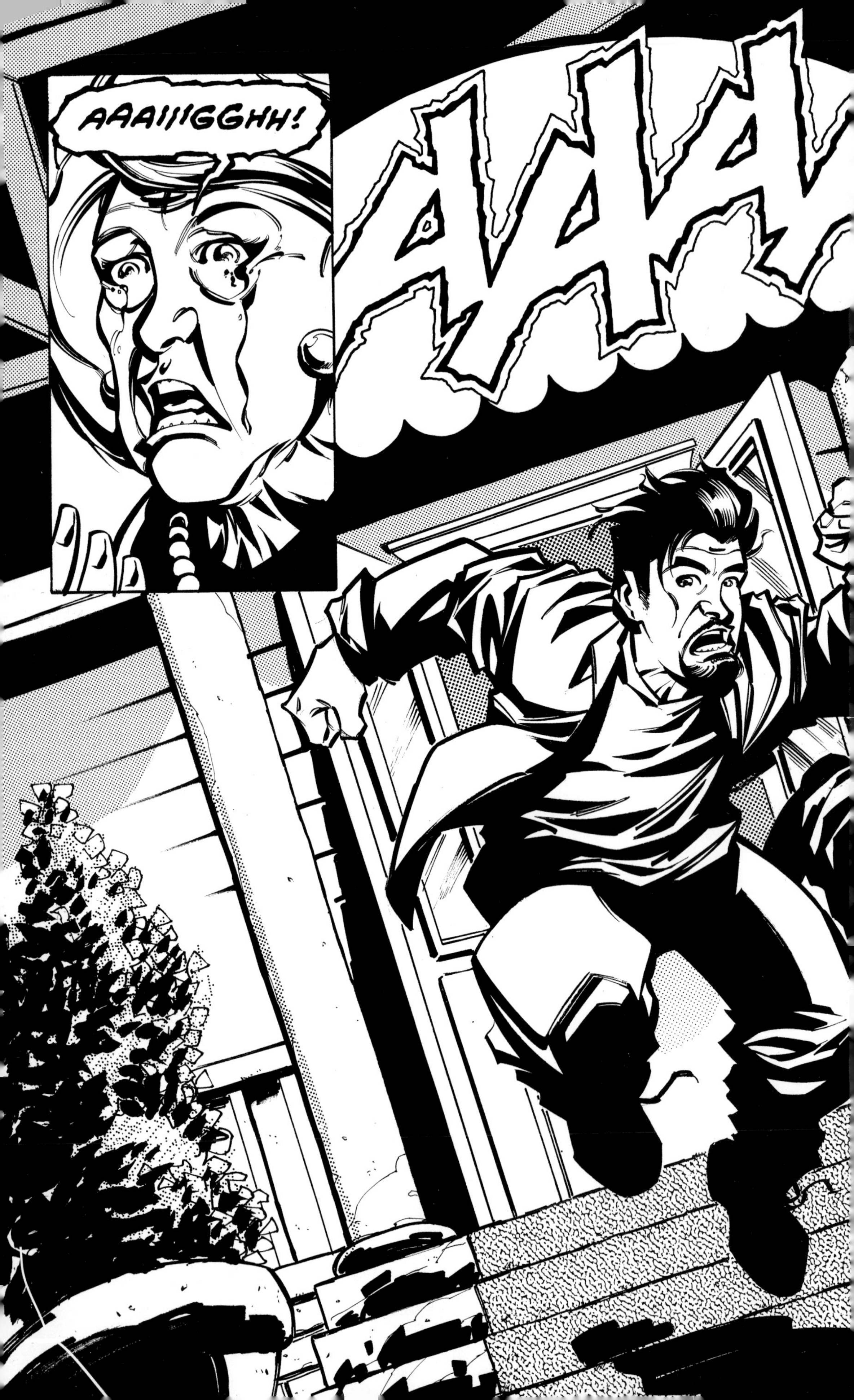
AAAIIIGGHH!

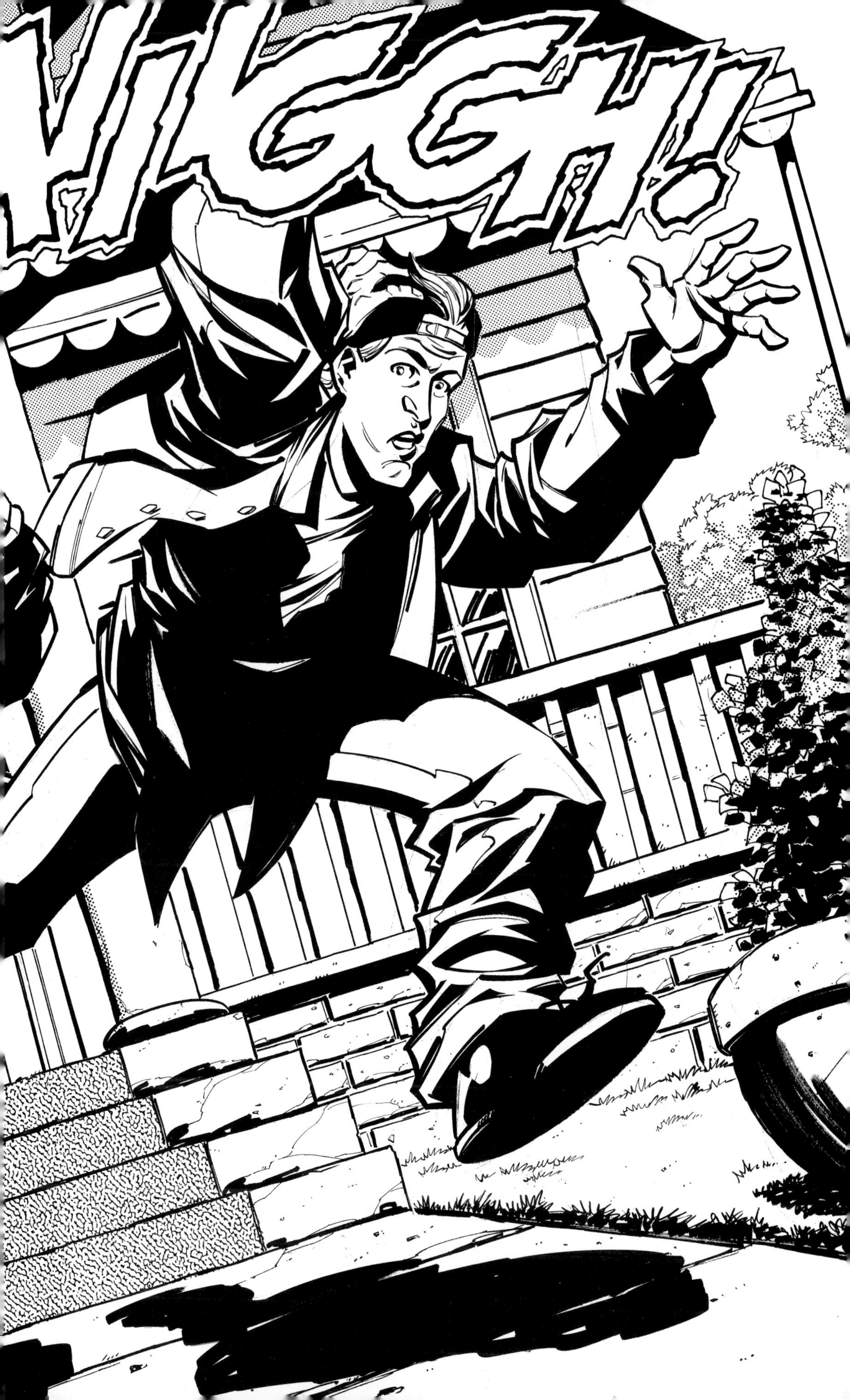

VIGGH!

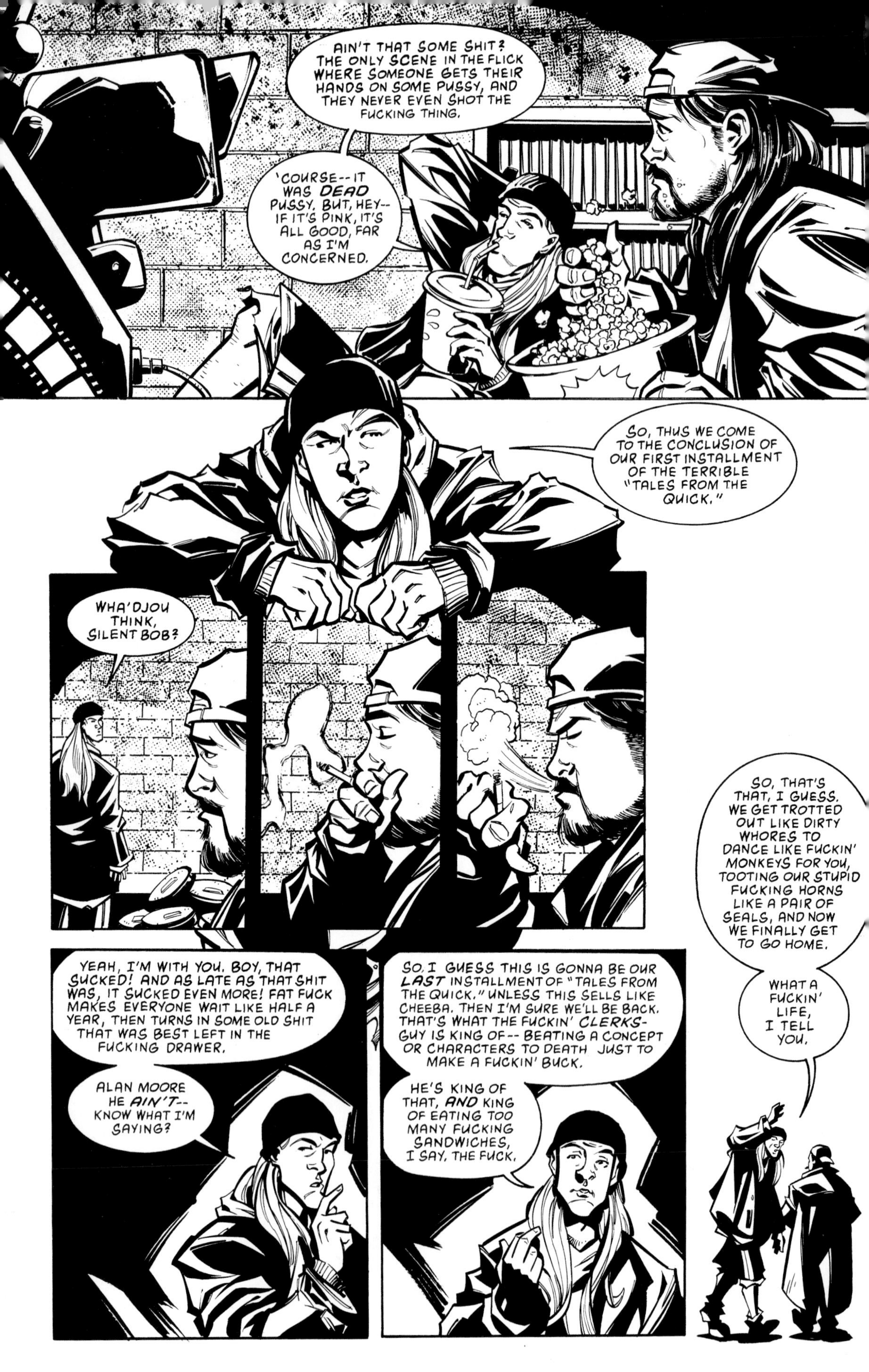

AIN'T THAT SOME SHIT? THE ONLY SCENE IN THE FLICK WHERE SOMEONE GETS THEIR HANDS ON SOME PUSSY, AND THEY NEVER EVEN SHOT THE FUCKING THING.
'COURSE--IT WAS DEAD PUSSY. BUT, HEY--IF IT'S PINK, IT'S ALL GOOD, FAR AS I'M CONCERNED.
SO, THUS WE COME TO THE CONCLUSION OF OUR FIRST INSTALLMENT OF THE TERRIBLE "TALES FROM THE QUICK."
WHA'DJOU THINK, SILENT BOB?
YEAH, I'M WITH YOU. BOY, THAT SUCKED! AND AS LATE AS THAT SHIT WAS, IT SUCKED EVEN MORE! FAT FUCK MAKES EVERYONE WAIT LIKE HALF A YEAR, THEN TURNS IN SOME OLD SHIT THAT WAS BEST LEFT IN THE FUCKING DRAWER.
ALAN MOORE HE AIN'T--KNOW WHAT I'M SAYING?
SO, I GUESS THIS IS GONNA BE OUR LAST INSTALLMENT OF "TALES FROM THE QUICK," UNLESS THIS SELLS LIKE CHEEBA. THEN I'M SURE WE'LL BE BACK. THAT'S WHAT THE FUCKIN' CLERKS-GUY IS KING OF--BEATING A CONCEPT OR CHARACTERS TO DEATH JUST TO MAKE A FUCKIN' BUCK.
HE'S KING OF THAT, AND KING OF EATING TOO MANY FUCKING SANDWICHES, I SAY, THE FUCK.
SO, THAT'S THAT, I GUESS. WE GET TROTTED OUT LIKE DIRTY WHORES TO DANCE LIKE FUCKIN' MONKEYS FOR YOU, TOOTING OUR STUPID FUCKING HORNS LIKE A PAIR OF SEALS, AND NOW WE FINALLY GET TO GO HOME.
WHAT A FUCKIN' LIFE, I TELL YOU.

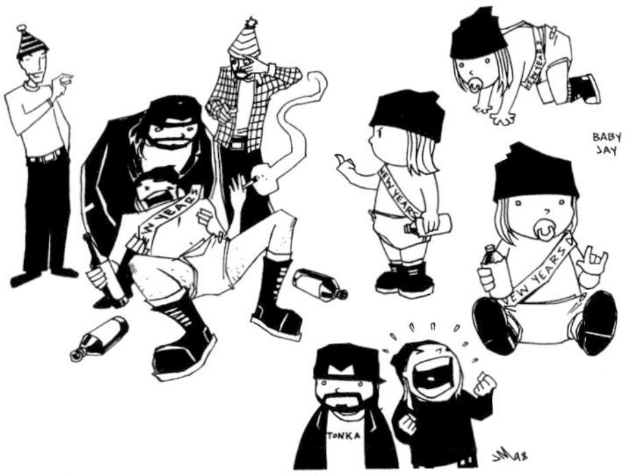
BABY JAY
TONKA

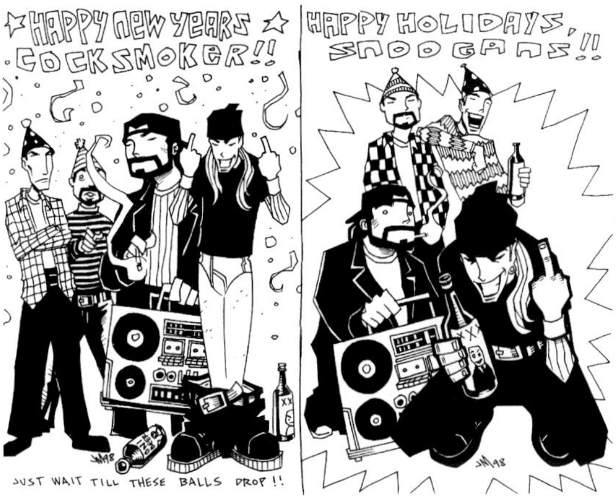
HAPPY NEW YEARS COCKSMOKER!!
HAPPY HOLIDAYS, SNOOGANS!!
JUST WAIT TILL THESE BALLS DROP!!

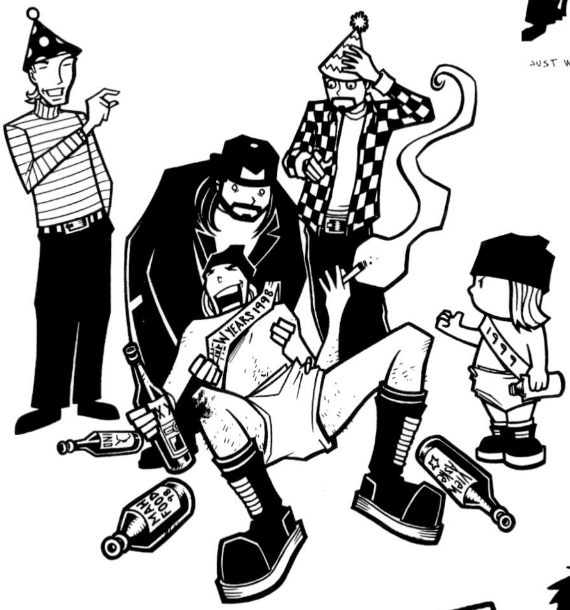

We've cracked open the pages of Jim Mahfood's sketch book to give you a peak at some of his initial drawings for this book.

Above and left: Designs for what would ultimately become a t-shirt and the 1998 Graphitti Designs/View Askew/Oni Press Christmas card.

Below and next page: Mahfoods earliest drawings for the View Askew characters, taking a more "serious" artistic approach.

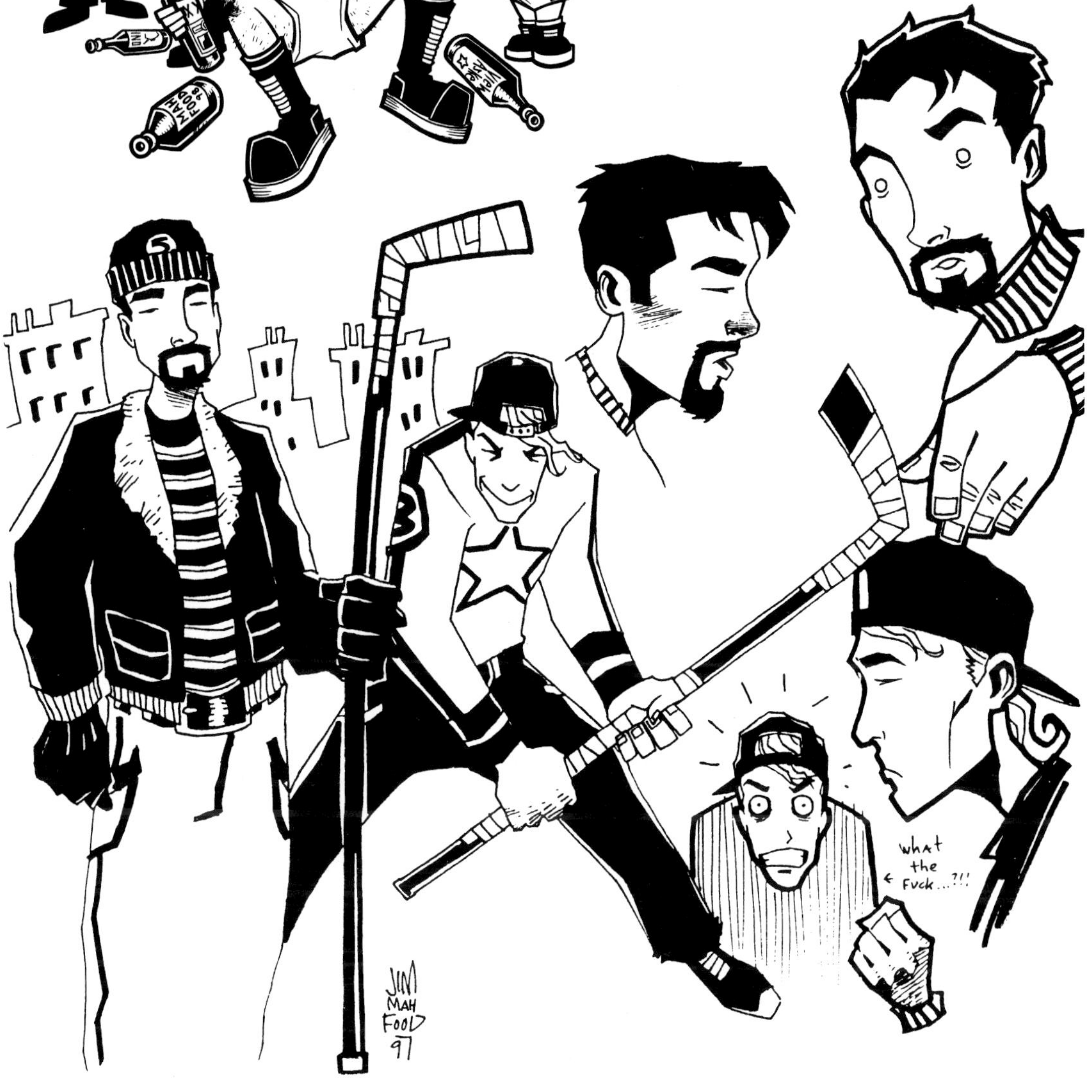
what the Fuck...?!!
JIM MAH FOOD 97

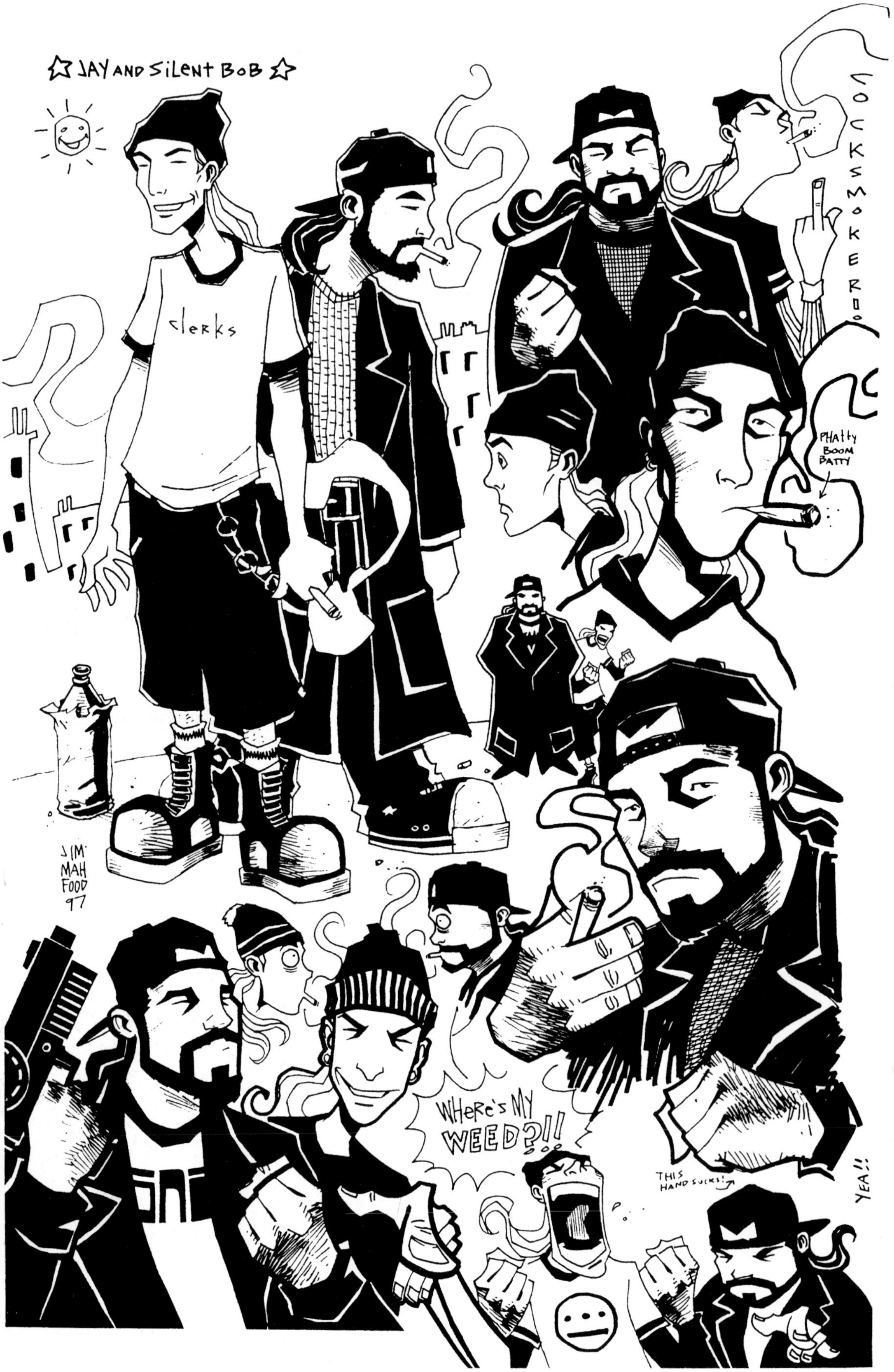
JAY AND SILENT BOB
clerks
SOCKSMOKER!!
PHATTY BOOM BATTY
JIM MAHFOOD 97
WHERE'S MY WEED?!!
THIS HAND SUCKS!
YEA!!